GRAD SCHOOL LIFE

GRAD SCHOOL LIFE

SURVIVING AND THRIVING BEYOND COURSEWORK AND RESEARCH

Jacqueline M. Kory-Westlund

COLUMBIA UNIVERSITY PRESS
New York

Columbia University Press
Publishers Since 1893
New York   Chichester, West Sussex
cup.columbia.edu
Copyright © 2024 Jacqueline M. Kory-Westlund
All rights reserved

Library of Congress Cataloging-in-Publication Data
Names: Kory-Westlund, Jacqueline M. (Jacqueline Marie), author.
Title: Grad school life : surviving and thriving beyond coursework and research / Jacqueline M. Kory-Westlund.
Description: New York : Columbia University Press, 2024. | Includes bibliographical references and index.
Identifiers: LCCN 2023037174 (print) | LCCN 2023037175 (ebook) | ISBN 9780231207843 (hardback) | ISBN 9780231207850 (trade paperback) | ISBN 9780231557146 (ebook)
Subjects: LCSH: Universities and colleges—United States—Graduate work—Handbooks, manuals, etc. | Graduate students—United States—Handbooks, manuals, etc.
Classification: LCC LB2371.4 .K67 2024 (print) | LCC LB2371.4 (ebook) | DDC 378.1/55—dc23/eng/20230925
LC record available at https://lccn.loc.gov/2023037174
LC ebook record available at https://lccn.loc.gov/2023037175

Cover design and illustration: Henry Sene Yee

TO RANDY, THE BEST HUSBAND A GRAD STUDENT
COULD ASK FOR,
AND
TO ALL THE GRADUATE STUDENTS WHO ARE
LOOKING FOR A HEALTHIER, MORE BALANCED LIFE

Contents

List of Exercises ix

Acknowledgments xi

Introduction 1

PART I. PLANNING YOUR JOURNEY

1. What's Next 9
2. Career Plans: Academia, or Not? 31
3. Money and Logistics 51
4. Making Grad School Work for You 67

PART II. GRAD SCHOOL SKILLS

5. Advisers 85
6. Labs, Classes, and Teaching 103
7. Research, Theses, and Dissertations 115
8. Managing Projects and Managing Time 143
9. Your Work and the World 164

PART III. THE REST OF YOUR LIFE

10 It's Just Grad School   191

11 Relationships and Family   207

12 Maintaining Your Sense of Self   224

13 Making Changes to Your School   233

14 What's Next, Revisited   247

Glossary   249

Notes   255

Resources   275

Index   301

Exercises

Exercise 1: Why Are You Here?   10
Exercise 2: Ranking Values   13
Exercise 3: Labeling Values   14
Exercise 4: Answer Questions Every Student Should Ask   29
Exercise 5: Life Goals   33
Exercise 6: Job Skills   44
Exercise 7: Make a Budget   58
Exercise 8: Make a Skill Plan   77
Exercise 9: Negotiation   98
Exercise 10: Who's on Your Team?   106
Exercise 11: Ideation   130
Exercise 12: Make a Degree Timeline   145
Exercise 13: Finding Your Rhythm   151
Exercise 14: The Point of the First Draft Is to Exist   180
Exercise 15: A Date with You   199
Exercise 16: Keep Tabs on Yourself   204
Exercise 17: Life Goals   209
Exercise 18: Build Your Relationships   214
Exercise 19: Who Are You?   225
Exercise 20: Revisit Your Reminders   226
Exercise 21: What Makes Life Meaningful?   230
Exercise 22: The Ideal Workplace   246

Acknowledgments

The journey from "Hey, I have an idea for a book!" to the polished final product you hold in your hands was not a jaunt down to the corner coffee shop. Years passed. So many years that I had two more kids at publication than I did when I first decided to start writing. But—thanks to the support and effort of far more people than would comfortably fit in my house for the dinner party I wish I could host for them all—here we are.

Thank you, first, to my agent Joe Perry for believing in this book's message. Thank you to Miranda Martin, my editor; Kathryn Jorge, who skillfully managed production; Ryan Perks, who copyedited with a close eye for detail; and the rest of the team at Columbia University Press who made this book a reality. Who knew it'd be so great to work with experts who can come up with better titles and better cover designs than I ever could on my own? I mean, I suspected.

I am grateful to the peer reviewers of the book proposal and the manuscript, first for agreeing to review an entire book in this busy age, and second, for not being reviewer #2. Your thoughtful, constructive feedback improved the book, as it should have.

Next, I'd like to list the people who influenced my perspective on all the many idea crumbs that I squashed into this book loaf. Ready?

At the top of the list, A+ for Amazing, is the Personal Robots Group (PRG) at the MIT Media Lab—especially my graduate advisor Cynthia Breazeal for crafting a incredible and supportive graduate school environment; Polly Guggenheim, the den mother of PRG; and Sooyeon Jeong, my longtime officemate and friend with whom I spent so many hours conversing about the state of our research, the academy, and the world. Every cup of tea was time well-spent.

Thank you to Roz for being a thoughtful, supportive committee member; for welcoming me to her research group in that interim year when Cynthia was on leave; and for introducing me to Martin Seligman's work on human flourishing. Thank you also to David DeSteno and Paul Harris for all the research mentorship, rigor, and expertise that shaped my projects and papers.

In these acknowledgements, I can dive back in time and thank people who shaped the path that led me to grad school in the first place. Isn't that fun? Thank you, Ken, Gwen, John, and Jenny—the Vassar College professors who saw my potential, gave me opportunities before I asked for them, and wrote me recommendation letters that I presume were great because I got into MIT.

More MIT people next: Thank you to Kristy Johnson, for being a shining example of academic motherhood in action. Also, the other Media Lab mothers who formed the first mom's support group I was a part of. We need these groups. If you're reading this and you're a mother and you aren't part of a mom's group, go find one today and thank me later.

Thank you to my PhD Crit Group—Laura, Jen, Jia, Cindy, and Amy—for the support, feedback, and solidarity as we slogged through generals, proposals, and defenses. Our paths have taken us such different places and they're all wonderful.

Thank you to my friends in SSOMIT and the Addir Fellows, with whom I had many amazing, thoughtful discussions about life, the universe, and everything, and who were part of how I found balance as a student.

Thank you to Dipa Shah and MIT's Kaufmann Teaching Certificate Program for the excellent introduction to teaching philosophy, syllabus design, and active learning.

Thank you to my colleagues at the Ronin Institute, especially the Women's IG+, who are embodying the kind of flexible, balanced lives I want more scholars to have. Special shoutout to Emily and Arika for helpful feedback on chapter drafts.

Okay, now we're getting close to the end. Hanging in there?

Thank you, Mom, for homeschooling me, so I never lost a love of learning and kept following my curiosity (to grad school and beyond). Thank you, Dad, for enabling her to stay home with us, and for being a role model in many things—like, as mentioned in chapter 1, career changes. Also for that advice, which I think you first dispensed when I was a kid and we were sneaking around unmarked hallways on a cruise ship, to act like you're supposed to be there... and no one will question you.

And the last one, because we always save the best for last in the acknowledgements: Thank you to my husband Randy for not thinking I was crazy to write a book about balancing life in grad school—which means maybe I got some of it right—and to my children, who are the center of my universe and the reason that life balance matters.

Introduction

When I started grad school, I had little idea of what to expect of my studies, less idea of how I would change and grow, and no idea how all my priorities would shift postpartum. Most of the advice I encountered focused on practical aspects of the grad school experience, such as finding funding, managing research projects and teaching assistantships, or how to write a good research paper. Very little talked about the *rest* of life. But the rest of life held my questions: how to build a life-school balance, positive ways to deal with colleagues and advisers, how to shape a career while starting and maintaining a family.

This is the book I wish I could have read when I started grad school.

Grad school is only one part of your life. I want to help you find balance, make the most of your time, and prepare for your career—whether in academia or beyond. Whether you are a current student or a prospective student, or simply someone interested in the realities of graduate student life, I hope to share methods for not only surviving the academic system but thriving in it as well.

When I applied to graduate schools, I had no long-term plan. I wrote in my personal statement, "I'm going to grad school because it'll be fun." Fun was my primary motivation. The fun part was learning. I liked learning so much that I stayed up until 3:00 a.m. doing data analysis for my senior undergrad thesis (abnormal behavior for me, the person who left college parties early so I could get a full eight hours of sleep). I liked learning, so I decided I wanted to do a PhD, because it would allow me to learn a slew of interesting things, pose interesting questions, and try to find interesting answers. Fortunately, that's the kind of person many PhD programs are looking for.[1] My first line worked. I was offered a spot in the program I was most excited about, and the rest, as they say, is history.

And, exactly like history, my journey through the MIT Media Lab's master's and PhD programs was neither easy nor straightforward. I did have fun. I learned plenty while programming robots to play with young kids, delving into educational psychology and child development theories, debating the ethics of technology use, and soldering wires onto motor control boards. But there were setbacks and challenges—some big, some small. My primary adviser took a leave of absence in my second year to start a company. I got married and had a baby. Robots broke, data collection had to be redone, papers were rejected. Lest you think my experience uncommon, I asked academics on Twitter what words they would use to describe their time in grad school: "fun" was there, right alongside "infuriating," "frustrating," "exhausting," "crushing," "defining," "expanding," "stimulating," "challenging," "enlightening," "fascinating," "exciting," "rewarding," and "valuable."

History is messy. Life is messy. Grad school can be messy too. The point of this book is to talk about that messiness with you. My hope is that by sharing my experiences and hard-won wisdom, I can make your grad school journey a little smoother—maybe even *fun*. I hope I can give you insight into the challenges grad students face, alongside concrete tips for facing those challenges—or, failing that, direct you to useful resources that *will* help you on your way. Not everyone needs the same advice! I'm only one data point. Advice that I think is awesomely helpful may not matter to you. To that end, I have included a list of related resources, such as books, websites, and podcasts, that may have the info you need. Many university libraries carry these books—and some public libraries have them too—so you don't have to buy them all yourself. If your library *doesn't* have them, most libraries have interlibrary loan programs that will let you borrow the book from elsewhere (for free!), and most libraries let you suggest purchases.

Given the inherent messiness of both life and school, one of my premises is that grad school isn't easy. (What worthwhile things in life are?) Grad school is even less easy when you're not the "traditional" student of yore: white, male, and upper-class. It wasn't all peaches and cream for me, even though I have some advantages. I'm a white woman. I grew up homeschooled in a middle-class suburban family. There were a few academics in my extended family—for example, on the Idahoan, potato-farming side, one of my grandmother's uncles studied dairy science and helped develop a new cheese. But my dad didn't attend college, and my mom earned her associate's degree about the same time I was completing my bachelor's. I got married while writing my master's thesis, had my first baby while working on my dissertation proposal, and was six months pregnant with my second when I defended.

While I include information in this book for the entire graduate student populace, I'm hoping to be especially helpful for the students who now, more than ever, have families and kids, are of color or identify with other underrepresented minority groups, come from lower socioeconomic status backgrounds, or are first-generation graduate students. According to the latest numbers from the National Center for Education Statistics, in 2017, 59 percent of graduate students were women, and 37 percent were non-white.[2] Nearly 10 percent of students were responsible for a child under twelve years of age.[3] And 21 percent had experienced discrimination, primarily related to gender or race.[4]

Another of my premises is that graduate school isn't often organized with life balance and mental health in mind. The stereotypical grad student is overworked, overstressed, and *over it*. A 2019 *Nature* survey found that 76 percent of students surveyed were working more than forty hours a week (with nearly half working over fifty hours)—and they weren't happy about their work schedules.[5] Half said their university culture often called for long hours and all-nighters. I understand working extra hard right before a deadline, but as a rule of life? Only 37 percent of students surveyed said their university supported a good work-life balance.

We need balance in order to thrive. Stress and overwork lead us into a negative spiral. An alarming 36 percent of grad students reported seeking help for anxiety or depression. Numbers like that make me wonder how many students are feeling stressed, depressed, and anxious but *aren't* seeking help. Unfortunately, only 29 percent said their university had adequate mental health services for PhD students. Some cope by dropping out. In doctoral programs, only half of entering students eventually get their degrees (in professional schools, 90 percent of students graduate—more on that in chapter 1, "What's Next").[6] Doctoral students in STEM (science, technology, engineering, and mathematics) fields are more likely to complete their degrees than students in the humanities and social sciences.[7]

If that picture wasn't bleak enough, grad students are entering a hostile and precarious job market too. The assumption baked into academic coursework and degree requirements is that students are professors-in-training—even though, as one estimate suggests, only 7 percent of people in PhD programs will succeed in that career path (more on this in chapter 2, "Career Plans").[8] Fewer people are being hired as full-time faculty than in decades past, and fewer students have jobs lined up when they graduate.[9] Short-term, part-time research or teaching positions provide little stability and less income. In some departments, as a result of the decline in full-time faculty positions, fewer students are admitted to their graduate programs too. These problems are worse in the humanities and social sciences than in STEM fields.

Can graduate school still be worth it, even with the difficulty and uncertainty? Yes. That's where this book comes in. If you want to know how to manage important personal relationships *and* a thesis, how to ensure grad school doesn't consume your life (and instead, how to build yourself up as a whole person), and how to find the people and resources that can help you succeed, this is the grad school advice book you're looking for. Throughout the book, I necessarily make generalizations—about life as a graduate student, and about life as a grad student in different fields. Students in STEM will have different experiences than students in the humanities, or in the social sciences. Even within these broad groups, there are differences—for instance, between lab scientists and theoreticians. Fortunately, there are plenty of commonalities too. This book is aimed at everyone in graduate school, regardless of field or program. I try to mention where different fields deviate. Even so, your specific graduate program or field may not match what's typical.

This book is designed to help you make the most of both your professional and personal lives, so you can do research and keep your sense of meaning and self intact in the process. To that end, every chapter includes one or more practical exercise that can help you answer questions about, for example, why you're in grad school, how to plan your grad school budget, and how to determine your ideal work habits. The exercises often involve journaling or writing. Personally, I've found that writing helps me clarify and organize my thoughts. You might not like writing. That's fine! Feel free to modify the exercises to suit your own style. Maybe you'd rather keep a voice log or talk through the exercises with a friend. You could also ignore the exercises altogether. I'm not one to claim that everyone needs the same information in the same format, or even in the same order. Read straight through or skip around. Learning is an individual journey, and I want to help you on your way!

Here's your road map. Part 1 is about planning your journey, starting in chapter 1, "What's Next," with some fundamental questions: Why are you in grad school? What's your motivation? What do you want out of your degree and your life? Chapter 2, "Career Plans," follows with important questions about your career path: Academia, or not? More than half of all PhDs, for example, get jobs outside of higher education. Knowing where you're headed will help you make the most of your graduate school experience. Then, we move on to pragmatic matters that make grad school happen: namely, all things money. Chapter 3, "Money and Logistics," covers acquiring funding to pay for school, moving, roommates, the two-body problem, budgeting, and more. Chapter 4, "Making Grad School Work for You," looks at how to ace grad school on your own terms—that is, how to get the most out of your experience. That chapter discusses four key skills: (1) keeping your goal in mind, (2) cultivating a learning mind-set, (3) seeking new skills, and (4) being picky about saying *yes*.

In part 2, we'll cover key skills that will help you succeed in grad school. Chapter 5, "Advisers," explains how to find, manage, and negotiate with the person who arguably has the most significant impact on your life in grad school: your adviser.

Then we get into the weeds. Chapter 6, "Labs, Classes, and Teaching," delves into the day-to-day: classwork, teaching assistantships, and research assistantships. This chapter also helps you think about who's on your team as you wade through the muck of graduate life. Following that, chapter 7, "Research, Theses, and Dissertations," covers how to come up with research ideas, find exam and thesis committees, and actually write your dissertation.

In chapter 8, "Managing Projects and Managing Time," I tackle how to do everything you need to do, in finite time. Discover your best work habits, learn to measure milestones, overcome failure, and figure out when to ask for help. Chapter 9, "Your Work and the World," follows with tips about communicating your research to the rest of the world via papers, presentations, blog posts, posters, and more. I include an overview of the different forms of academic writing, advice on the writing process, and tips for speaking about your work.

Part 3 covers your relationship to everything that's *not* grad school. Chapter 10, "It's Just Grad School," steps back to put your research life in perspective. We'll discuss the often elusive work-life balance, how grad schools often assume you don't have outside responsibilities (such as caregiving), and how not to put the rest of your life on hold for your career if you don't want to. Chapter 11, "Relationships and Family," narrows in on managing friends, dating, marriage, and children while in school—which are complicated enough without the added stress of graduate studies! In chapter 12, "Maintaining Your Sense of Self," I discuss how to live coherently—namely, by making your actions align with your values—and how to find or build a community of support. The message of these chapters is simple: The same stuff doesn't work for everyone. Build a life that is right for *you*. Don't put the rest of your life on hold for your career if you don't want to.

You may find that academia wasn't designed with you in mind (honestly, it probably wasn't). Chapter 13, "Making Changes to Your School," looks at ways we can make grad school friendlier for *all* students. The chapter covers such topics as student advocacy and student government. How do you convince your school to add a better maternity leave policy, or improve remote, part-time, and flexible working arrangements? The onus shouldn't be on students to propose and promote useful changes, but students can certainly get the ball rolling.

In chapter 14, "What's Next, Revisited," I return to motivation, life goals, life balance, and *you doing you*. There are infinite paths to success. Whether you're attending grad school for fun or for career advancement, out of a love for teaching or research, to address burning scientific questions, or working for the good of humankind; whether grad school is part of your road, or whether what you gain from this book is the knowledge that grad school isn't where you're headed—I wish you the best of luck. Finally, at the end of the book, you'll find a glossary defining a bunch of key academic terms that every student ought to know, but that they may not know to ask about. Flip there as needed! I will, of course, define all the terms I use as I use them, but it can be helpful to have all the definitions gathered in one place for reference. After the glossary, you'll also find the resources section that I mentioned earlier.

Enough preamble. On to the advice!

PART I

Planning Your Journey

chapter 1
What's Next

So you're going to grad school! Congratulations. What are you going to do when you're done?

Wait, you might be thinking. I just opened this book about how to get *through* grad school, and you're already asking me what I'm doing *after* grad school? Isn't that *mean*? Like asking seniors in college whether they have jobs yet?

It's not mean—it's pragmatic. I'm nothing if not pragmatic. (In college, one guy even called me "his pragmatic friend.") Asking you how you're planning to use your degree is asking you about your purpose. Hand in hand with that question is my next one: Why do you want to go to grad school? This question hones in on your motivation.

Motivation is why we start things, why we stick with things, and why we finish things. Whatever the thing, motivation is the driver that makes it happen.

I'm simplifying, of course, because motivation doesn't work alone. To get through grad school, as you may already know, you also need hard work and perseverance. Social support—friends and family. An adviser whom you can, at the least, tolerate, and who tolerates you; and at the best, one who has your back and shows you they believe in you. Sometimes you need thick skin. Sometimes you need a therapist. Money doesn't hurt, nor does good luck, but sometimes you have less control over these.

Whether you are motivated by burning questions, a specific career path, or if you're thinking about grad school because *why not?*, you need to know why you're in school and what you want to get out of school so you can make concrete plans. Having a concrete plan will help you get your degree on time while making the most of your experience, and will act as a buffer against the low points of school.

Before I talk more, though, let's get your initial thoughts and see where you stand.

> ## EXERCISE 1: WHY ARE YOU HERE?
>
> 1. Get a sheet of paper and a pen or open a blank text document.
> 2. For the next five to ten minutes, write down everything you can think of in response to the following questions:
>   a. Why do you want to go grad school?
>   b. If you've been accepted to a program, how did you feel when you got your acceptance letter? Draw a face to represent your feelings.
>   c. If you've started your program already, how do you feel about it?
>   d. What excites you about your grad program or potential grad program?
>   e. What do you want to do with your degree? List your top idea as well as anything you might consider as backup options.
> 3. Now look back at what you wrote. Do you see a clear goal? Do you see a clear motivation?

Keep your notes on hand—we'll come back to them momentarily.

If you were stumped by this exercise, don't fret. A blank page doesn't mean failure—just that you have some hard thinking and reflecting to do! Articulating your motivation and writing down your thoughts and feelings about grad school can be difficult. I have some advice just for you in a couple pages. Hang tight.

WHAT IS GRAD SCHOOL ALL ABOUT?

Ask different people and you'll get different answers, because the answer depends on the kind of graduate program you're in. Broadly speaking, there are two types of grad programs: (1) those focused on practice, gaining skills or qualifications, and professional advancement; and (2) those focused on research.

Practice-focused programs include most nondegree programs (such as certificates and micro credentials in, say, publishing, data analytics, or coding), most master's degree programs (MA in the social sciences and humanities, MFA for fine arts, MPH in public health, MSW in social work, MBA for business, and MS for sciences and math), and many professional doctoral degree programs, such as EdD (doctor of education), MD (doctor of medicine), and JD (doctor of law). You're more likely to pay for the programs out of pocket. They tend to involve a lot of classes and some independent study or practical application of the coursework. In master's programs, you'll generally have a final exam, project, or thesis. Master's degrees are one- to two-year programs. They come in three flavors: the so-called 4+1 program where you get a master's degree on top of your bachelor's by doing some extra stuff in your field at your bachelor's institution; a nonterminal program that's a step toward a doctoral degree; and a terminal or stand-alone program.

Research-focused programs, like most PhD programs, are about becoming a person who can evaluate ideas, come up with good questions, generate research plans and find resources to study those questions, follow through on those plans, and find answers—or at least find more questions. They're about producing new knowledge and ideas—and as a result, you're more likely than in a practice-focused program to get someone else to foot the bill. In some fields, the goal might be more about finding problems and crafting novel solutions to those problems than about asking questions, but the skills are related. And of course, you also learn many field-specific skills, facts, theories, and methods along the way. The structure and funding of PhD programs varies by field; in the humanities, you generally take more courses up front and independent research can take longer; in STEM fields, you often get started on research earlier, because you're often involved in a research group or lab.

Graduate degrees are useful or even necessary for some careers, especially college professors, physicians, and lawyers. Other professions, including teaching, industrial research, and museum work, also generally value people with advanced degrees or pay you more if you have one. PhDs, especially in the humanities, are often seen as a vocation: you're meant to be a professor, and this is how you get there! But by no means are you stuck on a particular career path. As I discuss in chapter 2, career diversity is real, even if many academic institutions and departments still lag behind in promoting anything other than "let's all be professors!"

What kind of program are you in, or planning on entering? Look at your notes from exercise 1. Does your motivation align with the program you're in? For example, if you wrote that you want to be a research professor or have a research-focused career, are you in a research-oriented program? You want your graduate degree to be a stepping stone, not a roadblock. Graduate school takes a long time, so make sure it's worth your while. The national median for years spent in graduate school for a PhD is 7.7 years.[1] In STEM fields, you may get away with 6.7 years; in the humanities, the median is 9.3. As Amanda Seligman wrote, "The best and most idealistic reason for going to graduate school is to learn in a relatively systematic fashion about a discipline that one simply wants to know more about."[2]

WHAT IF I DON'T KNOW WHAT I WANT TO DO AFTER GRAD SCHOOL?

You're not alone. Recent surveys of doctoral degree holders found that more than 25 percent of students don't have jobs lined up after their degree.[3] I was one of them. Based on my undergrad experience, I knew I liked research. I didn't know much about the differences between careers in academia, government, and industry. So I applied to research-focused graduate programs and assumed I'd figure the rest out along the way. That's a valid strategy. But if I'd had a clearer goal in mind from the get-go, I would have been better positioned to take advantage of all my school (MIT) and its city (Boston, Massachusetts) had to offer.

To figure out what you want to do in life, answer one key question: What's important to you?

Whether you're good at it is secondary. You can learn what you need to know if you're motivated. Other considerations, such as whether you can afford to make a big career change, whether your spouse or partner is on board with moving to a new city, or how to fit school in now that you have a baby, can be dealt with. I'm not saying they're not significant considerations, or even that you can definitely make everything work out perfectly for you (because sometimes you can't). Just that you need to think about your values *first*—because values matter most.

This is a big theme in one of my favorite job search and life-building books: *Designing Your Life* by Bill Burnett and Dave Evans. Live coherently. As they state, a coherent life is one lived in such a way that you can clearly connect to the dots between three things:

- Who you are
- What you believe
- What you are doing[4]

Increased coherency—increased connection between your values and your actions—leads to an increased sense of self, helps you create meaning, and generates greater satisfaction. As Burnett and Evans say, "Living coherently doesn't mean everything is in perfect order all the time. It simply means you are living in alignment with your values and have not sacrificed your integrity along the way."[5]

All the exercises in this book are geared toward increasing your life coherency. As Ayelet Fishbach argues in *Get It Done*, it's important that any goals you pursue are goals you set yourself—not goals that someone else suggests for you. If you set the goal, it means you have at least some interest in achieving it. So what goals do you have? What do you value, and what do you want to achieve?

EXERCISE 2: RANKING VALUES

Get out that paper again. This exercise will help you think through your values and determine whether grad school and your life-after-grad-school plan are in line with what you value most.

1. Here is a list of common things you might value or that may be important to you. (Feel free to add your own if you think a key value is missing.)
   a. Doing well in school, family (e.g., parents, children, spouse), religion and faith, friendships, career, mental health, money, hobbies (e.g., sports, writing, brewing beer).
2. Rank them in order from most important to least. Go with your gut instinct. Yes, these values are interrelated and some (e.g., mental health) are necessary for others to be possible. It's okay if you *know* something is important but generally prioritize something else. This is your list; no judgment here!
   a. For example, if I look back at myself when I was first wondering whether or not to apply to grad school, my order may have been academics, hobbies, mental health, friendships, career, family, money, religion and faith. At the time, I was very focused on getting my bachelor's. I wanted to pursue interesting ideas. I was a key member of the women's fencing team and dedicated to the

> sport. I had good financial aid from my college, etc. All these factors influenced what I prioritized and valued.
> 3. Evaluate: How does going to grad school support what matters to you? It might be obvious: for example, building a career as a pediatrician may be your top priority, so going to medical school is a clear step toward that goal. If family ranks first, maybe grad school indirectly supports that because it'll help you further your career, make more money, and support your family. It might not be obvious. Perhaps family comes first, but grad school is taking you to another continent and you have no clear plan on how you'll stay in touch or whether you'll move back when you graduate. This is important information, and we'll come back to it again in a few pages.

When discussing values, it's worth recognizing that following what you value, and attaining it, isn't a sure road to life satisfaction. You need the *right* goals. Psychology research following college students after graduation has found that people who held purpose-related goals (such as learning, growing, and helping others) and who felt they were achieving those goals were happy, satisfied, and had higher well-being and lower anxiety and depression than they reported in college.[6] Those who had profit-related goals (such as wealth or fame) were not any happier, and, in fact, were more anxious and depressed than they were in college.

> ### EXERCISE 3: LABELING VALUES
>
> Ranking values may have been helpful, or not. This next exercise takes a different stab at thinking about whether your values are in line with your life plan, by way of discovery and labeling, rather than ranking.
>
> 1. Below is a long list of values. Circle all the words that resonate with you (or write them down on another piece of paper if you'd like to keep this book pristine). Feel free to add your own if you think a key value is missing. The words you circle all relate to your personal core values.

Acceptance	Accountability	Achievement
Advancement	Adventure	Advocacy
Ambition	Appreciation	Attractiveness
Autonomy	Balance	Beauty
Being the best	Benevolence	Boldness
Brilliance	Calmness	Caring
Challenge	Charity	Cheerfulness
Cleverness	Collaboration	Commitment
Community	Compassion	Consistency
Contribution	Control	Cooperation
Creativity	Credibility	Curiosity
Daring	Decisiveness	Dedication
Dependability	Diversity	Empathy
Encouragement	Enthusiasm	Ethics
Excellence	Expressiveness	Fairness
Faith	Family	Flexibility
Freedom	Friendships	Fun
Generosity	Grace	Growth
Happiness	Health	Honesty
Humility	Humor	Inclusiveness
Independence	Individuality	Innovation
Inspiration	Integrity	Intelligence
Interdependence	Intuition	Joy
Kindness	Knowledge	Leadership
Learning	Love	Loyalty
Making a difference	Mindfulness	Motivation
Open-mindedness	Optimism	Originality
Passion	Peace	Perfection
Performance	Playfulness	Popularity
Power	Preparedness	Proactivity
Professionalism	Punctuality	Quality
Recognition	Relationships	Reliability
Resilience	Resourcefulness	Responsibility
Responsiveness	Risk taking	Safety
Security	Self-control	Selflessness

Service	Simplicity	Spirituality
Stability	Strength	Success
Thankfulness	Thoughtfulness	Traditionalism
Trustworthiness	Truth	Understanding
Uniqueness	Usefulness	Versatility
Vision	Warmth	Wealth
Well-being	Wisdom	Zeal

2. Next, from the values you picked in step 1, group all the similar values together. Group them in whatever way makes sense to you. Create three to five groupings. If you end up with more groupings, drop the one that feels least important. For example, you might group your words as follows:

<u>Group 1</u>

Adventure	Boldness	Curiosity
Enthusiasm	Fun	Growth
Learning	Open-mindedness	

<u>Group 2</u>

Beauty	Calmness	Community
Compassion	Collaboration	Empathy
Interdependence	Intuition	Love
Understanding		

<u>Group 3</u>

Balance	Creativity	Flexibility
Humor	Mindfulness	Optimism
Originality	Playfulness	Resilience
Versatility	Wisdom	

<u>Group 4</u>

Achievement	Ambition	Challenge
Contribution	Independence	Recognition

<u>Group 5</u>

Commitment	Dedication	Excellence
Motivation	Quality	Responsibility
Strength		

3. Choose one word within each group to represent the group. Don't overthink it—this is just a label to help you understand your core values. Here's an example:

Group 1
Adventure	Boldness	Curiosity
Enthusiasm	Fun	Growth
Learning	Open-mindedness	

Group 2
Beauty	Calmness	Community
Compassion	Collaboration	Empathy
Interdependence	Intuition	Love
Understanding		

Group 3
Balance	Creativity	Flexibility
Humor	Mindfulness	Optimism
Originality	Playfulness	*Resilience*
Versatility	Wisdom	

Group 4
Achievement	Ambition	Challenge
Contribution	Independence	Recognition

Group 5
Commitment	Dedication	Excellence
Integrity	Motivation	Quality
Responsibility	Strength	

4. Evaluate. Does your life plan—does going to grad school—reflect these values? How are you upholding these values in what you plan to study? Is your intended career aligned with these values?
5. Look back at your notes from exercises 1 and 2. Is your motivation in line with your stated values? For example, in exercise 2, you may have ranked family and money highest. You may have formed a grouping in exercise 3 around the concepts of family, contribution, or responsibility. Then, you may have written in exercise 1 that you are going to grad school to gain the skills needed to get a better,

> higher-paying job in a city closer to your parents—a motivation consistent with the ranking in exercise 2 and your values in exercise 3. That's just one example. This is an introspective exercise, and you're the only one who can determine whether your values and your actions are aligned.
>
> *Source*: This exercise was adapted from Barb Carr, "Live Your Core Values: 10-Minute Exercise to Increase Your Success," TapRoot Root Cause Analysis, April 11, 2013, https://www.taproot.com/live-your-core-values-exercise-to-increase-your-success/.

Before I move on, I have a bonus challenge exercise for you. Now that you have listed and prioritized your *own* values, consider the values of the institution or university you are at (or that you are considering joining). Do exercises 2 and 3 again: Rank and list your perception of the university's or grad program's values. Then evaluate whether those values are aligned with your own. It's okay if they are not! Academic culture, as well as the culture of individual universities, tends to impose a particular set of values; it's fine if your values are *not* aligned with those of academic culture at large, or those of your university—so long as you *know* that and can differentiate between what's expected of you and what you actually value doing.

WHAT'S THE OPPORTUNITY COST?

Some truths: Grad school may not line up with your values. Grad school is not compatible with all possible life paths. Grad school isn't a feasible path for everyone, even if it's what you desire most. Grad school is not necessarily the best way to further your career or your life. That's why I spent so much time talking about values: because you need to know what matters to you in order to choose what to do. Grad school might align nicely with your values, but is there something else you could be doing that aligns just as well—or, possibly, even better?

That's where opportunity cost comes in. If you don't go to grad school, what could you be doing instead? The jobs you're passing up are part of this opportunity cost—as are the money you might have made, the people you might have met, the town you might have been living in, and so forth. Opportunity cost is everything you lose by going to grad school. It's everything you *can't* do because you're going to school instead.

For example, you might be considering a master's program to gain new skills and qualifications, in order to advance your career, gain a promotion, make a better salary, and be better able to support your family. What are other ways you could achieve the same ends? Could you pick up a side hustle, take a shorter certification course, or even switch careers?

If one of your goals is to learn about something you are highly interested in, how else might you go about learning that thing? Are there more economical ways? Is a graduate degree necessary, or would online classes, video lectures, library books, local clubs, community college classes, or some other format suffice?

If you have a career path in mind, is grad school the best way to gain experience or qualifications for that career (particularly if your desired career is not in academia or in research)? Graduate school is frequently a high-stress, work-heavy environment, with a culture that often prioritizes dedicating all of one's time to one's work (and looks down on those with a healthier work-life balance), rather than promoting, you know, a healthier balance. This does vary by university, program, department, and adviser, though. (Chapter 5 dives into choosing and managing your adviser; chapters 11–13 cover life balance.)

Opportunity cost is an especially important consideration for PhD students in research-focused programs. Most practice-focused degree programs, as discussed above, are already aimed at non-higher-education employment. But many PhD students dream of becoming professors, and yet may not know the chances of becoming a professor—in a word, slim—or what *else* is possible. Chapter 2 will walk you through career plans. For now, simply consider whether you're thinking about heading into academia, or not.

If graduate school is definitely on your radar, do you want to attend immediately? There are valid reasons to jump right into graduate work, and equally valid reasons to get a taste of the real world first. For instance, if you've been employed or raising kids, you'll be far more mature and focused than students who are still in their early twenties, but you may have less energy. Recommendation letters for grad school applications can be harder to obtain if you've been out of school for a while. Starting right away means you'll still be in "school" mode; returning to school can be a big adjustment. Graduate students make very little money, as chapter 3 discusses; the upside is supposed to be that after a few years of low or no pay, you get the benefits of your advanced degree and rake in the dough. Entering grad school from a more established financial situation can be a huge benefit.

In the next sections, I'll share answers to some common questions: What if I'm in school, and second-guessing whether I should be? What if exercises 1–3 made me feel terrible, because I value some stuff but I *still* don't know what I want to do after grad school? (If that last one is you, I'm sorry. It can be downright maddening to feel unsure about the future—so there's a special section just on this topic. I hope it helps.)

Before that, however, I'm going to share the most important piece of advice in the chapter.

THE MOST IMPORTANT PIECE OF ADVICE IN THIS CHAPTER

You do not have to do the same thing forever.

Because that statement is so important, I'll say it again: *You do not have to do the same thing forever.*

It is unquestionably *okay* to change your mind about what you want to be doing—several times. Even after you're five years in and only a year away from a PhD. Even if you're five years post-school. Even if you've been in your career for twenty years, or more. A U.S. Department of Labor survey reported that people held, on average, ten different jobs before turning forty.[7] My dad, for instance, was an expert at the career change. His resume lists such things as ice cream scooper, owner of a punk rock recording studio, public relations spokesman for a big refinery, owner of a sailing school, and captain of a fancy billionaire's summer yacht. He was a great role model in that regard.

Values change. Opportunity costs shift. Unexpected events happen. People change what they are doing. It's important to be prepared—and the best offense, in this case, is a good understanding of yourself. I'll close out the chapter by giving you a list of questions to ponder that may help guide your decision making. My job is to give *you* resources. I want you to make the best decision you can for *you*.

WHAT IF I'M IN SCHOOL AND I'M SECOND-GUESSING WHETHER I SHOULD BE?

Do an online search for "how many people quit grad school" and you'll be inundated with articles about how quitting grad school isn't the end of the world—and in fact, how quitting can be a good decision in the right circumstances. Grad school isn't for everyone. You might discover that what you want to do doesn't require another degree. And that's okay! Lots of people are accepted to grad school. Some get a year, two years, even five years in, then leave without any new letters to tack onto their name. The experience of considering grad school, attending one semester or working at it for five years, might be exactly what you need to figure out that what you want or need to do next is something *else*.

If you're considering leaving, you're not alone. PhD programs in the United States have a 50 percent attrition rate,[8] and about 25 percent of PhD students leave in the first three years.[9] (This varies greatly by degree type, course of study, and specific university.)

It's not only PhD students leaving: 23 percent of STEM master's students left after two years, while MBA students had a 10 percent attrition rate.[10] After four years, 66 percent of STEM master's students and 86 percent of MBA students had received their degrees. Why the lower attrition for MBA students? Maybe they had clearer plans up front for how they intended to use their degrees. Master's students do tend to enroll in order to improve skills, or increase opportunities for promotion, advancement, or pay.

Common reasons to consider leaving school include the following: Grad school doesn't help you with your career and you want to switch to something else. You have a better opportunity coming your way. You have an unsupportive or abusive adviser. Your mental health is suffering. You can no longer afford to stay in school, or other financial stress. You have a new baby and want or need time off with your child (more common for women: after having a child, around 43 percent of women leave academia, compared to only 19 percent of men).[11]

In grad school, I heard about a past student from my research group, Jeff Lieberman, who was a researcher-engineer-artist. He was close to finishing his PhD when he received the opportunity to work on a big art-related project. Jeff had to decide: Take that opportunity and advance his career as an artist, or stick it out and get his doctorate? The was a once-in-a-lifetime opportunity—but so was his time in the PhD program. He had to decide what he wanted out of his career.

Which path would lead him where he wanted to go? Today, Jeff is not a doctor, but he *is* a highly successful artist.

Depending on the issue at hand for you, leaving may—or may not—be the right option. As Susan Basilla and Maggie Debilius wrote in *So What Are You Going to Do with That?*, "too many undergraduates head straight to grad school without a clear understanding of how few tenure-track jobs lie on the other side or of the debt they'll accrue along the way."[12] In the sciences, for instance, it can be a good idea to take a position in a related field (such as a lab tech or research assistant) for a year or two to help you figure out if you want to be in that science. Undergrad is a small slice of what's out there. Chapter 2 discusses career paths at greater length, and chapter 3 will walk you through grad school finances. Only you can decide which option is best for you. Consider all possible solutions before deciding. For example, you may be one of the many students struggling with mental health. Have you sought support or therapy? (See chapter 10.)

If your relationship with your adviser is a problem, skip ahead to chapter 5, "Advisers." If your concerns are financial, you're in luck: chapter 3, "Money and Logistics," talks financial woes. I cover mental health and work-life balance in chapters 10–12.

As Amanda Seligman wrote, students drop out of their programs for all kinds of reasons. Perhaps their intrinsic interest and curiosity in the topic has waned.[13] Perhaps they are attracted to higher-paying, more immediate work, perhaps they are leaving a bad adviser, or poor situation, or perhaps they have medical issues that mean a leave of absence or quitting altogether will be a better fit. She says, "Graduate school is not essential to anyone's life. Graduate school should be a pleasure, fun, interesting, and worth a student's time. When graduate school becomes just a grind and not a reward in itself, it is time to quit."[14]

RIGHT NOW, I THINK GRAD SCHOOL HELPS ME. BUT WHAT IF I CHANGE MY MIND LATER?

Everything changes. Change is the only constant. I will be the first in line to tell you that it's *really okay* to change your mind about your life or career goals. Change your mind multiple times! Even after you've been in school for five years! Even if you're five years post-school!

You change your mind when something happens to you, and your values or priorities change. That's normal. Honestly, you *should* change your mind about what's most important at least once in your life (and maybe more), because it means you're growing and changing.

As I've mentioned, one of my role models when it comes to career changes is my dad. His catchphrase was, "you don't have to do the same thing forever." And his resume reflects that. He didn't go to college. He got jobs and worked hard when he had to; he switched careers when he got bored and could make the switch work.

Maybe you're worried that going to grad school will lock you into a particular career path. You are not locked in. The skills you develop during a graduate program can open up other doors too. A PhD doesn't confine you to a professorship; an MBA doesn't restrict you to business. Depending on your field, it may take more, or less, effort to translate your expertise and experience into an "alternative" career—but it is doable, so long as you want to do the work to make it happen. Don't be discouraged.

If you change your mind later, revisit this chapter. Do the exercises again, reread the section about leaving grad school, explore the resources chapter for making a change.

WHAT'S IMPORTANT TO YOU CAN CHANGE: A STORY

When I entered my PhD program, I seriously considered pursuing tenure-track life. I'd lead cool new research, teach enthusiastic young people, pursue my burning questions. I had the requisite backlog of "future work" ideas. I was becoming adept at performing research in my field. I was committed to learning how to make better graphs and figures for every paper, and, get this, I even thought writing the first draft of a paper could be *fun*. (It's like putting together a puzzle! A fun puzzle made of bits of information!)

Then I had kids. It's a cliché, right? "After I had kids . . ." But the reality is, humans *are* mammals. There are some powerful biological mechanisms in place that mean we tend to care intensely about our offspring. Many of my priorities shifted.

I didn't suddenly decide that the pursuit of fascinating questions mattered not a whit in the face of baby gurgles. Rather, I recognized the humanity of my children and the deep-seated psychological need babies have for their mothers.[15] I could not, in good conscience, deprive my children of their mother during their most mother-needing, vulnerable time. "Family" had moved up to the top of my values list (exercise 2). So my husband and I reorganized our lives to center on our children, while still working on other things we cared about and making enough money to get by.[16]

That time in our lives involved numerous conversations about our values. My husband is a computer engineer; at the time, he was a part-time contractor and was working on a small, self-funded start-up. We realized that full-time, out-of-the-house work was not what either of us wanted. It was too strict. Instead, we wanted flexibility. We wanted to be able to take our son to the zoo on a Wednesday morning, take family vacations to the mountains in a random week in June, have picnic lunches at the park. Our income was a means to an end, not an end in itself. My research was fun and fascinating, but ultimately, if I had to choose between a tenure-track job and some other, more flexible arrangement that allowed me to spend more time with my kids, I'd pick the more flexible arrangement. And with that, I dropped the goal of being a full-time, tenured professor.

I began searching for opportunities that would advance my future flexible career. I enjoyed writing, so I attended a blogging workshop and wrote for MIT's graduate student blog. I wrote science communication articles about my research. I read books about negotiation, business sense, and managing money. I added a page to my website about possible consulting services I could offer. In short, I examined my values, and made sure my plan and my actions were in line with those values.

Before I move on, let's be clear: People leave the traditional academic pipeline for all kinds of reasons. Having kids is one reason. It's not the only reason, nor does having kids mean your priorities or life will shift as much as mine did. In addition, leaving full-time academia also does not mean you're out of academia for good. I still write papers as an independent scholar. Plenty of folks in industry do research and write papers. Some people leave academia and come back later—I had a computer science professor in college who had retired from IBM and, bored with retirement, decided to teach.

No matter what your background, your highest values, or your ultimate goals in life, if you want to do research, in academia or industry or for governments or independently, then do research. We need all kinds of people with all kinds of backgrounds and values doing research in all kinds of places. Different people will research different questions, in different fields, with different methodologies, and that is intensely valuable.

WHAT IF I STILL DON'T KNOW WHAT I WANT TO DO AFTER GRAD SCHOOL?

For some people, exercise 1 reveals that they don't know why they're in grad school or what they want to do with the degree when they're done. That's okay.

Some degree programs prepare you for specific careers. Others leave you with a remarkably open-ended future. For example, you might like research, but not know what research careers are out there. You might be unsure about choosing a job in academia versus industry versus government research. You might know you want to go into business with your MBA, but there are an awful lot of different jobs in business. If you're one of these people, here are a few ideas for figuring it all out.

First, you need to gather information. Your two best resources are (1) yourself, and (2) other people. By this, I mean that you should *(1) try new things* to determine what you enjoy doing and what you find fulfilling, and you should *(2) talk to other people* about their experiences doing different kinds of things.

Try New Things

Trying new things can take several forms. You can pursue new things independently. For example, pick up a nonfiction book at the library on a topic you know nothing about, read it, see if it interests you. Join a club to try out a new activity or volunteer to help with an event. Spend time thinking about what activities you find worthwhile and important. Helping people or animals in need? Engineering solutions to problems in the world? Making a lot of money so you can live the life you want?

You can try new things in a formal setting, such as a class, internship, or job-shadowing program. For example, in college, the reason I took my first computer science class was because one day, I looked at my laptop and thought to myself, *I don't know how you work at all*. I signed up for Computer Science 101. I was vaguely hoping that I'd learn something about the Magical Innards of Computers. I didn't—instead, I learned something about the Magical Incantations and Rituals for making little Java applications. I also learned that I find programming fun (usually), and that I'd probably enjoy further classes or work in that area. This contributed to my decision to pick a graduate program that included a heavy CS component (programming robots).

Depending on your graduate program and your personal situation, you may or may not have room for "extracurricular" classes that let you explore. If you do have room, fantastic. Take classes in novel areas. You can sign up for extra courses at your university, find an online course (many are free—see the chapter on resources), or take a class at a local community college or community center. If, after a few class sessions, you discover you hate it? Drop it. Try something else. Do keep in mind, however, that you may love a subject but dislike a particular professor, or love a professor enough to find any subject that person teaches interesting.

Internships can give you a good feel for working in a particular field or for a particular company. If you're currently enrolled in school, those summer months between semesters can be the perfect time. Some schools have fieldwork programs or internship programs built in. Taking a semester off, or even a year off, can also work for some. One of my friends spent a semester working at NASA, while one of my grad school labmates took two years off to work for a start-up before rejoining the lab. He gained a lot of useful experience and self-knowledge as a result.

Many internship programs require applications months ahead of time—anywhere from October of the previous year through May of the current year—so plan ahead. You'll need time to (1) find opportunities to apply for, and (2) actually apply, which may involve an interview or updating your resume or CV. There are many online databases of internship programs and summer research programs (see the resources chapter). If your university has a career development office or student careers office or career services office, they may be able to help you find opportunities as well as plan your application. Ask around.

Remember, if you do take a class, read a book, or find an internship, it's okay if you don't like it. Discovering that you *don't* like a particular field or a particular kind of work can be just as valuable as finding that you *do* like it. It helps point you in the right direction. It's also worth remembering that there are probably a lot of things you'd enjoy doing or would find fulfilling. You don't have to find *the best* one. You just need to find one.

Talk to People

You know lots of people. Those people know lots of people. Some of those people may hold jobs you're interested in, have careers in fields you're curious about, or might know other people who are looking for people to work for them. If you're thinking "Oh, right, networking," then bingo, you understand this section. But there's more to getting the most out of your network than just having conversations.

First, tell people what you're looking for. If they don't know, they can't help you or hook you up with opportunities they find. Are you looking for a specific internship? Information about a particular field? Are you hopelessly confused and need help? If your university has a student career services office, I'd suggest paying a visit. They have resources to help you—it is *literally* their job to have resources to help you.

Set up informational interviews. An informational interview is a brief conversation (often twenty to thirty minutes) during which you ask someone a bunch of questions about their job and their career trajectory, and then listen carefully to their stories. Most people are happy to chat about their lives; this is an easy way to learn about different jobs and fields. Chapter 2, "Career Plans," shares winning strategies for interviewing well.

If your university hosts a job fair, attend—even if you're not looking for a job. Ask recruiters what jobs are available and the skill sets desired to get an idea of what's out there.

In general, people *really like* talking about themselves. Use this to your advantage. Ask lots of questions: "So, what's your job like?" "Can you tell me more about what it's like to do X?" "How did you get to company Y?" "Why did you get interested in studying Z?" And so forth. Listen to the advice people share. (People also like giving out free advice.) You don't have to *take* any of their advice—not a word of it—but now and then, you might come across a truly useful gem of information.

Then What?

After learning about your options, stop evaluating which direction to go and just *go*. Maybe something you tried clicked and you're all set with your new career plan. If grad school is necessary for that career plan, great. If it isn't, great.

Maybe you like everything, and the sheer number of options is overwhelming. Or maybe you've concluded that *no* job will ever satisfy ... Okay, then, your options are to marry rich or find God. But seriously, in these cases, I would not suggest attending grad school. Instead, take a tolerable job that pays reasonably well in a location you don't hate near people you like. Go in *a* direction, at least for a while. If it seems okay, stick with it longer. If you hate it, move on. Reevaluate. Don't pick grad school simply because you have no idea what else to do, because, as I discuss in chapter 3, grad school isn't cheap, and the opportunity costs can be mountainous.

Remember, you don't have to do the same thing forever.

QUESTIONS EVERY STUDENT SHOULD ASK

In my third year at MIT, I remember leaning my elbows on the white table in a fluorescent-lit classroom with my cohort of PhD colleagues. My mug of tea was half empty already, but I could still smell the Earl Grey-scented steam. I took a sheet of paper from a stack being passed around. The paper read, "13 Questions Every PhD Student Should Ask."

The class was "prosem," the affectionate nickname for a semester-long seminar that my program required all PhD students take. This seminar was aimed at helping us understand what doing a PhD in the MIT Media Lab meant. We had read the Media Lab's founding documents; our professors had led informative Q&A sessions; and now we were in the midst of talking about what graduate research encompassed, what our expectations were (and what our professors' expectations were), and what the whole point of a dissertation was.

We read the question list. Then, we brainstormed our questions—whatever questions we thought we ought to answer before embarking on the long, arduous journey of the PhD. Prosem students did this exercise nearly every year.

EXERCISE 4: ANSWER QUESTIONS EVERY STUDENT SHOULD ASK

Here is the original list of thirteen questions, plus the best questions brainstormed by MIT Media Lab students. Answer some—they may help you clarify your purpose in graduate school.

13 QUESTIONS EVERY PHD STUDENT SHOULD ASK

1. What is the problem? What are you going to solve?
2. Who cares? Why do people care about this problem?
3. What have other people done about it?
4. Why is that not sufficient? What are the gaps and unanswered questions?
5. What are you going to do about it? (Approach)
6. What are you really going to do about it? (Methods)
7. What do you expect to find?
8. What did you find? (Findings)
9. What does this mean? (Conclusions)
10. So what? (Implications)
11. What are you going to do next?
12. Where are you going to publish?
13. What are you going to be doing in 5 years?

QUESTIONS FROM MEDIA LAB PHD STUDENTS

1. What do you want to learn?
2. What other skills should you be learning now?
3. Who should you interact with to learn more about your question, problem, or field?
4. How can you leverage resources around you?
5. What is the question or opportunity?
6. Why you—what uniqueness do you bring to your research?

7. Why do this in an academic environment?
8. Why is it not incremental? How are you changing the conversation?
9. What are some compelling examples that highlight the importance of this work?
10. What principles and values will guide your work?
11. Why will others be excited about it—how does it affect the world?
12. How can others build on your work?
13. How could you fail?
14. How do you define success?
15. Who do you want to share your work with and what's the best way to reach them? (Dissemination)
16. Do you have the right adviser to accomplish what you want?
17. Can you get this done in time? (Scope of work)
18. How can you balance your research with the rest of your life?

Source: "13 Questions Every PhD Student Should Ask," compiled by Professor Judy Olson, University of Michigan, for human-computer interaction graduate students.

ONWARD AND UPWARD

After this chapter, I hope you aren't feeling discouraged. The point of thinking about motivation, values, and life plans isn't to put you off from grad school, but to help you make sure you're going to grad school for a good reason. Time now could save your career or your family later.

The next smart steps are to think even more carefully about careers, and then to consider money and the logistics of attending grad school. These are the subjects of the next chapters.

chapter 2
Career Plans

Academia, or Not?

When signing off on my dissertation, one of my committee members told me, "Now we just have to get you a nice faculty position!" It was a nice sentiment, to be sure. The tenure track is the academic dream job: five to seven years as an assistant professor as you work toward tenure, then, if you're approved, lifetime job security. I appreciated that my academic mentors were invested in my career.

But at the same time, I heard the hidden assumption: that the academic track ought to be on my agenda. After all, I had previously expressed disinterest in launching a start-up immediately following graduation (pursuing a start-up was as common as candles on birthday cake among Media Lab grads). I was good at being an academic—research, publishing, mentoring undergraduates. So of course: academia it was. Or, failing that, perhaps a good industry research position. After all, what else was there?

CAREERS FOR ACADEMICS

In his book *Leaving Academia*, Christopher Caterine estimates that only 7 percent of people who enroll in PhD programs will eventually get a tenure-track professorship—and that's at any institution. Nine out of ten PhDs won't get tenure-track jobs. They'll do something else. Among STEM PhDs, one 2014 report suggested that 61 percent of STEM PhDs have nonacademic careers.[1]

If you're aiming to work at a leading institution, in the humanities for example, as low as 1.2 percent of doctoral students will get a tenure-track position. That's not very many. It gets worse: the academic job market, small as it is, is shrinking.[2] Fewer people are being hired as full-time faculty. Fewer students are graduating with job or postdoc commitments lined up.[3] From the late 1990s to 2017, the number of PhDs in tenured or tenure-track jobs fell from over 30 percent to just over 20 percent. In 2017, approximately equal numbers of PhDs landed jobs in the private sector (42 percent) as at educational institutions (43 percent—which includes postdocs and research scientists as well as tenured or tenure-track positions).[4]

Why the low number of professors? In large part, because universities are replacing full-time faculty with contingent faculty: non-tenure-track staff who may be hired full- or part-time, primarily to fulfill teaching and service duties.[5] They may be called lecturers, instructors, or adjuncts. Most are contract workers hired on a semester-by-semester basis to teach one or more courses—a precarious position with little stability, little job security, and generally no benefits such as health insurance or retirement plans. Tenure-track positions are decreasing, and 73 percent of college professors are now contingent faculty.[6]

Even if you squint at these statistics while turning your head sideways like an owl, they don't look promising. Realistically, probabilistically, you won't land a tenure-track professorship. You'll be doing something else.

Choosing to Leave, or Being Pushed Out?

Personally, my decision to leave academia was positive. I chose to leave because it aligned with my goals. However, for many who have their sights set on the academic world, leaving is difficult. If, like many academics, you love research, teaching, writing, and everything else that comes along with academic life (except maybe unpaid committee work), leaving that life can cause significant pain. This is especially true in the humanities, where PhDs and professorships are still seen as a calling rather than a career choice.[7] As Christopher Caterine argued, academics tend to see the tenure-track position as the sole determiner of happiness and success. This mind-set can lead to peer pressure from colleagues, who see leaving academia as failure.[8]

I don't want to dissuade you if your goal is to be faculty. Some PhDs do go that route. But approach that career path with your eyes open. Understand that despite all your hopes and dreams, you may not succeed at staying in academia. Willpower alone is not enough. There's too much luck involved and too much outside of your control—for instance, which schools are hiring and how many positions they are hiring for the year(s) you're on the job market, and who else in your field is on the market at the same time as you. Plus, there are inequalities entrenched in the academic hiring system—such as a penchant for hiring faculty from prestigious institutions.[9]

As discussed in the previous chapter, enter graduate school with a plan, even if you change your plan again later. Consider your options, whether in academia or out of it. Think about the obstacles you may face in achieving your career goals. Then work out how to overcome those obstacles—research shows that being optimistic about the future while also planning up front for how you'll tackle inevitable setbacks can improve your chances of success and improve your mental health.[10]

Before I discuss what will give you the best chance of meeting your career goals—whether in or out of academia—take a moment to think about what those career goals are.

EXERCISE 5: LIFE GOALS

1. What are your near-term goals for the next one to three years? What are your goals for the next five to ten years? Brainstorm a list of as many goals as you can. For example, you may want to finish your exams, pass a required class, teach a course, finish your dissertation, find a job, run a marathon, get married, have a baby, vacation in Spain, read two books for fun every month, start a blog, get in shape—your goals could span the entirety of your life.
2. Brainstorm constraints and concerns. For example, are you happy in graduate school? How's your motivation? How are your family and friends? Your life balance? Your finances? What does the job market look like in your field, in academia or out? What barriers are there to achieving your goals?
3. Reflect on what you've written. Do you have clear career goals? How might you overcome the barriers from step 2 to achieve your goals in step 1?

CAREERS IN ACADEMIA

Your professors during undergrad and graduate school are models for academic jobs, but depending on the institutions you've attended, that may not be the full picture. Different institutions require different amounts of teaching and research and have different expectations about how much external money faculty are expected to raise to support their research or salary (e.g., in the form of grants). Major research universities lean toward the "lots of grants, less teaching" end of the scale; liberal arts colleges and community colleges lean toward "more teaching"; regional colleges and universities are somewhere in the middle. Of course, these aren't the only factors that differ, just the most obvious—there are differences in prestige, departmental and school culture, service expectations, location, cost of living, support and community for you and/or your family, and so on. You'll want to weigh all these factors when deciding whether to pursue the tenure track, keeping in mind that, because of the scarcity of faculty jobs, you generally have to be less picky about where in the country you want to settle.

Numerous books explain the academic job-search process—check the resources chapter for a sampling of these. Rather than duplicate them, the focus of this section is on *why* you might choose an academic job, and some factors to consider along the way.

The Academic Job Market

Academic hiring is a long process that runs on an annual cycle. Jobs are typically posted over the summer or early fall, with applications due in November, since faculty are busy in December with end-of-semester finals. The applications are long: cover letter, CV, reference letters, writing samples, sometimes teaching statements or teaching portfolios, sometimes research statements, sometimes diversity statements, and multiple rounds of interviews. If you're a candidate on a university's short list, you may be invited to campus in the late winter or spring for an interview day, which can include meetings with colleagues, students, deans, and presidents; a presentation or job talk; tours of the campus; and informal dinners thereafter. Days or weeks later, you'll be told whether or not you got the job. (Probably. There are, unfortunately, known cases where university hiring committees simply ghosted the passed-over candidates.)

Up front, you'll need to set aside any arrogance you may have about how much better you are than other people on the market, because chances are, everyone who applies for the few positions available is equally well qualified. In addition, most hiring is done from within closed networks; the majority of faculty jobs go to alumni of a small set of prestigious institutions; and most fields have gender inequity in hiring.[11] Some jobs are only posted nominally; hiring committees may have someone in mind before the application process even starts. Sound bleak yet?

The process for finding an academic position varies across disciplines and departments. Positions may be posted publicly on the university website or online job boards, circulated on field-specific mailing lists, or spread by word of mouth. Ask your adviser and other professors you know in your field (and see the resources chapter).

Postdocs

In many fields, students complete one or more postdocs prior to getting a faculty position. A postdoc—which I was completely unaware of when I began grad school—is an intermediate job: someone who has finished their PhD and is now working with another professor or principal investigator (PI) to get more academic experience, training, and mentoring before running their own research group or lab.[12] Postdoc appointments are short-term contracts, usually one to three years long. Postdocs don't earn a lot; more than half earn less than $50,000; and 42 percent earn $50,000-$80,000.[13] Indeed, they are seen as a source of relatively cheap, highly skilled labor. In some STEM fields, there are higher-paying postdoc positions in government and industry labs. Postdocs primarily work on their PI's projects, since that's where the funding generally comes from; sometimes they also work on their own, related research.

Why do a postdoc? You're not going to get rich—the benefit must be in the additional training you receive and the connections you make that can advance your career. Peter Feibelman says when doing a postdoc, your goal is to finish a significant project in an area where you want to make your name, thus establishing your identity in that area in the research community and showing that you'll be a valuable colleague and faculty member.[14] You build up your CV with more publications, gain time to apply for funding or awards you need to start your own lab, and get specialized training in your subfield. Some people use postdocs as a time to switch subfields.

In STEM fields, doing a postdoc is almost required to become faculty. A 2020 *Nature* survey found that 48 percent of respondents had worked for three or more years as a postdoc, and many had completed two or more postdocs.[15] In the social sciences, arts, and humanities, however, postdocs often operate as a backup plan. If you go on the academic job market and fail to land a job, you may be able to find a postdoc to fill time while you wait for the next hiring cycle. That said, if you fail to land your desired academic job the first time around, Basalla and Debelius highly recommend pursuing a nonacademic job instead of a postdoc or adjunct job (see the next section).[16] It's a radical idea for someone looking to stay in academia, but you could earn more money (and pay down debt), live where you want to live, use your free time (which you will have!) to work on academic things if you want (like teaching a class or writing a paper), and then, when it's time to hire again, you can jump in the market—or decide you're happy where you are.

The chapter on resources lists places to search for postdoc positions. You can apply for postdoc funding on your own, or with your PI/postdoc supervisor, or they may already have funding available—you'll have to ask. If you want to postdoc immediately after defending, start looking one to two years out from your defense date.

What are the alternatives to postdocing? If you're not planning on being faculty, you can look for a job anywhere—more on that below. If you want to explore, then a fantastic option is a fellowship or internship in government, industry, or with a nonprofit. You'll gain work experience and build your network outside academia, which can lead to future jobs and opportunities.

Adjuncts

Adjuncts are also called ad hoc, contingent, or temporary faculty. They teach one or more courses on a semester-by-semester contract basis, at one or more institutions. Most people choose to adjunct if they think it will be temporary, a job to keep them busy or build up teaching experience on their CV while they go on the academic job market. That's a significant bet to make. Christopher Caterine explains the difficulty that many part-time faculty experience: over a quarter are recipients of public assistance in the United States; most receive no benefits or health insurance; most work long hours for low pay; most never receive the tenure-track job they desire. It's a precarious situation.[17]

However, some people choose to adjunct if they enjoy teaching. This can work if they have a partner with a stable job that provides benefits such as health insurance, if they have other work that pays the bills, or if they are employed at an institution that pays adjuncts well.[18]

Tenure Track

Tenure-track jobs are the academic dream. You are hired as an assistant professor. You spend five to seven years working on the Three Pillars of Academia: research, teaching, and service to the institution. At the end of those years, you undergo tenure review, during which you're evaluated by people internal to your institution as well as other researchers in your field on your contributions to the Three Pillars. If you pass review, you're granted tenure—that is, you're promoted to associate professor and you get lifetime job security. If you fail, you have to find a job elsewhere.

The requirements for being granted tenure vary across institutions, so check what specific activities, service, and publications are counted so you know where to focus your effort. You'll be establishing your own research agenda and research program, perhaps by applying for grants to support your work. You'll teach courses. You'll serve on committees, mentor students, and generally be a good academic community member.

Many people have written about the tenure process and their unique approaches to it; see the resources for further suggestions.

Professional and Administration

Universities also employ PhDs in many other positions: student affairs, admissions,[19] teaching and learning support, research administration, science and technical operations, research staff, institutional analysis and policy, publishing, libraries, program administration, and many more.[20] These jobs can be appealing because you're still in the university context, simply working at it from a different angle.

LEAVING ACADEMIA

Former academics, academic refugees, post-academics: whatever you call them, they went through some or all of graduate school and now have or are seeking careers outside the academy. These careers—variably named post-academic careers, alternative academic careers, or simply *careers* (#postac, #altac, #careerdiversity)—can be in any industry, or no industry at all. People who leave academia do wonderful, fulfilling work in research, business, nonprofits, government, policy, education, health care, arts administration, journalism, publishing, writing, media, life coaching, and consulting. Some become entrepreneurs, found tech companies, or start art or design studios. Some stay home with their families. Some work part-time, balancing unique situations (such as medical or caring duties) in their own unique ways. Many, especially those holding PhDs, report higher levels of job satisfaction than people who stayed in academia.[21]

Why Leave?

Why leave academia? Well, what keeps you there? What can you get from an academic career that you can't get elsewhere?

Many people are afraid that when they leave academia, they will leave behind intellectual work and academic interests, and that they will be constantly alongside people they think of as intellectually inferior. This is absolutely wrong. As Susan Basalla and Maggie Debelius explain, "few post-academics completely abandon their academic interests. Rather, they find creative ways to continue a trajectory that started long before graduate school. Instead of making a U-turn in the middle of their lives, most of these alumni followed up on a lifelong interest or a half-forgotten talent by traveling a parallel path to an equally fulfilling destination."[22] Outside academia, people frequently study obscure topics for the sheer joy of it during their downtime. Others have formed careers around generating ideas, solving problems, testing solutions, and other highly intellectual work. What you love about your academic work may also be realized working for a company, nonprofit, or museum.

If you have spent very little or no time away from the academy, how are your assumptions about outside life affecting the way you see a change of career? How much time have you spent with people who aren't academics? The vast, vast majority of jobs and people are not part of academia. Do you know anything about what they are like? Can you find out? For example, outside of academia, much work progresses at a faster pace.[23] The quality of work is different since the heuristic is often to get as much done as well as possible in a shorter time—but the upside is that you may feel like you are actually accomplishing something meaningful each day. Compensation will vary by role, but many government and industry jobs pay more than academic positions.

Because academia is often seen as a vocation rather than a career, many people worry that they don't know who they will be if they cease to be academics. They may be afraid of hurting their career by changing trajectory. When you've put so much time and energy into a dream of a career you love, it may feel like a significant failure to abandon that dream, even if there's something more lucrative you could be doing. But you can still leave—the sunk costs fallacy is sticking with a decision simply because you've sunk a lot of time and energy into it. Every former academic interviewed by Caterine or by Basalla and Debelius was happy they left. None regretted their decision. Some missed parts of academic life, such as teaching, but all of them appreciated their new jobs. Any pains around leaving or feelings of disappointment and failure eventually fade. It takes time to forge a new identity and figure out who you are, and this can be a challenging period of self-reflection and self-creation. But it can be worth it.

Are you facing pressure to stay in academia? Mentors who see a professorship as a vocation don't understand why you'd leave; they may outright tell you that you're throwing away your career. Or they may want you to stay to keep their department numbers looking good—women and minorities, in particular. You may be concerned that if you leave, you'll be just one more of the "leaky pipeline" statistics—for example, women are 19.5 percent more likely to leave academia than men.[24] And 43 percent of women versus 19 percent of men leave academia after having children.[25] Women are outnumbered at high academic ranks, despite often higher levels of productivity.[26] Will you be "lost to science" if you leave? There's pressure to stay and prove that you can make it.

But a reframe is needed here. If the issue in academia is one of retention—that women, and others, leave academia because it doesn't suit them or doesn't support them—then why stay? Many women, and other caregivers, desire flexibility; they may want or need to stay home full- or part-time.[27] Other careers and unconventional paths may suit them better (see chapter 13).

Fortunately, the conversation around career diversity has expanded in recent years. A plethora of books delve into alternative careers of all kinds (see the resources). Career diversity is more common in the sciences, likely because there is so much industry research that STEM PhDs can slide into. Among STEM PhDs I knew, even at the beginning of our graduate programs, equal numbers intended to join start-ups or pursue industry research as were interested in being professors.

Once you decide you're leaving academia, as Christopher Caterine points out, you have a great deal of freedom in deciding where to go, both in terms of what kind of career you seek, and where you live.[28] You can decide whether you want to go abroad, change states, move closer to family, or follow your partner to a new city. You can find a job doing something related to your research, or something completely unrelated. There may be a learning curve; you may feel like you're starting over on the bottom of the career ladder. Or you may immediately feel at home. Regardless, there is freedom.

As Bill Burnett and Dave Evans emphasize, there are many, many possible lives you could live, all of which could be equally satisfying to you.[29] How are you going to design your life to live coherently with yourself, your goals, your values, and your beliefs?

How Do You Decide?

What do you love about academia? What do you dislike? Notice when you are happiest, when you are most frustrated, the kinds of work that excites you, and the kinds of experience you want to avoid. Look inward. Assess your values and goals, as discussed in the previous chapter. Then, you can plan for the life and career that makes you feel most fulfilled.

There are numerous strategies to guide your observations. Christopher Caterine recommends a career journal. In the first entry, write about why you entered academia and how you feel about leaving it. What do you want out of life? What do you want out of a career? How can you best align the two?

Basalla and Debelius suggest making a pro/con list of everything you love and hate about academia. For example, you may love the flexibility, intellectual engagement, mentoring students, teaching, campus life. You may hate academic writing, the geographic limitations of academic work, grading papers, or the tenure system. What drew you to your current field of study? List experiences in your life that have given you the most joy, and what kinds of activities you did during those experiences. What do you do when no one is watching you? What are your favorite activities and hobbies? How do you procrastinate? Sometimes your choice of procrastination and distraction reflects your preferences, skills, or interests. Usually, what leads you into a post-academic job is not subject matter, but skill set. It's the things you like doing, the activities, and skills, that turn into future jobs. Not necessarily your passion for Chinese history, Romantic philosophers, or testing neuroscience theories on lab rats.

Burnett and Evans recommend keeping a "Good Time Journal" for a few weeks, in which you track when you're feeling engaged or disengaged and whether you're feeling energized or drained by every activity during your day. The goal is to discover what activities feed into a sense of flow and bring you energy, and which activities bore you and drain your energy. They use the AEIOU observation framework to consider different aspects of each activity that could feed into engagement and energy: activities or actions you take, environments you are in, interactions you have, objects involved, users or other people in the space.[30] Your goal is to end up with more engagement and more energizing activities, so you need to know which activities to keep or increase, and which ones need work.

Your mind-set matters. If you believe you won't be happy outside academia, you won't be. If you believe you can find interesting work, you will. Remember that it is also never too late to change careers—you don't have to do the same thing forever!—and a return to academia is possible later in life.

Keep an open mind. Don't limit your options by assuming your degree dictates the kind of job you must get. There are no rules! Yes, it may be harder to transition to some careers based on your starting point, but no career is completely closed to you.

How Do You Make Time for a Job Search?

People make time for the things that are important to them. If finding a job is important, there is time. As Basalla and Debelius explain, you may feel like your adviser owns all your hours, but they don't. They don't police the lab; they're too busy. You could use early morning, late evening, or weekend hours. If you have children, work when they are asleep, or involve them in the process. There's time; you just have to decide that exploring careers is more important than something else you could be doing. (See chapters 11-13 for more on life balance.) It may take a long time to find the right job—Caterine, for example, spent two years on his move from academia to a new job outside. Stick with it. It'll be worth it.

How Do You Find a Job?

Jobs are everywhere. The key is finding one that fits you. (I'm dwelling in more detail on the nonacademic job search process because graduate advisers and academic mentors may not be as helpful here.)

First, reframe. Burnett and Evans suggest reframing from "pursuing a job" to "pursuing job offers." It's a small but important difference, as it opens space for curiosity and authenticity: you're seeking out opportunities to evaluate offers rather than trying to mold yourself into a specific job description. Remember, careers most often develop in unexpected ways.

Then, prepare. Do your research and get your materials in order, such as a personal website and resume. After that, talk to people and try stuff.

Job Skills for Other Careers

Make no mistake, you are valuable outside academia. The work you do—research, writing, analyzing, and teaching—is valued. As Leonard Cassuto writes, "Ph.D.'s typically have an exceptional ability to organize and analyze large amounts of information. They understand the need to read and learn widely and deeply in order to understand something (including looking beyond the immediate subject area). And they can carry out that task with minimal supervision. They can manage long projects and work on their own—and of course their dissertations demonstrate their ability to finish these projects."[31] The key is communicating your value.

To make your skills and contributions clear, you need to learn *skill translation*—that is, how to translate your experience into the language of the business world in your resume, job application materials, and during interviews. The biggest pivot is from talking about *what* you did to talking about *why and how* you did it. Surprise: your dissertation is not, in fact, your most valuable asset outside of academia. Most people care more about your skills and interests than about the narrow topic you wrote so much about. Here are some examples.

Teaching. Teaching and training are applicable everywhere, in every field. Teaching experience translates into communication skills, such as public speaking, distilling complex concepts into simpler terms, delivering multimedia presentations to large groups of people, setting an agenda and leading discussions in meetings, and balancing stakeholder interests—those of students, department, the field, and yourself—when planning and teaching a course. Teaching uses mentoring skills, emotional intelligence, working with students in and out of the classroom, the ability to guide people during conversation, interviewing and diplomacy skills, and helping others design and execute projects.

Completing a dissertation. Working on your dissertation involves project-management experience, including detailing what you need to do to accomplish a complex, long-term goal, mapping requirements onto a schedule, attention to detail, and following through on the project with minimal oversight. It involves analytical and writing skills, such as making sense of complex information, learning new subjects quickly, assessing major areas of thought around a question or problem, conveying information efficiently, applying style guides, finding tools and determining whether those tools are applicable for the problem you're solving, resource allocation and budgeting, assessing results, and highly specialized techniques related to your specific field, such as lab skills, proposal or grant writing, designing experimental protocols, and using particular equipment or machinery.

You can translate taking courses into a love for learning, since every field requires you to learn new things to stay on top of novel developments. Service on committees or experience organizing professional meetings, workshops, or panels can be translated into a slew of organizational and interpersonal skills. Managing a course website can translate into technical and web-design skills.

> **EXERCISE 6: JOB SKILLS**
>
> Begin your list of experiences, skills, and qualifications. Once you have this foundational material, you can massage it into a resume. This exercise is adapted from Basilla and Debelius.
>
> 1. List every activity you've ever done: everything academic, summer jobs, internships, temp jobs, part-time work, full-time work, work studies, volunteer positions, contract gigs, and so on. Also list what you do on a daily basis currently, such as being a teaching assistant or being a research assistant.
> 2. Describe each activity in as many ways as possible. What tasks do you perform during these activities? What tools, techniques, or methodologies do you use?
> 3. Write down skills associated with each task. List both broad and specific skills. Include computer programs you've used (you don't have to list how *well* you've used them!).
> 4. Now, use this material when creating a resume.

Prepare Materials: CV to Resume

Most jobs outside academia require a resume, not a CV. These are two completely different formats for explaining your relevant experiences—a resume is not a CV scrunched up into one or two pages. A CV is self-oriented. It showcases *what* you've accomplished: your credentials; work history (both academic and nonacademic); publications; awards and honors; conference presentations and speaking experience; teaching experience; and service to your department, university, or discipline. A resume is an other-oriented, persuasive document that highlights your work history, skills, and accomplishments in a way that convinces someone else you'd be valuable on their team. Resumes are commonly organized into a reverse chronological list of your work history—useful if you do, in fact, have relevant work experience—or in a skills-based format, which can be useful if you've had an unusual career path or are pivoting in your career.

Christopher Caterine says the challenge is showing that you're neither over- nor underqualified. You want to convince your resume readers that you're not only a narrow subject-matter expert and that your academic experience is a bonus, not a downside. The best way to do that is to focus on how you work, not what you work on. Be brief and write concise summaries. Focus on knowledge areas and skill sets. Demonstrate value by using concrete examples and vivid verbs. Don't list every course you've taught when simply saying that you've taught college-level classes will do. Cherry-pick experiences too. A resume is not meant to be exhaustive. Pick the most interesting and relevant bits of experience for the particular job you are applying for.

A resume is accompanied by a cover letter, which is generally the first thing potential employers read. Keep it short and simple—less than a page. Highlight a couple key experiences related to the job you are applying for; don't talk about your choice to leave academia. The goal is to sell yourself as having relevant experience and interest in the job.

Solicit feedback on your resume and other application materials from people you know. Reach out to career counselors at your university—most institutions have some kind of career center for students. They can give you advice on the kind of language you want to use, how to present yourself, even how to format a resume to make it easier to read. Try to ask at least a few people outside academia for feedback too. Finally, to really dig deep into the nitty-gritty of translating your academic experience into relevant, brief, compelling summaries for a resume, see the resources chapter.

Your Public Persona

How are you presenting yourself on your personal website and on any public social media accounts? What story are you telling about yourself? Are you consistent?

If you don't have a website, consider setting one up. There are many website-building platforms that make it easy. You can showcase your work and talents, such as writing, coding, graphic design, or photography. Academics tend to highlight publications; outside academia, focus on skills and projects. Having an online presence can be useful in the job market. You can share all your professional accomplishments in one place and make it easy for potential employers to find out who you are and what you've done.

In all your public-facing media, it's never a bad idea to stay positive and polite—there's enough anger and vitriol online already. Finally, there's no need to relate all your content to your work—we're all human and have lives too! Talk about hobbies, interests, friends, and family to your heart's content.

Talk to People

Your network is your key to a job. Up to 85 percent of jobs are filled via referral or networking.[32] Burnett and Evans argue that talking to people is *the* way to get job offers. Sheer number of resumes sent out? Nope, not a success metric. Offers in hand are what you're aiming for. Even if you customize your cover letter and resume, applying to tons of online job listings won't get you many hits. Plus, many interesting jobs at large companies, as well as most jobs at small businesses, are rarely posted publicly—at least not until after trying to fill them via word of mouth and internal social networks.

Expand your network by having conversations with interesting people.[33] This technique, known variably as an informational interview, a journalistic interview, or a life-design interview (search these terms for more techniques and tips), involves reaching out to people who interest you and asking if they'll meet you for half an hour to tell their story while you buy them a cup of coffee. Then meet, ask questions, and listen. Because these interviews are framed around hearing someone's story, not you looking for a job, many people are amenable to them. People like talking about themselves and how they got where they are. Most people are, at heart, helpful; they want to share their perspective and advice.

Who Do I Interview?   Find people whose careers or lives you want to emulate. Search through your undergraduate and graduate institutions' online alumni databases (not all have them, but many do). At every interview, explicitly ask for suggestions for other people to talk to. People may also spontaneously offer to connect you to other people.

How Do I Contact Them?   Ideally through a mutual acquaintance or a referral. Barring that, email is fine. Keep it brief. Introduce yourself, offer a sentence about how you found them or how you're connected, ask if you can chat with them about their journey to where they are today. That's it.

What Do I Ask? Here's a list of questions you can ask at this kind of interview:

1. How did you get to where you are now? What was your career path like?
2. How did you get the necessary expertise for the work you do now?
3. What skills do you wish you'd had before you started this work?
4. Tell me about a typical workday.
5. What do you like and dislike about your work and life?
6. How do you find balance between work and the rest of your life?
7. What have other people in positions like yours gone on to do later?
8. What steps would be involved in someone like me exploring how to be a part of your organization or company? (Or something similarly open-ended.)
9. Who else should I talk with to learn more about this company/field/job/area?

Asking about balance is important because you want to get a sense of whether their career and work is possible with the particular life balance you're aiming for. Some people love their careers, but at the expense of everything else.

Burnett and Evans say question 8 from the list above is critical for job offers. Because it's open-ended, it allows the interviewee to suggest not only jobs currently open at their workplace, but other opportunities that might lead in that direction or that might be similar. For example, they might tell you their company isn't hiring, but this other, similar one is, and they can connect you to someone they know there.

Caterine reminds us that your interviewee will ask questions about you, your story, and where you're going. It's worth developing your personal elevator pitch: who you are in a sentence, why you're considering switching careers, and why you're interested in what they are doing. Keep it short and sweet.

Finally, don't forget to thank every interviewee for their time! Try to send a follow-up thank-you note within a couple days of your meeting.

EXERCISE: SET UP AN INTERVIEW

1. Find someone you'd like to interview about their career.
2. Reach out! Set up the interview! Use the suggestions above to guide your questions.

Try Stuff

Hands-on experience via job shadowing, an internship, a part-time job, or even volunteer work can give you a taste of different career paths. You may have an opportunity to pursue one of these options during the summer as an undergraduate or graduate student. During my senior year of college, I was undecided about grad school, so I sought out a research position for the following year that I thought could give me the experience I needed to decide.

Not everything you try has to be clearly related to your future career. Pursue hobbies, campus clubs and tutoring, and other interests. Sometimes, careers go in unexpected directions and one of your other hobbies will turn into a career. You'll gain new skills, ideas, and experiences from anything you explore.

Job Interviews

When you do find yourself in a job interview, remember that interviews are two-way events. Basalla and Debelius say you need to prove you can do the job, while the organization wants to determine whether you are a good fit. You also need to find out whether you *want* to do the job.

Do your homework up front: find out as much as you can about the job and company before the interview. Practice your brief self-introduction, prepare answers to standard interview questions (you can find lists of typical questions online, or you can ask at your university's career center). Prepare questions for your interviewer, like these, adapted from Basalla and Debelius:

1. What are the biggest challenges you face in your position, and what are ways you address those challenges?
2. How could the person you hire help solve those challenges?
3. What do you see as the greatest threats or opportunities for this organization as a whole in the next ten years?

For a first interview, focus on big-picture questions, such as how you will fit into the organization and how you can help them, rather than delving into whether they are the absolute perfect fit for you.

Negotiation

Everything is negotiable in the business world: your salary, your benefits, relocation expenses, the flexibility of your hours, even some responsibilities and the promotion path. For example, the organization is likely to offer a salary that is *less* than they would be willing to pay. Look online to find out what appropriate salaries in the field are. The key is to approach a negotiation in a friendly, constructive way—how can we make this work for both of us? For a fantastic, engaging primer on negotiation, I highly recommend *Never Split the Difference* by Chris Voss—see chapter 5 for a short overview.

INTERNATIONAL STUDENTS

The advice in this chapter about building a career should be applicable even if you are an international student. The primary differences will have to do with immigration laws and regulations around employment eligibility and work visas. You may have already talked to someone like a director of international services at your university, but if you haven't, now would be a good time to start. They can guide you to the relevant information.

International students, as well as students from minority or underprivileged groups, may feel out of their league when it comes to communication and interpersonal skills, especially if English is a second language or if their home culture is very different. They may engage in code-switching to speak in academic language or business language, especially if they were not raised in a family of academics, or if they come from a working-class family. Honestly, there's no magic cure that will make a student feel comfortable. It takes time and practice, and no small amount of faking it 'til you make it. (See the section on imposter syndrome in chapter 4.)

GAINING NEW EXPERIENCE AND FINDING TIME

During your job search, you may find you don't have the necessary skills or experience to get the job you want, in academia or out. In chapter 4, I describe the learning mind-set and how to get the experience you need—through classes, online courses, professional training programs, certifications, volunteering, part-time employment, personal creative work, and more.

Remember, the same life won't suit everyone. Whether you stay in academia or leave, whether other people are disappointed with your choices or offer their full support—you are the person living your life. And you are the person who needs to be satisfied with how you live it.

chapter 3
Money and Logistics

My first semester started in less than a month, and I didn't know where I was going to live. I was visiting Boston for a few days trying to find a place. I'd lined up showings at a dozen apartments—I'd been told to search near the red line train, because it had stops at either end of MIT's campus, but beyond that, I only knew a scant handful of facts about different Boston neighborhoods and where the "good" places to live were—all sourced from Wikipedia. Most of the showings got canceled. The places had already been rented.

I wasn't thrilled about moving to a city where it was hard to find a place to rent, let alone an *affordable* place. Boston came in hot as the fourth most expensive city in America (behind New York, San Francisco, and Honolulu). Typical rent was over $2,000 per month. I couldn't afford that. Grad students aren't known for making bank. Not even in STEM fields, not even at Ivy League schools, not even with full funding or fellowships. Plus, most places in Boston required a *huge* chunk of cash up front: first month's rent, last month's rent, and a security deposit. No way could I afford that for a more expensive place.

I went to the few showings I could set up. After two days of despair, I talked to a realtor. In Boston, a good chunk of the market was rented via realtors, who generally took a month of rent as payment for finding their clients a tenant and finding you a place to live. The realtor drove me to a couple places: a shoebox on the third floor of a big apartment building, a couple blocks from a train stop; another shoebox; a second-floor apartment with the landlady downstairs, a mile from the closest train stop but in the right price range. Plus, it had wood floors and bay windows. I took it.

Finding housing isn't the only financial challenge grad students face, but you *should* have a roof over your head and enough to eat, no matter what school or program you're in. If you manage your money well, you may even be able to save up for your future. Let's talk shop.

PAYING FOR SCHOOL, OR BEING PAID?

First, costs. Let's assume you've been admitted to a school. Yay! You pay tuition to the school: for a master's degree, on average, $66,340, for a doctoral degree, $114,300.[1]

But that's not everything—you've also got living expenses, such as rent, groceries, childcare, health care, commuting, the occasional night out, and so on. Is this sounding expensive yet? It should.[2]

In this scenario, summarized as "you pay for everything yourself," you're paying money out of pocket for tuition and all your living expenses for the duration of grad school. This money has to come from somewhere—perhaps your savings. Maybe student loans. Forty-eight percent of people with PhDs have student loan debt from graduate school, carrying an average of $111,702. Sixty percent of people with master's degrees owe student loan debt too, carrying an average of $55,351.[3] If you're in a graduate program part-time, you may still be working, so you can use the money you earn to pay for all this. Or you may have a partner who rakes in the dough, and who is supporting your schooling.

Graduate Assistantships

Fortunately, that's not the only scenario. As Amanda Seligman writes, "The standard advice for doctoral students . . . is not to enroll in a Ph.D. program unless someone else . . . is financing their education and underwriting their basic living expenses."[4] The mission of universities is to produce research. Producing research is easier with relatively cheap labor—that is, graduate students. In STEM fields, graduate students conduct the majority of the actual *work* of research. Thus, universities have some systems in place to ensure they keep that cheap labor while you get, well, not quite as broke as you would have been otherwise. The most common setup is a research assistantship or teaching assistantship, in which you perform research or teach classes for the school—more details in chapter 6—and they pay for some or all of your costs. Their payment may include some or all of your tuition, a stipend (i.e., money paid out from the school to you to help cover living expenses), and benefits such as health insurance, subsidized subway passes, access to campus sporting or gym facilities, or even subsidized or on-campus childcare.

Research assistantships are more common in STEM fields; teaching assistantships are more common in the humanities and liberal arts. Both are more available for students in doctoral programs than for students in master's programs. Stipends average $36,390 per year,[5] but the range is wide, anywhere from $6,000 to $50,000 or more—it varies by institution, program, and location.[6] Some assistantships are part-time, such as ten hours/week for a smaller stipend and half of your tuition paid; some are full-time, such as twenty hours/week and all your tuition paid.

How do you get a graduate assistantship? These positions are most commonly offered during the admissions process as part of your admissions package. You may have to fill out an additional form or write an extra essay when you apply to be considered for a position. Some programs do not finance first-year students, saving their resources for students who have "proven" themselves.

Funding availability varies. STEM programs often have more funding. Humanities, well, it depends. You're likely to go into debt for law school or medical school, as well as for many master's programs. Talk to students and administrators in the program you're entering to get an idea of what's typical.

Fellowships, Grants, and Scholarships

The third option is to obtain a fellowship, grant, or scholarship. Usually, you submit applications to external funding organizations, including government bodies such as the National Science Foundation, the National Institutes of Health, and the Department of Defense, nonprofits, private companies such as Microsoft and Facebook, or your employer (many companies will finance continuing education for their employees); you may also apply for internal funding from your own university. If the organization likes your application enough and thinks you and/or your research have merit (and even this involves a lot of luck, as it turns out, not just skill in applications), you get some money, paid out on a schedule (e.g., monthly, semesterly), that you can use to cover costs such as tuition and living expenses, traveling to conferences or field sites, paying for access to data sets, or spending semesters working on your research instead of teaching. You may have to submit reports or take employment in exchange for the money. Often, your school helps administer and pay out these funds; if it does, the school keeps a percentage of the money to cover its costs. Some schools give fellowships to particularly promising students.

What's the difference between fellowships, grants, and scholarships? A scholarship is the most general. It's money awarded to you, based on merit, need, or some other qualifying factor (it could even be the result of an essay contest), that you can use to pay for your schooling or living expenses. It always involves money. You don't have to repay the money—it's akin to a grant, not a loan.

Grants also provide money, but they're more specific—they're usually investments in specific research projects or even particular parts of a project. Many professors, for example, fund their research using external grants, covering the costs of equipment, personnel, and even parts of their own salaries.

Fellowships are more about investment in you as a person and researcher, rather than investment in a particular research project—money you get from organizations to pursue your specific academic interests. But they don't always involve money; they may provide networking, mentoring, and personal support. Some give you an affiliation with an institute or university, or opportunities to work on certain topics or with certain organizations without receiving money from them. Fellowships are almost always merit-based. You are frequently required to submit yearly reports on your progress through school. Many have other strings, such as a commitment to work for the organization during the summer for an internship or after school for some number of years, or a requirement to carry out a particular research project, but on the whole, they have fewer rules and constraints than grants.

Fellowships, grants, and scholarships let you focus more energy on your own research, rather than on someone else's. Money and time can be traded for one another. With more funding, you may even be able to pay other people to do tedious or "shallow" work, such as transcribing interviews, allowing you to use your energy on the things only you can do.[7] That said, if your goal is to become a university professor, then some of these other activities, especially teaching, can be useful career preparation.

While some fellowships have stipulations that you cannot take another major fellowship at the same time, many funding options are not mutually exclusive. Often, the money received by working for a school as a research assistant (RA) or teaching assistant (TA) is not sufficient to cover all your living expenses. The addition of a fellowship or outside work can top it off (e.g., other teaching, consulting, a side hustle).

I was lucky that my graduate program at the MIT Media Lab provided tuition, a stipend, and health insurance in return for students working as research assistants. The stipend was adjusted each year to reflect the increasing cost of living in Boston, and was just enough for a thrifty student to make do. When my husband's self-employment and consulting income was added on top, we were comfortable—but instead of spending his income, we saved and invested it, because we had a dream of someday owning a home and having a little garden in our own backyard.[8]

WHEN SHOULD YOU APPLY FOR FUNDING?

You have two options: you can apply for funding when you apply to graduate school, or you can apply after you've enrolled. They're not mutually exclusive. Personally, I did both. I applied for a handful of big fellowships when I applied to graduate school, since I knew if I got one, it would give me more options—for example, I might be able to attend a school that I couldn't otherwise afford. After that fellowship ran out, I applied for other funding. I also applied for various travel scholarships to support conference travel.

Applying early can double the number of applications you need to submit in an already stressful application season (more essays, more forms, etc.). Most academic fellowship applications are due about the same time as graduate school applications, in the late fall or early winter. But if you know funding is going to be a critical factor in determining which school you attend, or whether you can attend at all, then it's worth applying early. You also get an extra shot, since if you don't get the fellowship you're hoping for, you can often apply again the following year.

Or you can wait. Many fellowships let you apply in your first year or two of graduate school. You'll have a stronger application, a clearer research plan, and, hopefully, more guidance and feedback on your application materials from your adviser or campus career center. Your adviser may also know of appropriate funding sources for your field that aren't widely advertised. I had several friends who applied for fellowships in their first or second years to great effect.

Regardless of when you apply, I recommend finding someone in the academic world who can advise you—a previous undergrad mentor, a potential supervisor, a graduate student friend. Ask about the best funding options for your field and for feedback on all your application materials—especially your research plan and other essays. When asking for feedback, make sure you give them enough time to respond. No one likes last-minute requests. Also factor in time for revision based on the feedback.

Personally, I did not seek much guidance; mostly, I read articles online and looked at sample application essays people shared. I tracked everything I applied for in a spreadsheet. Jessica Calarco recommends tracking the names of what you're applying for, eligibility requirements, the amount of the award, deadlines, application materials required, who you're getting to write your recommendation letters and whether they've received or responded to the request, and links to the agency providing the funding.[9] Pay attention to the timeline and deadlines—you miss a deadline and you're out. Ask for recommendation letters way in advance. Plan to submit the application at least a day or two before the deadline in case you have technical problems with the application website. Put effort into the essays—make sure you tell a compelling story (see chapter 9).

I adapted my grad school admissions essays for the fellowship applications. Having heard that the research plan was especially important, I poured energy into crafting a solid research plan, even though I knew it probably wasn't what I'd end up researching, since at that point, I had no idea who my PhD adviser would be. I was lucky enough to be awarded an NSF Graduate Research Fellowship. Luck is huge. Like with graduate applications, there are more qualified applicants every year than there is funding. Some of the decision comes down to chance. You may not get lucky, and that sucks. However, many successful, amazing scientists and researchers didn't get prestigious fellowships in graduate school. It's not what defines a good researcher.

The resources chapter contains links to databases of fellowships, articles about applications, and more. Good luck!

HEADS UP: LOANS, STIPENDS, TAXES

Fellowships, scholarships, stipends: in the United States, these are taxable income. Depending on how the money is paid out to you, you may receive a W-2 (i.e., a tax document showing how much money in wages an employer paid out to you and how much money was withheld to cover other taxes, such as social security). Or you may not, which means you'll have to pay quarterly estimated taxes. Be sure to research this early, because there are financial penalties if you don't pay your estimated taxes on time. There may also be tax credits you can get for education or for your student loan payments. The U.S. tax system is complicated, so it's worth investigating up front to ensure yours are handled correctly. Consult the resources for places to get more information.

In addition, check when any loan payments are due, and stay on top of payments. If you're carrying student loans from undergrad, you may be able to defer payments until you're out of grad school too. But check whether interest keeps accruing; if it does, I recommend putting money toward payment now, even if you aren't required to, just to keep the amount you have to pay back lower. For some loans, the federal government will pay interest while you are in school, so you can safely ignore them until you graduate.

BUDGETING

You may already keep a close eye on your finances. Or you may wing it every month, noticing money disappear as you pay bills, but not really caring so long as everything gets paid for. I admit, I started out more like the latter. I had enough income to cover living expenses, so I didn't pay too close attention to exactly how much money went to everything. My account was in the green; that was good enough, right?

Wrong. While you *can* get by like that, you won't *prosper*. You won't buy a house when you graduate—which might sound improbable, or downright ludicrous, but that's what I did. Eight months before I handed in my dissertation, my husband and I flew cross-country to house hunt. We arrived in Idaho on a Tuesday, twenty-month-old son in tow. We crashed at my mom's place (our goal was to live near family, in a family-friendly town, with a cost of living lower than in Boston). The next morning, a realtor took us on a whirlwind tour of house after house after house. The market was racing. Half the houses we lined up to see were already under contract before we could tour them. Then we found one: a nice three-bedroom with a verdant yard and the *perfect* spot for my future garden. We put in an offer.

On average, it takes over a month to close on a house, mostly due to the processing time for the mortgage loan. At the end of our two-week trip, we held the keys to our new abode. How? We paid cash. A deal can close like a cheetah if you pay cash—no loans to process. We combined frugal living, saving, and investing with my husband's non-grad-student income to go from a couple hundred dollars in the bank to the $200,000 we needed for our first house. Without our miserly money mind-set, we could have easily blown through his income too.

If you want a chance at meeting financial goals, such as buying a future house, paying off your debts and living debt-free, or even saving for retirement, the first step is to live within your means and track your money. That's called budgeting.

Budgeting doesn't have to mean clipping coupons or carefully dividing your paycheck into envelopes earmarked for different bills (though the envelope system *can* help some people succeed). Budgeting just means tracking how much money you get, from where; and how much money you pay out, to whom. That way, you can easily see where your money goes, which expenses may be unnecessary, how much you spend, and how much is available to save or invest.

Evaluate your budget early in your graduate career—before you apply if you can!—because you need to know whether you can afford graduate school. While you *may* get the funding you apply for, there's no guarantee. Rejection is a staple of academia. If you can't afford school, you need to make alternate plans.

Some top-rated budgeting apps are listed in the resources. Try them out and see which you like. Or maybe you get lucky and your spouse, like mine, decides that budgeting apps don't cut it, and so learns how to use accounting software himself (e.g., GnuCash). Then decides he likes accounting. And even subscribes to an accounting podcast.

But you don't have to be that rigorous. Even a basic budget will get you pretty far.

EXERCISE 7: MAKE A BUDGET

1. Pick a budgeting method. A simple spreadsheet will suffice, or you can try a budgeting app.
2. Identify monthly income. Where does your money come from? List all wages, tips, stipends, side hustles. For example, you may receive $1,000 per month as a stipend from a fellowship, plus $200 from tutoring. Or you may receive $1,200 from your teaching assistantship and your spouse gets $2,300 a month from their job.

3. Estimate monthly expenses. Write down the amount spent on the items listed below in each of the past three months. Add up the three months and divide by three to get the average. Use this average as your estimated monthly expense for that item. For example, you may have spent $25.43 on your gas bill last month, $22.02 the month before that, and $26.80 the month before that. Added up, that's $74.25, which divided by three is $24.75 per month.

   You can use more than three months if you'd like a more accurate average, but three is respectable.

   Feel free to add additional categories below if there's something you feel is missing!

   a. Housing
      i. Rent or mortgage
      ii. Property taxes
      iii. Housing upkeep
   b. Utilities (if you rent, you likely don't pay all of these separately)
      i. Phone
      ii. Internet
      iii. Water/sewer
      iv. Trash
      v. Oil
      vi. Gas
      vii. Electric
   c. Transportation
      i. Car payment
      ii. Gas
      iii. Bus or subway or train tickets
      iv. Vehicle upkeep (bike, car)
      v. Parking permits
   d. Food
      i. Groceries
      ii. Dining out
      iii. Drinks

e. Childcare
   f. Health care
      i. Health insurance
      ii. Ongoing medication expenses
   g. Pets
      i. Pet food
      ii. Pet sitters
      iii. Pet supplies
      iv. Vet bills
   h. Other debt payments
      i. Student loans
      ii. Medical debts
      iii. Other
   i. Stuff (clothes, shoes, gifts, etc.)
   j. Other

4. Using your estimated expenses, you can plan for how much money you will spend next month.

Evaluating Your Budget

Now you can see the money coming in and the money going out. Hopefully, the first number is higher than the second. If not, big red flag! First, evaluate whether all your spending is necessary—which spending is for *needs* versus for *wants*? If, even after you cut any optional spending (and you may have very little optional spending), you still come out losing money, don't panic. Grad student stipends aren't exactly designed with getting rich in mind, let alone getting by. We'll talk below about how to cover the shortfall.

If you make more money than you spend, fantastic. That means you have money available to save. The first pile of savings to aim for is an emergency fund: enough cash to pay for three to six months of expenses. Use your budget to estimate how much money you would need to cover such a period. Set that money aside in a savings account. Some people like to set up a separate savings account just for their emergency fund, to ensure they don't touch it unless there's an actual emergency, while other people feel comfortable keeping everything together in the same checking or savings accounts. It's up to you.

After you have your emergency fund, then you can begin using money for other goals, such as paying down debt, or saving for a future car or house. In my case, after I had an emergency fund, my husband and I began investing whatever little bits of income we could, saving up for that future house. The resources point to a couple good primers on investing.

What to Do If Your Budget Doesn't Add Up

If you're not adding in a partner's or spouse's income, chances are, money is tight. Unfortunately, situations where students worry about paying for both rent *and* food in a given month are not uncommon.[10] That's one reason we spent so much time in the previous chapter thinking about whether graduate school was, in fact, your best option to get the career or life you want. So, if you want to make graduate school work, what can you do?

Can you find a cheaper place to live? Unfortunately, time and money are often traded for one another, so cheaper housing usually comes with the cost of a longer commute, a less desirable neighborhood, and/or more roommates. If it means you can eat, though, it could be worth it. I lived farther from campus than most of my colleagues, but I paid less in rent too.

Can you increase your income? Some students add a side hustle: consulting, coaching, tutoring, additional teaching, babysitting, editing, delivering pizza. The *Personal Finance for PhDs* podcast, listed in the resources, has fantastic interviews with graduate students about how they found and managed side hustles (some of which turned into full-time jobs!). Some graduate programs make you sign an exclusivity statement saying you won't take other employment while enrolled (mine did), so double-check that before seeking a second income. Since I wasn't allowed to have a side hustle, my husband worked extra hard to up his income, essentially taking on the side hustle for us both.

Can you get help from family, friends, or local or federal programs? There are state-level and federal-level assistance programs in the United States to provide access to health care, food, and other basic necessities. You may be eligible for Medicaid, SNAP (the Supplemental Nutrition Assistance Program), WIC (nutrition assistance for women, infants, and children), or other programs—an online search will help you find what's available in your state. Public libraries often have toiletries available. Join a local Buy Nothing group. If you're in a college town, you may find free items on the sidewalk at the end of the spring semester when students leave. If you have a part-time job, you may be eligible for some benefits, such as employer-subsidized health insurance, which may be cheaper than paying for student health insurance.

You may be able to visit food banks and women's centers in your city, or your institution may have a food pantry. Sometimes local farmers markets will sell produce at reduced prices just before closing; if you or a friend work at a grocery store or restaurant, you may be able to take leftover food or purchase food at a discount. You may also find resources, advice, and assistance from your campus's counseling center or the campus ministry. If you are pregnant or have a young child, you may be able to seek assistance with diapers, formula, and other basic baby supplies from local pregnancy resource centers or churches. Also, talk to your campus financial aid office to see if there are any options you haven't yet explored for covering costs.

MONEY PRAGMATICS

Who to Live With and Where to Live

Once you've thought about your budget, it's easier to answer pragmatic questions about attending grad school. Let's start with housing.

Housing ideally makes up 25–30 percent or less of your budget. Realistically, it may be up to half or more—it was for me. Housing impacts many other costs, such as utilities, transportation, and local amenities such as schools and grocery stores.

Housing has two parts: who you live with, and where you live. The logistics of *who* you live with may already be decided: You may be married with a family, cohabiting with a partner, caring for an elderly relative at home, or raising one or more kids as a single parent. Or perhaps you're on your own and wondering whether you ought to find roommates to keep costs down.

Who you live with provides constraints on *where* to live. Are you staying in your current location, or relocating? Perhaps you've chosen to apply to suitable graduate programs nearby so you can stay near your child's current school, or so your partner can stay in their current job. But for most people, attending grad school means relocating.[11] You may have applied to schools all over the country, or perhaps you've restricted your applications to schools near family or near certain medical centers that can provide specialized treatment for you or someone you're responsible for. Either way, picking up your life and taking it somewhere else can be daunting.

What's the cost of living? Cities are more expensive; suburbs and small college towns in the literal middle of nowhere are cheaper. While some schools in cities will compensate for higher costs of living by providing higher stipends (mine did), you can't count on it. Also consider the tradeoffs: For instance, what will your commute be like? Housing farther away from campus can be cheaper, but the commute may take more time and money. Jessica McCrory Calarco, in *A Field Guide to Graduate School*, explains how she ultimately decided to attend a school an hour from her parents' house so that she could save on costs by living at home, even though it made her commute much longer.[12]

Will you be able to afford living near campus for the duration of your educational journey? Even if you're entering a degree program near where you already live, you may be taking a pay cut to do so, which affects your overall housing budget—can you stay where you are, or will you need to find somewhere cheaper? And will you have to move again after you graduate to pursue your career? Go back to chapters 1 and 2 and look at your career plans: Where in the country, or the world, will you need to be to pursue them? Moving, especially moving long distance, is expensive. If you can minimize moves, you'll save time and money. When renting, you often have to pay both first and last month's rent and a security deposit up front, which means you need a lot of cash on hand every time you move.

How will your well-being be affected by living there? Maybe you know that living up north seriously impacts your mental health in the winter, or that living in a predominantly white, Protestant town in flyover country will be difficult. Will you be able to find the community and other resources you need? For instance, you may need to be walking distance from a synagogue or an easy drive to a good elementary school. Can you handle living close to, or far from, key people in your life? (Also see chapters 10–12 for more on life balance.)

You may be in a position to entertain living on campus versus off. Many schools provide on-campus dorms, single apartments, shared apartments, or family apartments, which have the benefit of being close to class, work, and campus clubs and activities. Sometimes they're cheaper than off-campus housing, though not always, and the rent is pretty much guaranteed to go up every year. There's also usually far more students than available on-campus housing. If you're single, you may be able to live with other students, which can be a ready-made social group. However, there may be less privacy, more noise, and less flexibility. You may have the option of a nine-month lease for the school year. There may be unusual options on campus too: one of my friends, for instance, was a graduate resident adviser for an undergraduate dorm, which meant that in exchange for living in a small apartment in the undergrad dorm and mentoring a small herd of undergrads, she got free rent and a moderate stipend.

Off campus, you have every regular housing option available: apartments and houses; with roommates or without; within walking distance of campus or with a longer commute. You'll have more flexibility and more privacy. You will, however, be more likely to be locked into a twelve-month lease. Will you be staying for the summers? Will you be allowed to sublet if you're not?

Personally, I lived off campus with my boyfriend turned husband. We lived in a small second-floor apartment of a multifamily home all six years we were in Boston. It took seventeen minutes of brisk walking to reach the closest subway station, where I rode the train to campus—fifteen minutes on a great day; significantly longer when a train caught fire, or during rush hour, or in winter. Despite the frequent delays and average forty-five-minute (or more) commute, off campus was cheaper and helped me maintain balance—more on that in chapter 10.

Where you live comes down to your personal situation and preferences. I had friends who loved on-campus life. One single mom in family housing appreciated the on-campus amenities and being able to walk to her son's preschool. Other students liked being within a short walk of campus in an area with some restaurants and nightlife, as well as the opportunity to roll out of bed, pop into a local coffee shop, and be in the lab five minutes later. One of our postdocs, however, always drove to campus because she had to drop off her kids at school along the way—even though driving in Boston is never fun, and parking on campus is a nightmare.

Paying Down Debt and Saving Money

If you hold debt, one of the best things you can do for your financial situation is to get rid of it. Dave Ramsey—a radio personality famous for monetary advice—argues for the "debt snowball."[13] List all the debt you have. Make minimum payments on everything *except* the smallest debt. Throw everything else you have at the smallest debt and get rid of it. Then move on to the next smallest. It doesn't matter which debt has the highest interest rate—what matters is getting a fast win, making visible progress on paying back debts, and snowballing the amount you can pay, thus getting rid of all your debts faster.

Besides paying down debt, if you're trying to save money, every time you could buy something, ask yourself, "Would I die if I don't buy this?" If not, don't buy it. Some things are necessities (food, water, shelter); fewer things are necessities than we often think. Put yourself in a frugal mind-set. That's what my husband and I did. For example, if you pay for heat, turn down the thermostat by a couple degrees and put on a sweater. If you pay for electricity, remember to turn off the lights. If you pay for water, take a shorter shower. Get a laundry drying rack and instead of spending money on a dryer, drape your clothes over the rack. They'll dry themselves!

Be inventive and buy less stuff in general. Need an end table? Have a box of random junk, books, computer parts, or summer clothes that you have to store anyway? Take the box. Set it next to your couch. Drape a nice-looking piece of fabric or a blanket over it. Bam! End table and storage, all in one! Even Ikea can't beat that. Don't have a good desk chair? Take a pile of textbooks, stack them on your desk, and make it an ergonomic standing desk instead. While these suggestions might sound silly, I've done both.

If you do need to buy, buy used when you can. Shop discounts and sales. Shop at thrift stores or dollar stores—you can find deals on furniture, clothes, silverware that doesn't match, kitchen and cleaning supplies, decent-quality dishes, and much more. Walk when you can. Some schools may subsidize or partially subsidize train or bus passes. Combine errands and other trips out so you spend less time and money on transportation.

Learn to cook. A lot of simple, nourishing dishes can be made on the cheap. Rice and beans, anyone? Frozen vegetables are cheaper than fresh. Pasta is cheap. Cook in bulk and bring leftovers for lunch all week instead of eating out. I did all of these things. Check the resources for more budget-friendly ideas.

The Cost of Doing Research

In an ideal world, all the costs of doing research would be covered by your institution as part of the graduate student package. We don't live in an ideal world.

Graduate students sometimes have to pay out of pocket for various research expenses, such as conferences, workshops, access to data, and required books for courses and research. And, even when costs like these *are* covered, there's usually a burdensome reimbursement process that means you're basically giving the university an interest-free loan for months on end.

Academic conferences, for example, are expensive—thousands of dollars for registration fees, travel, hotels, and food. They're expensive because of the time and effort it takes to organize one, the cost of reserving space at a conference venue or hotel, swag they give out, food they provide, and so on. Academic conferences can be important to attend if you want an academic job; not only are they a hub for networking, in some fields, the first round of interviews take place at conferences. You can gain valuable feedback on your research and stay on top of what's current in your field. You can reduce the costs some—for example, don't stay for the entire conference, split hotel rooms or other lodging with other students, don't stay in the official conference hotel, take public transit, avoid the hotel bar, hit up a grocery store instead of eating out.

You may be able to get internal funding from your university or program to attend a conference—even a few hundred dollars will help. Professional organizations in your field may have graduate student scholarships, and the conferences themselves may offer to cover registration, travel, or hotel costs in exchange for volunteering at the conference—which can be a good way to meet people in your field. I once attended a workshop at a conference that provided travel funds for students. Sometimes your adviser or coauthors will have funding earmarked for conferences. Mine did, because in our field, certain conferences are nearly as prestigious as journals. Professors can sometimes get conference funding as part of other grants they get for research.

Similarly, these same sources may have grants or scholarships available to help students cover other research costs. It's worth asking your adviser, other graduate students, and admins in your department whether they know of any field-specific opportunities you ought to apply for.

chapter 4
Making Grad School Work for You

In my third year, I met with one of my professors to ask her who I should pick for my general exam committee. Passing my general exams was my next big PhD milestone (described in depth in chapter 7, "Research, Theses, and Dissertations"). I was in the midst of explaining the research areas that seemed relevant for my exams when she interjected, "What are you thinking, career-wise?"

I was caught off guard. Why did that matter now? I was busy trying to figure out who had expertise in developmental psychology and the ethics of technology use with children. "I'm not sure," I stuttered. "I like research . . . maybe academia. Or maybe industry research."

She nodded sagely, then explained that picking a committee is an opportunity to make strategic connections. It wasn't just about expertise. Was there someone relevant to my future career who I wanted to connect with?

Lightbulb. Grad school is *preparation for later*, not just *cool research now*. Yes, I admit realizing this in my *third year* says something about the privileged academic program I was in at MIT (as well as about my murky motivation for attending grad school in the first place—"fun"). But hey, you get insight when you get insight.

That's when I began thinking hard about my future research career and started looking for opportunities that would help me get there. For example, my school's learning center offered a teaching certificate program every semester. I signed up. I was funded through a research assistantship, with no teaching required as part of my degree, but if I wanted to stay in academia, teaching would be a major component. My school organized a yearly two-day seminar for women considering the academic career path. I attended. And so on.

The message of this chapter is simple: You're in grad school for a reason (I hope). Use your time in grad school to work toward your goals. Seek activities, workshops, events, classes, and other learning opportunities that will help you build the skills and knowledge you'll need to do what you want to do later. Keeping your mission in mind will help you prioritize what to say yes to and what to pass over.

However, lest I sound too certain here, remember that *your plans might change.* For my first four or five years of grad school, I was pretty sure I wanted to be a professor. I prioritized learning about teaching, researching, running experimental studies, writing papers, organizing a lab, and all that jazz. Then my plans changed. I had kids. I wasn't so sure that I wanted a full-time academic job. I wanted more flexibility. I visited one of my school's career counselors, who connected me with a list of alumni who had independent design studios. I began looking at other career directions. What else did I enjoy besides full-time research? What was it about research that I enjoyed? I liked writing, so I wrote public-facing posts communicating my research. I attended a workshop on blogging and wrote for MIT's graduate student blog.

Be proactive and flexible. Learn what you'll need, and also what interests you. Many people gravitate toward jobs that involve what interests them, regardless of whether those jobs are what they initially trained for. Aim for your postgrad goals, and also remember that missing your target could lead you in an exciting, unexpected new direction.

Okay, you may be thinking, that's all well and good, but how do you actually *do* all that? Keep your mission in mind? Figure out what to learn? Prioritize? Here are four tools.

KEEP YOUR MISSION IN MIND

To get you wherever you want to go, you need to remember that grad school is a means to an end. Ayelet Fishbach, in *Get It Done*, her book about achieving goals, writes, "When you find yourself facing a goal that's highly important, framing your progress based on what you haven't yet accomplished may be more motivating than thinking about what you've already done."[1] People reminded of *why* they work will work harder.[2] You need to remember your postgrad goals, especially when you're saying yes or no to different activities (more on that below). How do you keep your mission in mind?

The first strategy is easy and low-tech. Write your goal on a piece of paper. Tape the paper to the wall behind your computer monitor, above your desk, on your fridge, or anywhere else you'll see it. Notice it periodically. The paper is a visual reminder that grad school is a means to an end.

Second, add a regular slot on your schedule to check in with yourself. Make it a date—whether every month or once a semester; the frequency matters less than it being a regular date and ensuring you don't stand yourself up. Revisit your goals. You could do the exercise from chapter 1 again, or just look back at what you wrote down. Are your goals still the same? Is grad school still a useful step in getting where you want to go and doing what you want to do? If so, you'll have just reminded yourself of your purpose in attending school. If not, schedule another date with yourself in the near future to reconsider your plans. Think hard about whether grad school is still helping you, or whether you want to get out.

Fishbach discusses the role of social support in achieving our goals—such as how we feel connected to people who support and/or share our goals. Friends, especially those in your student cohort, can be great support (more on friends in chapter 11, "Relationships and Family"). Schedule a regular check-in session with a friend or two, and hold each other accountable for thinking about your goals and whether you've made progress toward them. I had a support group in grad school composed of four other women in my PhD cohort; we met monthly to share progress, struggles, and wins (see chapter 6, "Labs, Classes, and Teaching," for more about who's on your team).

You could use any of a number of productivity and scheduling apps (there are lots; a search of the app store will show you what's current). Some are designed to remind you about important tasks, snooze ideas for a while and ping you later when it might be an opportune time to revisit, or otherwise help you not forget stuff you've decided is important. Personal preference will matter a lot in choosing a productivity app, so experiment with a few to see what works for you. (See chapter 8, "Managing Projects and Managing Time," for more on managing goals and maintaining motivation).

You could also try reverse psychology. There's a well-known social psychology study that came out of Daniel Wegner's lab, in which participants were asked to verbalize their stream of consciousness for five minutes. Some participants were told not to think about a white bear. Guess what? A white bear popped into their minds more than once a minute. What's more, being told *not* to think about a white bear led to *more* thinking about a white bear later, during a second stream-of-consciousness verbalization session, than being told *to* think about the bear! Try it. Tell yourself *not* to think about your goal... maybe you'll start thinking about it more.[3]

Really, use whatever method you like—the main point is to regularly revisit your goals so you don't forget that you have them.

As a final note in this section, time to degree is not the only thing that matters. Yes, your mission is to complete your studies. But as Leonard Cassuto discusses, students who complete their degrees fastest are not rewarded with the academic jobs they desire.[4] Staying longer provides opportunities to do additional teaching or publish more articles—the kinds of activities hiring committees like. Quick finishers are penalized on the job market, even if you'd think they'd be seen as having greater potential (it's ridiculous; hiring committees: do better!). The point being, when you plan your graduate years, take into account the kind of experience you expect to need to pursue the life you want—know your goals, so you can choose your actions.

A LEARNING MIND-SET

The next tool is what I call a learning mind-set. The university's job is not to educate you, but rather to offer you opportunities to learn. Learning is an active process. If you *actually* want to learn, *you* have to learn. You, like everyone else, learn best and learn most when you're intrinsically motivated and curious—when you have what I call a learning mind-set. It's the mind-set that kids adopt naturally as they explore the world around them, asking, *What's that? How come? Why?* It's a state of wonder, play, and exploration. And our understanding of it is rooted in decades of psychology and education research.

First, there's your motivation for learning. Motivation runs on a spectrum, anchored at one end by intrinsic motivation, the things you do because they give you joy, build up a relationship, or contribute to something you value. At the other end are extrinsic motivators, like grades and paychecks. Fun fact: extrinsic rewards can actually decrease your intrinsic desire to pursue an activity![5] (But there's nuance—more on that in chapter 8, "Managing Projects and Managing Time.") A learning mind-set means you engage in learning activities because *you* want to—because you're intrinsically motivated, not because someone told you you'd get a gold star if you did those activities. Intrinsic motivation is associated with deeper learning and satisfaction. You master a subject because you want to master a subject.

Second, a learning mind-set involves knowing that you *can* learn, change, and discover if you put in practice and effort—what's known as a growth mind-set.[6] A growth mind-set is contrasted with a fixed mind-set, in which you believe that intelligence is more like a hand of cards you're dealt, and you can't change it. While a learning mind-set requires a growth mind-set, they're not identical; a learning mind-set is an entire approach to life.

In psychology, there are two well-known theories about learning and challenge. Igor Vygotsky championed what he called the zone of proximal development;[7] Mihaly Csikszentmihalyi developed a theory of flow.[8] Both rely on similar foundations: At any given time, some things are too hard for us; others too easy. In between, where you feel challenged—not bored, not frustrated—is where you learn most. That's where you feel flow and are engaged in the moment. A learning mind-set is oriented toward this kind of challenge.

A learning mind-set is also an orientation toward mastery and competence. I tend to think of this attitude toward mastery as part of your general attitude toward *success* versus *excellence*. The best explanation of the difference between success and excellence I ever heard came from George Platt, my first fencing coach. He'd stand solidly with this gaggle of sweaty teenagers around him, regaling us with the story of some other young fencer, let's call him Jesse, who loved fencing, like we all did. Jesse went to tournaments and fenced hard, but never won a bout. He came to practice like clockwork. He even took private lessons. But Jesse was, quite honestly, a terrible fencer. His determination, though! After years of work, Jesse went to another tournament and finally, *finally* won a bout. This meant that he didn't come in last place! This was the pinnacle of Jesse's fencing career, and that, George would tell us with a chuckle, was excellence.

Put another way, success is how good you are in relation to the rest of the world. Success is winning medals in competitions, good grades, and gold stars. Excellence, on the other hand, is how good you are in relation to how good *you individually* can be. Achieving excellence is being the best you can be, regardless of how good anyone else is. It's you improving and achieving your individual level of mastery. In the context of a learning mind-set, it's the pursuit of knowledge and skills because *you individually* want to learn. You, yourself, want to improve.

I like the success-versus-excellence framing because it drives home what my goals in life really ought to be. Am I going to be satisfied with a medal, an award, or a prestigious paper? Maybe, but I'll be more satisfied with what I accomplish if I'm aiming at stuff that satisfies me, personally, regardless of external perception of those accomplishments. I pursued my PhD in a social robotics lab because I wanted to learn more about people, perception, learning, and robots, not because I wanted fancy letters to tack onto my name.

How Do I Cultivate a Learning Mind-Set?

Practically speaking, how do you cultivate a learning mind-set? How do you realign yourself from seeking success to pursuing excellence? One of the first steps is to take a step back. "Deschool" a little. Try living life as if school doesn't exist, even if just for an afternoon. What would you be doing if you didn't have to study for an exam, write a paper, run an experiment, or attend class? Take an afternoon and do that. Reconnect with what interests you. This can help you recharge and refocus. (Flip to chapter 10, "It's Just Grad School," for more on building life balance.)

Remind yourself to ask *why*. Why are you studying? What was the impetus for you choosing this degree program? Why are you trying to learn new skills? Why are you running this particular experiment? Why are you in the library today?

Ask questions. A postdoc I knew often told stories about how he had begun as a psychology student, then switched to tech-heavy machine learning. When he switched, there was a *lot* he didn't know. He made a point of asking anytime he didn't know something, even if he thought it might be a dumb question. Sure, he was a white male, so it was probably easier for him to get away with showing his ignorance, but being willing to admit that you don't know something and being willing to ask for help can be the difference between graduating or not graduating—and can remind you that you're here to learn.

Rediscover curiosity. Some Zen meditation practices suggest practitioners look at the world with "beginner's mind"—that is, with an attitude that is curious, open, wondering, and able to see many possibilities. If you were five years old again, what about the world would fascinate and puzzle you? Visit the library and pick out a book that looks interesting—not one that is necessarily useful, but one you think you'll enjoy reading. When was the last time you read a book just for fun?

Curiosity goes hand in hand with creativity, play, and doing things that intrinsically motivate you.[9]

Play. According to James Carse, games are either finite or infinite.[10] In a finite game, you follow the rules in order to win. Play, however, is an infinite game. It stays fun and rewarding so long as you follow the self-imposed rules of play, which means the incentive to do the activity is doing the activity itself. Play is something you're intrinsically motivated to do. Playing can bring you into a state of flow. Being in flow helps your brain associate enjoyment with focused attention, practice, and hard work, and reinforces the behaviors that lead to the experience of flow: directed effort, learning, and attention. These are all components of a learning mind-set.

Why Does a Learning Mind-Set Work?

Does a learning mind-set work? You bet. In one extreme example, a study of kids in Sudbury schools (a type of democratic school that emphasizes interest-driven learning) showed that, when intrinsically motivated, the kids could learn the entirety of the American K–6 math curriculum in about twenty hours—that's seven years of math in less than a day![11] Kerry McDonald, in her book *Unschooled: Raising Curious, Well-Educated Children Outside the Conventional Classroom*, shared several anecdotes about kids who, once they decided reading was a relevant skill to know, learned to read like cheetahs run. One nine-year-old learned to read and write in the span of a week because he wanted to write letters to a girl he liked. That time scale isn't uncommon among unschoolers. Another boy started reading on his own the day his dad wasn't available to help him read the text in a video game.[12] Given resources, like a literacy-rich environment, and motivation, kids are capable of teaching themselves to read.[13]

In a totally different domain, parents have found that toilet training a toddler can take upward of a year if you start when they're eighteen to twenty-one months old and have no idea why you care where they poop.[14] But if you start when they're closer to three years old, when they are motivated to be a competent individual, you can get away with a lot less training—on average four months, but incredibly, as little as a single day. The eldest son of a mother I know was three when he decided he hated diapers. She gave her son underwear and said, "If you have an accident, you're back in diapers!" He didn't have an accident. Motivation is everything.

One last note before moving on to the next tool in our toolbox: changing your mind-set can be difficult. It would be great if we could flip a switch and magically start acting in line with our goals: Be the best you can be. Learn what you enjoy learning. Put effort into the things that are important to you. Be curious. etc. But, like most things, it's not as simple in practice. Failure to achieve success can dissuade us from continuing to pursue excellence—not only because it's a discouraging emotional experience, but because we're often measured by our external successes: classes taken, exams passed, papers published, studies run, and so forth.

Changing your mind-set can also take time. Like anything important, a learning mind-set is a practice. You practice it. You get better. You keep practicing.

How Do I Deal with Imposter Syndrome?

Imposter syndrome is the feeling that you've been mistakenly admitted to your program, that you're not smart enough to be there, that you don't fit in. You may feel you need to put in *more* effort and be *more* perfect to prove you belong. After all, it may feel like it's only a matter of time before everyone realizes you're not cut out for academic life. If you feel this way, know that you are *far* from alone. Many, many students feel the same—perhaps even some of your own classmates or friends.

Feeling like an imposter isn't your fault. As Christine Liu writes, "by framing feelings of inadequacy as a personal flaw that needs to be worked on, we let the toxic culture in academic research off the hook."[15] Academia has a culture of overwork, under-compensation, and the same sexism and racism as the rest of society. These factors cannot be overlooked when trying to understand why so many young researchers feel they don't belong—it's not that they lack confidence (though some do); it's that the system works against them.

Beating imposter syndrome can be tough, but it's possible. You can, for instance, reframe experiences. For example, a student may think, "Oh no, I didn't learn this material in a class!" and jump to "Maybe I'm not supposed to be in grad school." Reframe the lack of knowledge: "I didn't learn this material because courses never teach us everything we need to know. I learned how to learn, and I can learn this too." Courses don't cover everything. Everyone enters graduate school with a different foundation. You'll know things your fellow students won't, and vice versa.

Write a list of positive affirmations on a sheet of paper and tape it above your desk. Include a summary of your education and work experience, five things you're proud of, your top five skills, and examples of positive feedback you've received.[16]

Keep a folder of all the amazing things that happened that made you smile—doesn't matter if it's digital or printed. Star emails with your accomplishments, such as grad school acceptance letters, paper acceptances, or messages from friends or family. When imposter syndrome is dragging you down, look back at these reminders. They'll tell you that the work you're doing is going somewhere. People *do* believe in you. You *can* achieve.

Remember that the system works against you. Remind yourself of your worth. Here are a few mantras: Your feelings aren't facts. Perfect doesn't exist. It's okay not to know everything and to ask for help. No one knows everything—and no one knows exactly the same things you do, nor will anyone else think about your research questions the same way you do. You provide value. You worked hard to be where you are. You deserve to be where you are. You're enough.

Practice saying these phrases to yourself in the mirror. Other people's accomplishments can be inspiration, rather than competition.

SEEK NEW SKILLS

Every degree program has requirements to check off before you graduate: required classes, lab rotations, exams, teaching, a proposal, a thesis, a dissertation. Many people assume that if they finish all the requirements, they'll be all set to succeed at whatever career their degree is supposed to prepare them for. Unfortunately, in practice, the requirements won't necessarily be comprehensive or useful. The classes might not provide you with the information you need to run experiments. Knowing that you need to write a thesis doesn't help you learn how to actually *write* a good thesis. If you're in a PhD program, you're being trained for an academic career—even though, as discussed in chapter 2, most PhDs don't become professors. And you're not even getting *all* the training you'd need to succeed as an academic! Generally, there's no training in project management, grant writing, mentoring students, managing budgets, or even teaching.

So, instead of assuming you're golden if you do what you're told, take charge. Graduate school comes with an expectation that you *will* go out and learn on your own. As Amanda Seligman explains, "graduate students do most of the learning on their own, essentially self-directed."[17] The goal is to create independent researchers, so it makes sense that much of the time, you're on your own. So be proactive! You're armed with a learning mind-set. You're thinking about what you want to do after grad school. It's time to find opportunities to learn.

Fortunately, you're in luck: opportunities abound! Besides providing classes (which you can learn about via course catalogs online and by asking other students), universities host workshops, lectures, and talks on all manner of topics. Some useful learning opportunities will also be hosted by student groups or other on-campus organizations. For example, the blogging workshop I attended was hosted by the student editors of MIT's graduate student blog. The topics aren't limited to the scholarly—many cover career planning and life skills. I once attended a panel during which four professors discussed how to get a postdoc. Another time, I was invited to be on a panel about dealing with stress as a student. For a couple years, some students in my department hosted a daylong Festival of Learning, in which anyone from the department could sign up to teach a workshop on absolutely anything (yes, anything: research methods, web development, yogurt making, poker, bicycle maintenance, cardboard forts).

You can discover campus resources and events by asking people in your department (students, staff, and admin), talking to a librarian (a truly underrated resource), wandering the halls and looking at the announcements stapled to the announcement boards, chatting with people from other departments, and signing up for relevant mailing lists on campus (departmental, clubs, special interests, local organizations). Read books and articles. If you want to learn to teach, seek teaching assistantships (sometimes you can volunteer) or teacher-training workshops. I knew a couple grad students who, with a professor's sign-off, created and taught their own class on designing and fabricating technology inspired by science fiction. Most campuses have a writing center that can give you feedback on all kinds of writing, including the ideation stage, and many host events on writing, teaching, and learning. Some institutions have research support offices.

Your classmates and colleagues are a source of learning—ask them for help. In my research group, we gave practice talks and shared paper drafts, with the goal of helping each other become better presenters and writers. We helped each other debug code, fix robots, and learn the day-to-day research skills needed to succeed in the lab.

Off campus, take advantage of the surrounding town or city. Look for local meetups and clubs. For example, if you'd like to improve your public speaking, a Toastmasters club could be something to try. I know students who regularly volunteered with local STEM outreach organizations, after-school programs, museum events, and Boys and Girls Clubs. Student groups often organize volunteering efforts too. Local organizations may host talks or workshops, many of which are advertised in local newspapers, mailing lists, or on Facebook.

We're living in the information age, and you probably already know that the Internet is full of useful resources. YouTube videos; all kinds of tutorials; blogs and personal sites with stories, walk-throughs, and advice; Reddit threads; online webinars, courses, and classes, some of which you pay for and many of which are free... there's so much available! If you prefer a more structured learning environment for picking up an academic subject, try MOOCs (massive online open courses) taught by university professors from around the world (many are free). If you have specific unanswered questions, asking on social media, such as in an appropriate Facebook group, can get you up-to-date answers.

One challenge you may have in looking at learning opportunities is deciding which opportunities and skills are relevant to you and to what you want to do with your life. That's where our next exercise comes in.

EXERCISE 8: MAKE A SKILL PLAN

What skills do you want to learn during grad school? What skills and tasks matter to you and engage you? How can you learn those skills? Let's create a skill plan. The plan will have three parts: *skill → action steps → timeline*.

Review: Make a Skill List

1. Review your life goals and career goals, which we talked about in the introduction. Think about where you want to be and what you want to do.
2. Brainstorm skills you need. Get a piece of paper or open a blank text document. Write down everything you can think of in response to the following questions: What do you need to know to achieve your goals? What skills, degrees, or qualifications are

required? What do people with the job you want do? What do they know? How do they do what they do?
3. Brainstorm skills you like. Continue writing: What tasks are you doing when you feel energized? Who are you with? Where are you? What about those tasks do you enjoy? What skills do those tasks build up?
4. Here's some additional inspiration. This is a list of some "real-world" skills people often learn in grad school without realizing that these are what they are learning:

- Teaching, presenting at conferences → public speaking
- Working effectively in a team
- Writing skills
- Making decisions and solving problems
- Planning, conceptualizing, organizing, and prioritizing
- Accessing and processing information
- Analyzing quantitative/qualitative data
- Having technical knowledge related to the job
- Proficiency with computer software programs
- Creating and/or editing written reports
- Forming an argument/providing supportive details
- Organizing/managing data
- Managing projects
- Leading/motivating others
- Setting goals and objectives

Assess: What Needs Work?

5. Where are you at now? Look at the list you just generated. What skills do you have already? Which ones need work? Be honest with yourself. You're the only one looking at your list. You won't learn and improve if you don't think you need improvement. What are you learning right now? How are you learning those things?

Plan: Develop Action Steps and a Timeline

6. For each skill you listed above, write down at least one way you can learn or practice that skill (more is fine). These are your action

steps—concrete ways to work on the skill. For example, if you decided you need to work on your writing skills, you could take a writing class, start a writing group, or schedule in consistent time to practice writing (e.g., every day or every week).

7. Next, fill in the *timeline* column: *when* you might work on the skill. Can you make progress this semester? Can you make progress this academic year? Could you, say, take a class in the spring or attend a workshop scheduled for two months from now? Are there prerequisite skills? Do you need to finish the course on introductory statistics before you can work further on your data analysis skills or on learning how to make nice figures for your paper? You can set deadlines if you like, or just make notes about when opportunities to learn each skill might arise.

SAY YES STRATEGICALLY

The fourth and final skill in this chapter is learning not to say *yes* to everything. You will be asked to do many things in grad school. Some are optional. Some are not. Every research group, every adviser, and every academic program has different expectations for what you ought to do with your time. To get a feel for what's typical, ask other students in your cohort or research group. Ask academic social media (see the resources chapter), which can net you responses from a wider range of people. Knowing what's typical can help you determine whether you're obligated to say yes, or whether the request is an opportunity that may, or may *not*, be useful for you.

For example, if you're working toward a career in academia, it's useful to learn how to peer review research papers. Invitations to review papers for conferences or journals in your field can give you practice (more common for grad students in STEM fields than in the humanities). It's a great learning opportunity—you learn how a good research paper is put together, how to give feedback on writing, and you also get to hear about the cutting edge in your field before it's officially published. Plus, if you're submitting your work to a conference or journal, it's polite and often expected that you review other people's work submitted to the same venue. But beyond that, review requests can pile up. Reviewing papers takes time away from your other, often more important work. It's also unpaid labor. So beyond a certain amount of reviewing that's probably useful and/or required, saying no is justified. Especially if you know that when you graduate, you're going to join a biotech company or curate a museum and never review another paper in your life. But how do you say no?

Let's put this on the record: When requests are not a wise use of your time, you *can* decline. It's okay. I want you to be picky. I know it can be hard. One way to start: Don't say *yes* immediately. If a lecture or on-campus activity looks interesting, make a note on your calendar. Take a picture of the flier. But don't commit to going right away. You can decide later whether you actually want to go and whether you actually have time. If someone asks you to do something, buy yourself time to decide whether the task is worth it. Say, "Thanks for considering me. Let me think about it." Say, "Let me check my calendar first." Say, "I'll get back to you about this tomorrow." If it's a request submitted via email, you can simply let the email sit for a day or two while you think it over before replying.

Then do think it over. You can set aside time every day to consider requests and upcoming events. But do think before you commit. If your default is saying yes, ask yourself *why* you would say yes. What do you get out of doing the thing? How does doing the thing contribute to you reaching your life goals? Are you required to do the thing? Are you expected to do the thing? Are you expected to do the thing, but you are already doing many other expected things, with no time left over for more things? Who asked you to do the thing, and are you under any social obligation to do the thing for them?

Some requests you can simply delete or ignore without consequence. For example, I've gotten emails from random people I've never met whose work is not really related to my research field for comments on their papers, funding I don't offer, and postdoc positions in my research group (yes, even when I was a master's student . . . it baffles me too).

Some requests you will feel you must agree to. Often, these are requests from your adviser. They hold a particular position of power over you and your academic future, so yes, it's wise to consider their requests carefully. However, advisers and supervisors may not be keeping track of how much they have already asked you to do. They may be unconsciously assigning all administrative work to women students. They may not know what is a reasonable workload for you. They may have forgotten that tasks that take them twenty minutes may take a trainee two hours. And so on. As such, if a request from an adviser or supervisor feels unreasonable... it may very well might be unreasonable. (See chapter 5, "Advisers" for strategies for managing your adviser.)

Say yes when a request is necessary, interesting, or helps you. Say no otherwise. Don't overwork yourself for the sake of appearing nice and helpful, unless you actually want to be nice and helpful in that instance. For example, my labmates and I sent each other paper drafts for feedback. This was a nice, helpful thing for us to do for each other. Because it was reciprocal, it worked out just fine. I set boundaries though: if a labmate wanted my feedback, they needed to send me their draft with sufficient time for me to review it and for them to incorporate my feedback... in other words, not the day of the deadline.

Say no when you have too much on your plate. Say no when the request isn't interesting and doesn't help you. You can set personal policies to help you remember to say no. For example, you may decide you will only review a certain number of conference papers or only review papers that look really interesting. You might decide you can only travel a certain number of times a year. You might decide that you will only schedule and attend meetings during regular business hours (an especially useful policy if you have children). You might decide that you will not agree to anything extra until you have finished your dissertation proposal, because all your time needs to be focused on that.

You can also step back after the fact if you need to. Perhaps you've volunteered to help run clubs, events, or committees. If you want to cut back on hours, perhaps you can pass the torch to someone else. Jessica Calarco recommends avoiding big service commitments while working toward major milestones—such as exams or teaching your first class—and limiting yourself to one major service commitment at a time.[18]

Say no strategically and politely. Decline by simply saying, "No, thank you." If that seems too short, you can expand it: "Thanks for thinking of me. This opportunity sounds great, but I have a prior commitment." You do not have to explain why you are unavailable, but you can if it seems prudent: "I appreciate your invitation. However, I am in lab meetings from 9 a.m. until noon every Wednesday, so I am never available at that time."

Decline by volunteering someone else for the job. State that you are unavailable or explain why you are not the right person for the job—for example, "My expertise does not fall in that area, however..." Then suggest someone else who is competent, more relevant, more likely to be available (or underutilized), and who may actually appreciate being volunteered. Gigs you personally don't want or don't have time for, such as being on a conference panel, giving a guest lecture in a class, or reviewing a paper, may be a desirable gig to someone else. If it's less desirable work, such as being the notetaker for group meetings, you can suggest that first-year Bob ought to take on that role, because he's very detail-oriented and doesn't have many responsibilities in the group yet.

Saying no is a skill to work on. It can take a lot of gumption. Chapter 5, "Advisers," includes a primer on negotiation, including tactics shared by Chris Voss—who was a lead FBI kidnapping negotiator—in his book *Never Split the Difference*. Use these tactics to negotiate down a workload and invite whomever you're negotiating with to help you find a solution.

USE YOUR NEW TOOLS

You won't be in grad school forever. The point of grad school is to learn, so learn! If you keep your mission in mind, you'll be in a better position to prioritize activities and take advantage of learning opportunities. Cultivate your curiosity. Proactively seek interesting and relevant activities. Revisit your goals and your skill plan regularly. Be picky about what you agree to do.

PART II
Grad School Skills

chapter 5
Advisers

One chilly February morning, I paced outside the blocky psychology building on the Notre Dame University campus. I peered at my still silent phone. *Tap tap tap.* I turned the volume up. I put the phone in my coat pocket, checked that my notebook and pen were cozily nested in my other pocket, and fished my phone back out. It rang.

Flinching at the jolt of noise, I answered. The voice on the other end said, "Hello, Jacqueline? This is Cynthia."

Dr. Cynthia Breazeal, potential graduate adviser. I wriggled out the notebook, wanting the comfort of all the hopefully convincing answers I'd jotted down in response to potential hard questions about why I was a fantastically qualified fit for her lab at MIT.

But my pre-call jitters were misplaced. The conversation wasn't an intimidating, FBI-level interrogation. Instead, Cynthia wanted to gauge my interest in her lab group while selling me on her research vision. Which, if I'd been wise to graduate admissions, I would have known. Finding an adviser is a bit like dating. You're both trying to find a good match. Cynthia wanted to know whether I was interested in her ongoing projects and whether my attitude toward working and learning fit the kind of person she wanted in her lab. I wanted to know what kind of adviser she was, and whether she could support the research I wanted to learn to do.

Advisers use students' application packages and subsequent interviews to curate who they take on. Graduate students should be just as careful—or even more so—in choosing their adviser.

WHAT DOES AN ADVISER DO?

Arguably, the most important person in your graduate school career is your adviser (sometimes known as your supervisor or your PI, principal investigator). They are probably a professor with a PhD or similar advanced degree.

Your adviser has the most direct control over your academic life. Their role is to guide you through your graduate program, train you, help you achieve your goals, make sure you have opportunities, provide resources and strategies, and help you secure funding (or provide funding for you). Initially, they help you pick classes. Later, they supervise your research (more so in STEM) and help you find a job. Ideally, your adviser is clearly on your team. They should promote your development as a researcher and be a good mentor. The advising relationship can last long past your time in graduate school; they may mentor you for your whole career. Having good mentors is a top indicator of graduate student success.[1]

Unfortunately, many advisers are not ideal. Professors are people too; they are just as fallible as every other group of humans. Some of their failings may be due to lack of training—professors-to-be don't habitually receive training in management, mentoring, teaching, or advising, even though a huge part of their job is exactly those things. But most of their failings, well, that's on them. They may have bad time-management or organizational skills, leading to absences or delays when you need them—such as in replying to emails in a reasonable time frame, writing a recommendation letter, or giving you feedback on a paper. They may make sexist or racist remarks, show outright hostility, make unwelcome and unprofessional advances, or even simply give you bad advice. This all falls under what Jessica Calarco calls "mis-mentoring and under-mentoring," and the consensus is it happens all the time and none of it is your fault.[2]

Personally, I got lucky. While I can attribute *some* of my luck to the hard work of applying to programs, good advice from my undergraduate mentors, and careful interviewing and vetting before accepting an offer, let's be real: I wasn't *that* awesome at figuring people out. I was lucky that my adviser was not only an excellent researcher, but a star adviser.

HOW DO YOU GET AN ADVISER?

In some programs, particularly in STEM fields, you pick an adviser when applying to graduate school. You are admitted to work with a particular professor in their research group off the bat. In other programs, often in the social sciences and humanities or terminal master's programs, you are admitted to a department, then either are assigned an adviser or pick one after a year or two.

Choosing an adviser is a major decision. While you can change advisers later (and people do for a variety of reasons, as I describe in this chapter), it's not always easy. So it is critical to do some legwork up front to ensure you find someone compatible with you personally and academically. You will want to interview potential advisers, as well as their students and postdocs. More on that in a moment. First, let's talk about what you're looking for.

THE IDEAL ADVISER

Advisers vary in their approaches to work, management, research, and life. When choosing an adviser, assess (1) research area, (2) research skills, (3) practical logistics, and (4) mentoring skills and personal fit.

Research area. Your adviser's expertise should align with your general interests. They should know what to study in your field and how to study it. They should be familiar with the key debates in your field, and whether any research you want to pursue is actually interesting and important enough to pursue.

In the arts, humanities, and social sciences, you generally don't want an *exact* match with your research interests—you'll be coming up with your thesis or dissertation on your own, so if your topic is too similar to your adviser's research, some people may assume your adviser handed you the topic. In STEM fields, however, your research will almost always build off your adviser's work, and it is expected that your topic will relate—often very closely—to your adviser's work.

Research skills. Does this adviser use the methods you want to use? (You may not know what you want to use yet, and that's fine.) If they don't, that's okay, so long as they have a healthy respect for your intended methods. You can seek methods help from another committee member or a more advanced graduate student. If the adviser disdains your methods, find someone else. For example, if they're all about quantitative approaches and look down their nose at that soft, fluffy qualitative mush, but you want to try a qualitative approach... that's an invitation for conflict down the road.

Practical logistics. Pick an adviser active in teaching and research who will likely still be at the university when you finish your degree. For example, you may not want to pick someone who is unlikely to be granted tenure, or who's looking to retire or leave academia. Is your potential adviser overburdened—for example, by having too many students or too much service and committee work? It varies how much a person can handle, so eke out an individual sense of this when interviewing. I've seen extremely well-run research labs of thirty-plus students in which each student met individually with the professor every week, and groups of three or five who saw their professor once a semester if they were lucky.

Mentoring skills and personal fit. Ideal advisers give constructive feedback on your work. They are timely, give you the attention you need, answer your questions, and listen. They're supportive. They invest in your career—they see potential students as mentees, as investments, not simply cheap labor. They can give you strategic advice, help you plan your career, and are well connected and well respected in your field, so they can introduce you to people you need or want to know. They genuinely want to help you.

Some people have all the right skills and qualifications but rub you the wrong way. It is almost always better to find someone who jibes with you and can support you than to settle for the perfect research fit or a prominent hotshot. After all, you can seek research support from non-advisers too—such as your committee, covered in chapter 7—and you may change your mind about the specific topics you want to research anyway.

You probably won't find an adviser who can do everything. That's normal—everyone has their strengths and weaknesses. Prioritize the most important qualities: supportive, helpful, constructive. With those qualities, your adviser will be on board to help you find whatever *other* support you need—whether research advice, help crafting papers, or detailed feedback on your methodology.

Interviewing Potential Advisers

When interviewing, ask questions like an obsessed six-year-old: relentlessly. But do your homework first! Don't waste time on questions with easy-to-research answers. For example, you may be curious about the composition of the current lab group or who has graduated from the group. Is there a website? Many research groups list all current lab members (including race/gender breakdowns) on their websites, as well as all alumni. Also, before trying to set up an interview with a faculty member, try to discover whether they are even open to new advising relationships—sometimes, they'll mention on their website that they're looking for new students or not admitting anyone to their research group this year.[3]

Logistics
- How many students and postdocs do you have currently? What's typical?
- How is your research group structured? For example, who will I work with? What are the expectations regarding collaboration between students or collaboration with other researchers?
- How is the group funded? For example, will I be expected to work on projects for grants?
- How many students have finished the master's or PhD program? If they didn't finish, what did they do instead?
- What kinds of jobs do your past students have? (This can give you a sense of whether this adviser supports nonacademic jobs.)
- How long did it take them to graduate? Is that average for the program? Does it vary by race or gender? (This can help you determine whether students like you finish their degrees, and what they do next.)
- What do you teach currently? And how often are these courses offered?

Managing Student Research
- How often do you meet with students? What are these meetings typically like? What other meetings does your research group typically have? For example, lab meetings or project-specific meetings.
- What progress do you expect from a student during a semester? How do you measure and evaluate that progress?
- What do you do when students are struggling? How have you helped struggling students in the past?
- How do you know when to advise a student to stop working on a project or pivot on a project?
- When you publish with grad students, what does the division of labor typically look like?
- How do you help students prepare for their careers?
- What are you working on now? What kinds of projects can graduate students be involved in?
- How often do students attend conferences?

General/Campus Life
- Do you value diversity? How do you support diversity?
- What would you change about this town, university, or department?
- How often do students take time off? What kinds of lab or department outings or events are there?
- How do you enable life balance for your students?

Interviewing Potential Departments or Research Groups

In addition to interviewing potential advisers, you should also talk to current students and postdocs, as well as recent graduates from the adviser's research group or from the department. In most STEM fields you will be first and foremost part of a research group or lab group headed by your adviser. You may have a lab rotation prior to signing on for the long haul, which means you get to try out different advisers and lab groups to see where you feel you fit best, both socially and academically, before committing. In the humanities, usually you're considered part of the department. You have an adviser, but the cohort of students you work with or see regularly is different and, often, limited. Humanities research tends to be more solitary; in STEM fields, it's more collaborative.

Try to get a sense of the department or research group culture, as well as whether the adviser is the kind of person you would want to work with long-term. Academic cultures can feel vastly different—more collaborative versus more competitive; more relaxed versus more stressed. Students are often open and honest with their opinions. Some potential advisers will actually *suggest* that you talk to their students—this is a good sign. It means they trust their students. Ask a lot of questions—see below (and do your research first so you don't waste time on things you could learn online!). As Jessica Calarco recommends, try to find out what the experience of students like you is.

My undergraduate adviser, John Long, told me to speak with students, because "My first criterion is this: are the graduate students happy? If they aren't, you're in trouble, since it's most likely you'll be unhappy too. If they are happy, that's a great sign: happy people do the best work."[4] Are your future graduate student peers *happy?* If the other students are miserable, what makes you think you won't be too?

Research
- Which professors do you work with and how did you start working with them?
- Are there any professors you avoid, and why?
- What are faculty demands on time like? Do they follow the rules? How do faculty generally treat grad students?
- What autonomy do students have over their work? What decisions do students make?
- What does it take to be successful in this program?
- What kind of microaggressions have you encountered? What does the campus feel like? Do you feel comfortable there?
- What's the culture like? Do students help each other or are they more competitive?
- Who do you go to for help when you're not sure about something in grad school?

Practical Stuff
- What are students required to do to get funding, such as teaching or research?
- How much debt do students typically accrue during the program?
- Where do students typically live? How do students get to and from campus (e.g., public transit, cars), and how much does that cost?
- What are options for school and child care for children?
- What do students do for fun?
- What are your favorite things about this town, university, and department? And what would you change?

You may also have the chance to ask department admins some questions. That can be a good time to ask about funding and timeline logistics, such as

- How are students typically funded, and what is included in the funding? Is there funding for health insurance, vision, dental, relocation, conference travel, summers? How are taxes handled? Can I do any work outside of graduate school while I am enrolled? What happens to me and my funding if my adviser leaves?

- What is the expected timeline for completion? What happens if someone takes longer? What happens for students who are struggling to stay on track?
- What kind of support is there for students' career planning and job searches, in academia or out?

MANAGING YOUR ADVISER

Expectations, Boundaries, and Communication

Once you have an adviser, you'll need to manage your relationship. Advisers are busy people. They usually have lots of people to advise and supervise. They have research to do, grants to write, committee work to do, administrative minutiae to attend to, and that's just the on-campus stuff. They often have families and dependents of their own, hobbies, their own boundaries and their own balance. On your part, you want the answers and direction you need to get on with your research and your career. Set expectations up front: tell them what to expect of you and ask what to expect of them—regarding work (research, classes, teaching, etc.), communication, and boundaries. Setting expectations early on in the relationship can go a long way toward keeping things smooth.

Find out what their work expectations and boundaries are. Some of the answers you need you can glean during conversations with current or past students. Some you can ask about directly. Never underestimate the power of a direct question! A simple "So, do you prefer that I email you or come to your office when I have a question about X?" can go a long way. Even if it's not *your* favorite means of communication, adapting to your adviser's preferences can mean you get the information and support you need faster.

Does your adviser expect to see you in the lab eight hours a day, or do they care more about you getting the work done whatever the hour? How often will you meet, and what kind of progress and updates do they expect? What do they think your timeline could, or should, be? What are their expectations around collaboration, mentoring other students, helping with research projects, obtaining funding, and so on? What's the best way to get a hold of them—email, texts, video calls, in-person meetings, a quick chat in the hall? Make sure to tell your adviser what to expect of you too. For example, if you run marathons and thus go for a long run every day at noon, or if you can't be in until 8:00 a.m. after you drop your kids at school, share that. That way, they don't expect to find you in the lab at those times. Make and share your proposed timeline for your degree, and get their feedback (more on timelines in chapter 8).

The key is to share enough relevant information with each other to know what to expect. Be up front about who you are, what you do with your time, and what you want to get out of the situation or the relationship. This way, no one's left wondering. If everyone knows what to expect, you won't get into a situation where someone is upset because they didn't get what they were expecting.

Communicate both when things are going well *and* when they're not. Give regular updates on your progress, whether you've achieved awesome results or are stuck in a rut. Honestly, it may be even more important to share when you're stuck, because part of your adviser's job is to help you get unstuck! One person I once worked with said, "If you don't update me, I'll assume you're not working." While that's not a particularly gracious attitude, it is important to ensure the relevant people—like your adviser—know what you're up to (and more on that in chapter 7, where I talk about committees).

Remember, people generally assume too much. They'll build up their own image of you *whether or not you tell them anything.* So be proactive. Be your own advocate. Make sure they build up an image that correctly reflects reality.

Generational Expectations

Advisers who are significantly older than you—from a different generation—may have drastically different views from you about how much work, compensation, and balance is appropriate for students to have. Many current students feel underpaid and overworked. They feel their advisers are too demanding. Many advisers, on the other hand, feel that students are acting entitled.

There is truth to both claims. When compared to peers in the workforce, many students *are* underpaid and overworked. But grad students are not *just* employees like their peers. They are also students getting an education, in training for a highly specialized career in research. As professors from the older generation generally argue, part of their compensation is not in salary or benefits, but in the training they receive.

But it's hard to judge the monetary value of the training. Are students being fairly compensated? If you were likely to land a tenure-track job when you graduated—which was often the case for members of the older generation—then maybe! High future salaries and job security is how many people justify the debt incurred in medical school, for instance. But given the state of academia, the shrinking number of people who get professorships, the number who have to switch career paths (see chapter 2), the changing demographics of students to include women, minorities, and parents, coupled with the rising costs of living in so many parts of the country, and so on—maybe the compensation students are getting is *not* sufficient. Chapter 13 covers this topic further, including discussion of student unions, benefits, and flexibility.

When dealing with your adviser, remember that every generation has its differences in view and values from earlier ones. These differences will inevitably cause conflict. That conflict does not imply malicious behavior or intent on anyone's part; both you and your adviser are reflecting the values and expectations of your respective generations, based on your own experiences of graduate school, academia, and the world in general. Empathy on your part, and theirs, will make it easier to find a solution that works for both of you.

Sometimes, of course, when you feel your adviser is acting unreasonably, they *are* being unreasonable. I'll give you tools for dealing with that later in this chapter.

Making the Most of Meetings

Do your part to make it easy for your adviser to help you. Send direct questions—bold the most importance sentences and put the most important questions at the top of your emails. Make an agenda (and share it ahead of time) for your meetings. Come to meetings prepared with the questions you need answered.

Beyond the Immediate: Discussing Your Career/Life Plans

Speak frankly about your plans for the job market, your personal goals, and your career ambitions. Once your adviser has some idea what your plans are, they can help you out—or not (and then you can find other help). For example, if you're trying to line up your postgraduation job, your adviser could help pick a final date to turn in your dissertation, so you can plan your start date. If you're leaving academia, maybe they can find a way for you to produce a shorter dissertation that lets you graduate and move on. The key: Your adviser can't help if they're in the dark. Shed some light.

Asking Questions

When in doubt, ask a question. For example, if you're not sure you understand something or if you want to verify you have the requirements or expectations right, restate what you think you understand, then ask, "Is that right?" Asking for clarification is usually seen as a sign of intelligence and being on top of things, not a sign that you're not smart enough.

In practice, it can be difficult to ask questions, especially for students who may think—for whatever reason—that asking a question will reflect negatively on them. For example, that if I ask questions, it will prove that I am not smart enough to be here; that asking questions shows I don't belong; that I don't trust this person enough to ask them that kind of question, etc. There's no easy way to become more comfortable asking questions other than practice. Is there someone else you can ask? Can you ask over email instead of in person?

How Do I Ask for a Recommendation Letter?

Be respectful, appreciative, and efficient in any request you make. Don't ask for last-minute favors; professors are busy people. Ask at least two weeks in advance; two months is better! Acknowledge that it's okay if they say no—sometimes, they just aren't able to add one more thing to their plate. Include a copy of your most recent CV, and any other pertinent information, such as the application's specific instructions to recommendation writers and how to submit the letter. Offer to follow up in person or with a phone call if the recommender has questions.

SOLVING ADVISER PROBLEMS

When you're in a dissatisfying situation, you have four options.[5] First, you can *exit*: leave the situation entirely. At the most extreme, this may mean finding a new adviser or leaving graduate school. Second, you can *persist*: decide it's not worth the effort of changing, so grit your teeth and get through it. Third, you can *neglect*: similar to persist, you're deciding not to try to change the situation, so you stay, but reduce your involvement and effort to the minimum viable amount. Fourth, you *voice*: that is, actively try to change the situation in some way, such as having the hard conversation or escalating the conflict to your department head.

Which option you pick will relate to your level of control and commitment. Can you effect change, or are you stuck with the status quo no matter what? Do you care enough to try to change the situation? All the options can be hard, but exercising *voice* can take the most skill—but it's also the option that is applicable for *most* situations.

The first step is to take stock. Assess your circumstances, collect facts, and take an attitude of curiosity. Assume honest mistakes until proven otherwise, unless patterns of past behavior indicate you shouldn't be so generous. Are there misunderstandings about roles, responsibilities, and expectations that can be cleared up by asking questions and having dialogue? The first stage in solving problems is to communicate—ask for a meeting, respectfully lay out your concerns, propose how to improve or deal with the situation, and as Chris Cramer recommends, point out that you're not trying to be a problem, you're simply looking for a solution that works for you.[6]

If a conversation doesn't resolve the conflict, are there any other active ways you can try to remedy things? Or do you need to pick another option—exit, persist, or neglect? Not all conflicts involve harassment or abuse; sometimes, you really just don't jibe with someone's style or personality. Can you escalate? Can you negotiate? Can you grit your teeth and bear it?

If you choose to escalate, determine who to talk to first. Initially, this will probably be the faculty in charge of your department's graduate program, such as the director of graduate studies, or a department head. Ask for a confidential meeting to discuss the situation; if they agree that further discussion or intervention could be beneficial, they will help you plan next steps, such as a joint meeting with them, you, and your adviser. Depending on your department's structure, you may also talk to an admin, or your institution may have an office for conflict resolution, mediation, or an ombudsperson or ombuds office that may be able to help you out.

If you're facing an abusive adviser—which is unfortunately not as rare as it should be—then you may need to jump the gun straight to escalation without confronting your adviser first. Students in these situations are victims on the wrong side of an extreme power differential; they are vulnerable and may rightly fear retaliation. *Exit* is the correct strategy. You will need to decide how far out to get—change advisers within your department, leave the department, leave the school? You will also need to decide how much to escalate while getting out. You may feel an obligation to go on the record or go public with your story to protect future students, or you may worry that losing your anonymity will be harmful. If you wish to report the case, since graduate students are an unusual class of person, being both student and employee, you may have to determine whether to file your grievance with an office related to student affairs or related to employment. Finally, reach out to your campus's mental health services if you need to. (And see the resources chapter.)

In all cases where you escalate, collect written documentation. Keep copies of relevant texts and emails. If you negotiate some outcome, such as particular hours to work or the duties allowable as part of your research assistantship, make sure the agreement gets written out and signed. Having a record can protect you. For example, you could use your documentation to show that your adviser violated your institution's faculty code of conduct, or other relevant rules or laws.

In the next sections, I cover a few skills that can be useful regardless of the kind of conflict, and how to deal with some common issues with advisers.

A Brief Introduction to Negotiation

Whether you are dealing with major issues or are simply trying to push back against heavy-handed suggestions about the direction you should take your research, learning basic negotiation tactics can help you manage your adviser—and everyone else.

Chris Voss, who was a lead FBI kidnapping negotiator, explains key tactics to use.[7]

1. Be empathetic and build rapport using two proven techniques: mirroring and labeling. Mirror your counterpart's speech selectively, by repeating their words back to them, especially the last few words of their sentences. They will often feel drawn to respond and expand. Summarize and label what you're hearing, using phrases like "It sounds like . . . ," "It

looks like you're concerned about . . . ," "It seems like you . . ." If your counterpart feels understood, you'll hear a "That's right." If you get a "you're right" instead, ramp up the empathy!
2. Slow down and try out your "late night DJ" voice—that is, smooth, composed, even, calm. Nothing escalates a situation faster than voices that are obviously nervous, stressed, angry, and loud.
3. Proactively list the worst issues or outcomes before your counterpart says them—what Voss calls an "accusation audit." It can help your counterpart feel like you understand their position. Adam Grant, in his book *Originals*, explains how this tactic has been used effectively by starting sales pitches with why investors *shouldn't* invest![8]
4. Give your counterpart the opportunity to say no rather than yes. Saying no makes people feel safer and more in control (autonomy is one of our three most crucial psychological needs);[9] saying yes makes people feel defensive, like they know you're trying to sell them on something. Rephrase: "Is it a ridiculous idea for . . . ," "Would it be horrible if . . . ," "Is now a bad time for . . . ," "Do you disagree?" "Are you against . . ."
5. Voss's favorite negotiation question is "How am I supposed to do that?" Use a calm, questioning, nonconfrontational tone; don't be accusatory. The question invites your counterpart into your shoes, to consider how their demands affect you. It gives them the illusion of control. Ask how and what questions. Ask, "What's an example of an outcome that would work for you?" Let them offer suggestions on how to fix the situation. If it's their idea, they're more likely to go along with it.

You can practice these techniques—especially building rapport through mirroring and labeling—in everyday conversation. That way, when the time comes to negotiate something important, you won't feel completely in the dark.

> ### EXERCISE 9: NEGOTIATION
>
> Try out Chris Voss's conversation and negotiation tactics. Mirror during conversation to get your interlocutor talking. Practice your "late night DJ" voice. Ask, "How am I supposed to do that?" And see how the conversation develops!

Suggestions Versus Requirements

Your adviser will, commonly, have suggestions for you: which courses to take, who to have on your committee, what direction to take your research. My adviser, for instance, was a visionary. She was known among her students for "feature creep"—that is, suggesting all kinds of additions to projects that, honestly, would be awesome directions to take the research, but, also honestly, would have extended the time frame for those projects tremendously. She was showing her enthusiasm for the topic by wondering aloud, "Hey, wouldn't it be cool if we added . . . ," or, "What about comparing that to this related thing, or looking at it through this lens?" Take notes if your adviser does this! These ideas are great for those "future work" sections of papers, and as seeds for actual future projects.

But, these are, ultimately, *suggestions*—not requirements. They may not *feel* like suggestions, and it is often in your best interest to take your adviser's suggestions to heart, especially when your adviser is generally a good adviser who seems to have your best interests in mind. However, even the best advisers can suggest too much. Use negotiation tactics to push back: "How am I supposed to do that?" Give reasons for why you can't add the new feature right now and invite your adviser to help you find a way to satisfy both of you.

What Do I Do If My Adviser Says, "Don't Do X!" But I Know It Will Help My Career?

Do it anyway. You're the person living your life; you're the person who needs to be satisfied with it. You may also want to ask your adviser why they think you shouldn't do X—perhaps they actually have good reason for their advice—and it may not hurt to get a second opinion from another mentor or a career counselor at your school as well. But ultimately, it's your life, you need to make yourself happy, and you don't have to live your life according to your adviser's whims.

How to Have Hard Conversations

Hard conversations can involve asking for something, such as requesting accommodations while you take maternity leave; sharing difficult information, such as explaining that you're leaving academia or that your results didn't pan out; or negotiating a dissatisfying situation, such as the schedule you work.

Plan what you want to say about the issue or situation, why you're concerned, and what's working or not working. Line up the facts. Try to be direct, clear, and empathetic. Then, what are the options for improving or dealing with the situation? Make a list. Rehearse with a friend. For example, if you're going on maternity leave, can you turn a paper in early, line up your substitute teachers and lesson plans ahead of time, or schedule your experiment for before or after leave?

Second, schedule a meeting so there's time set aside for the conversation. If you're not comfortable in your adviser's office, try a public or neutral location like a coffee shop. If you think you need witnesses or would like help with the conversation, ask someone from a campus ombudsperson or ombuds office, or a mediation or conflict resolution office.

During the meeting, stay calm if you can. Remember to breathe. Listen in return. Use the negotiation tactics discussed earlier.

What Do I Do If My Adviser Isn't Responsive?

Sometimes advisers are slow-moving or indecisive. Sometimes they don't answer emails or phone calls; sometimes you're positively neglected. And sometimes you think they're ignoring you, but it turns out, it's a long weekend or they're home with sick kids, and they'll get back to work when they can. Some advisers like to give students room to work independently, but if you feel you need more support, when you do get a meeting, bring up your concern and ask for more support.

First, try to contact them again with your most direct, urgent questions. Email again. Professors often get hundreds of emails a day, so they may not have *meant* to ignore you. Then call, text, or track them down in person. If your adviser teaches a course, can you snag them for a quick question before or after? Do they have office hours? If they still don't respond, escalate, as outlined above.

What If My Adviser Makes Unwelcome Comments?

No matter why the comments are unwelcome—sexist, racist, intolerant, etc.—that's not okay. You could confront them directly; they may brush it off. Record the incident if you can; keep copies of texts or emails. Escalate as discussed above.

How Do I Break Up with My Adviser?

Students change advisers. Sometimes it's intellectual fit, sometimes it's about personality and style. Depending on the circumstances, you may feel angry and bitter, or you may feel more amiable. While you may feel like this is a bridge to burn, it is still probably best to be diplomatic. After all, you still may encounter your adviser at your institution—in classes, in the hallway, at department events—and they may still have some impact or input on your future career in the field. It's a politically tricky situation, as Amanda Seligman acknowledges.[10]

In an ideal world, you would be able to politely explain that your adviser isn't a great fit and that someone else is a better fit, they'd smile and say, "Great!", and we'd all move on. The world isn't ideal, but you can do your part: schedule a meeting. This counts as a hard conversation—follow the steps above. Keep the meeting brief. Stay professional and explain that your new adviser is a better fit for your work.

How Do I Find a New Adviser?

Even students who don't want to leave their adviser may have to find a new one—sometimes advisers will leave the university because they are denied tenure, or are retiring, or are simply moving to a job at another institution. In the latter case, you may have the option of following your adviser to their new institution. If not, however, you'll need to find someone else. Who else in your department has expertise in your area of interest? Who have you taken classes with, and liked? Flip back to the section on choosing an adviser. Do you know anyone at your institution who could serve? Set up an interview to discuss the possibility.

OTHER PROFESSORS

Although your adviser is the most important professor in your graduate career, they are not the only professor who matters. You may take classes from other professors, you may work with them, you may see them at department events or seminars. It is worth getting to know at least one or two of them reasonably well—well enough to ask for a letter of recommendation, well enough to be a backup option if your adviser turns out to be a bad fit for you, well enough to have other academic guidance available should you need it. You may also seek out other professors for research assistant or teaching opportunities; you can check their websites to see what they're working on now or stop by during their office hours to inquire.

Classes, especially smaller classes and seminars, departmental events, and rotations (for students in some lab sciences) are good ways to get to know other professors and for them to get to know you and your work. For example, in the second year of my master's program, I knew I needed a letter of recommendation from a second professor within my department to apply for the PhD program. But I didn't know anyone well enough to justify asking. Time for strategy: I selected a suitable professor, enrolled in one of her fall courses, and punched the work gas. Effort in, rec letter out.

chapter 6
Labs, Classes, and Teaching

In Somerville, a couple stops up the red line train from MIT, a little southern-themed restaurant served every kind of barbecue imaginable. The walls in its basement dining area were painted with modern, vibrant, bizarre cityscapes, dogs, futuristic robots, and surfing gods. At least once a semester, my lab group pushed tables together, ordered good food on the lab dime (the fried pickles were excellent), and spent a couple hours hashing out ideas, discussing research and life, and generally becoming better friends.

In the grand scheme of graduate schools, the MIT Media Lab was unusual in the amount of cash available for events like graduate student social nights. But my adviser knew that graduate school is a team sport, especially in our interdisciplinary field of human-robot interaction. While a dissertation may be the most independent, individual thing you ever do, you're still standing on the shoulders of giants; you may collaborate with labmates or build on fellow students' work; you will need advice and support from many people. My adviser wanted to foster a particularly supportive culture in her lab, and part of doing that was funding the occasional lab social night.

Who's on your team as you go through graduate school? Your adviser, yes, but they are far from the only person who matters in your graduate career. In this chapter and the next, I delve into your daily grind—coursework, teaching assistantships, research assistantships, and your path through your research program—with an emphasis on the people you encounter along the way.

WHO'S ON YOUR TEAM?

Throughout all your classes and daily activities, whether teaching or conducting research, you interact with many of the same people year in and year out: students, administrators, faculty. Some of these people are on your team—the people who most closely support you and work with you as you progress through your graduate program. Jessica Calarco lists numerous roles graduate students need to have filled on their team: (1) a topic/field/area expert to help you figure out what research to pursue; (2) an expert on your field's research methods; (3) someone to help you with writing and editing; (4) someone to help you strategize about your research and career; and (5) someone you enjoy talking to and can help you work through problems and stay balanced.[1] I would also add (6) someone to help you stay on track and get work done. These people may be graduate students, faculty, or even people outside academia entirely, and they may overlap—for example, roles 1 and 2 may be fulfilled by your adviser.

Students and Postdocs

Other students are good candidates for general support. Research on first-year grad students has found that the boot camp quality of many graduate programs can create strong bonds between students.[2] Peer mentoring programs can reduce student stress and improve student welfare.[3]

Who is in your core student group? In STEM fields, many faculty lead a research group or a laboratory with postdocs, PhD students, master's students, and undergrads. When signing on to work with such an adviser, you join the research group; they are who you see and work with most often outside of classes. The culture of your particular research group will significantly influence your research life, and your group mates will teach you as much or more than your adviser.

If you are in the humanities, your core student group will likely be classmates in your department. You may share an adviser with some of them, but your individual research will go in different directions, and you probably won't work closely outside of class. The farther you get in your program, the higher the potential for isolation. Regardless of your discipline, even when students start a program at the same time, in the same cohort, they certainly won't all graduate at the same time—some research will take longer, some students may take a leave of absence or leave entirely for illnesses, care work, to have babies, or for other reasons.

Students and postdocs may be able to give you feedback on your writing and research, and help you stay on track. When I started my PhD program, I formed a crit group with a handful of other women in my cohort.[4] We met monthly to discuss our progress, give practice talks, critique papers and proposals, hash out ideas, and generally support each other on the long road toward being #PhDone. We were in different fields and different research groups, but we traveled together in the program—a good reminder that we weren't in it alone. It lessened the isolation of being farther along in the program, when there were few or no classes, lots of independent time working and writing, and uncertainty about whether we were making sufficient progress.

Admins

Academic departments are composed of more than just faculty and students—they're also filled with administrators and support staff. Every department has admins who manage finances and budgets and help with purchasing and scheduling. Many science labs have research scientists, lab managers, and other staff who perform research-related work on a daily basis. The exact structure varies by department and by university, so make a point of finding out who the key people are at your institution. Ask more advanced students or your adviser. See who sends all the reminder and announcement emails about upcoming talks and deadlines.

Being on the good side of the admins is in your best interest. If you're nice to them, they'll be nice to you. Some admins function as department grandmothers; my research group's admin, for instance, liked to chat and provide social support for the students in addition to her administrative functions. The admins know the rules; they know the ins and outs of the university; they know what's going on in the department. Being able to ask them questions can be very helpful. But be respectful of their time. Do your homework before asking questions or barging into their offices: Is your question something you could answer with a quick website search or by actually reading past emails they've sent out? Sometimes the best way to stay on an admin's good side is being polite and following the instructions they send. For example, the program administrator in my department was a stickler for deadlines. So I turned in my paperwork on time—or early!—and stayed on her good side forever, understandably, since not having to track me down made her job that much easier.

EXERCISE 10: WHO'S ON YOUR TEAM?

Do you know who's on your team as you work toward your degree? Pull out a piece of paper!

1. Make a list of people you rely on—for academic support, social support, financial support, etc.
2. Next, note beside their name what you rely on them for: Advice about your career? Help with statistics? Questions about how academia works? Child care?
3. Now look back at the five roles listed on page 104. Do you have someone filling each role? If not, brainstorm who you might be able to reach out to for support.

Knowing who you rely on and where the gaps are—if any—can help you ensure you have the support you need to finish your degree. Knowing about a potential problem is the first step in addressing it.

COURSEWORK

Classes compose the majority of master's programs. PhD programs are heavier on classes for the first couple years, and then taper off into dissertation land. Graduate programs vary in their required classes; in most cases, all students follow the same course with a few electives or variations based on personal interest. Unlike an undergraduate degree, however, when classes end for the semester, graduate work often doesn't, which may be confusing to friends and family. Most students do a significant amount of work between semesters on papers, manuscripts, readings, and their own research.[5]

Classes are a mix of methods and content. Methods are ways people in your field approach research and answer questions or test hypotheses; content is the facts, information, theories, and the general subject matter you're supposed to know in your field. In social sciences and humanities, classes are where you learn how to conduct research; in STEM fields, you may have special methodology classes or lab sections, and also learn skills hands-on in a lab or in the field outside of class.

Graduate-level classes usually consume more time than any class at the undergraduate level. However, if you imagine the most difficult, demanding undergraduate class you took, many graduate classes are at about that level.

Grades and GPA matter relatively little, beyond maintaining whatever GPA is required for your program (often a 3.0 on a four-point scale). Occasionally, a program's funding decisions may consider GPA rankings. Once you have finished graduate school, GPA will matter not a whit.

Which Classes to Take?

When you have options in your course schedule, always pick the class that interests you more or is taught by the professor whose classes you enjoy over a class you think you ought to take because it better serves your degree or career. Going with what interests you leads to greater motivation and better performance.

Doing the Work

Think about how you learn best in classrooms, especially if it has been a while since you've been in a formal classroom setting. For example, I prefer to sit front and center, as it minimizes the distraction caused by other students and lets me focus on the lecture. Do you prefer to take notes in a notebook or on your laptop? Do you need special accommodations, such as someone to take notes for you? Accommodations can take time to get, even if they shouldn't, so ask early—your institution should have an office with a name like "Student Accommodations and Support Services" or "Educational Support Services" or "Student Disability Services."

Find a system for keeping track of assignments and deadlines (more on deadlines in chapter 8). The best system is the one you actually use. For example, tape the syllabus to the wall over your desk so you can easily reference the assignment list. Add assignments and exam dates to your daily planner, your calendar (whether paper or digital), a dry-erase board hanging on your wall, or a scheduling app.

For classes you find difficult, form study groups with other students. Peer tutoring can be incredibly effective.[6] You may also have access to campus resources such as tutoring centers for math, writing, and other subjects.

In doing assignments, Amanda Seligman points out that there are two general directions you can go.[7] One way is to make every class project and paper feed into your dissertation or thesis research, or these could even be writing or projects that are *part* of your thesis. The other is to explore widely in classes, which may give you the broad foundation you need to develop interesting dissertation ideas. Obtaining a broad knowledge base can also be important if, for instance, you aspire to a teaching-oriented job.

Group Projects

Some classes or research projects may involve group work. You might have bad memories of group projects from college or earlier schooling; often, there's at least one group member slacking off while the rest of you work harder to compensate. This is the *social loafing* problem. Ayelet Fishbach, in her book *Get It Done*, explains that when working with others, people often feel a motivational deficit, because they feel the others in the group can help out.[8] She suggests several remedies. First, when people are recognized as contributing to the group, they feel more accountable and responsible. In your group meetings, call out what everyone is doing; ensure everyone knows what everyone's responsibilities are and divide up the chores accordingly. Second, you may feel the work is more worth it when you contribute early—and are seen as a role model—than when you wait to contribute. So try speaking up earlier and getting your ideas heard. Third, if the group is large, break it into smaller subgroups, since this can make contributions feel more personal and more important.

Effective, Efficient Reading

Graduate classes have piles of assigned reading—more than you'll ever have time for. Seminar classes, in particular, are reading-heavy. Students are often expected to find additional reading (papers, articles, books, etc.) when doing assignments and writing papers—not to mention all the reading you may do for your master's thesis, exams, and dissertation.

Read strategically. No one does *all* the reading. Pick and choose what to read in depth, what to skim, and what you can get away with not reading at all. Weird advice, right? But in academia, there are thirty thousand different journals that researchers publish in and over three million new articles published per year.[9] A 2010 estimate put the total number of scholarly papers at fifty million—and that was over a decade ago![10] No one can keep up with reading everything published in their field. Part of what you learn in grad school is how to manage an overwhelming amount of information—so pick and choose.

To read strategically, first determine what your goal is. Why are you reading this article or book? What do you need to learn from it? That will guide your reading. For instance, you may want to learn about the central arguments and themes, the research questions explored, the data and methods used, or the limitations of the work. Start with the abstract or table of contents, introduction, and conclusion. Then choose other sections based on what you're looking to learn.

Take notes as you read. Jessica Calarco recommends keeping track of the citation as well as a couple bullet points of key background information; bullet points about the data or methods, the research question, the argument or contribution of the paper, and its implications for the field; and finally, a couple points about key findings, key patterns in the data, and limitations or unanswered questions.[11] It's up to you whether you opt for hard copies or digital notes, highlighters and stickies, notebooks or text files full of information.

How Do I Keep Track of References and Reading Notes?

As an undergrad, you may have written papers in which you had to cite or reference other works (papers, books, articles, etc.). As a graduate student, you definitely will.

To organize and keep track of references, use reference-management software (also called citation-management software or a citation manager). Some software will link the reference to the pdf (if you have it) and to your notes, let you add tags and create folders of references to share, or integrate with other tools such as Evernote.

When you write a paper, you can use the software to insert citations into your paper—for example, by using a word processor plug-in that gives you a special reference-management toolbar. You can also generate a bibliography automatically and change the formatting of all your references with one click. While the software isn't perfect, using it can definitely speed up your writing and referencing process. Many options exist, including Mendeley, EndNote, Zotero, RefWorks, and PaperPile; all have pros and cons. Try one; switch to another later if you don't like the first.

Should I Print Out Papers, or Annotate Them as PDFs? Or Is There Some Third Alternative That Works Even Better?

This is entirely your personal preference. I liked the ease of reading a printed-out paper on the train during my daily commute. I also liked being able to digitally search through my notes, so I read many pdfs on my laptop while taking notes in text files.

TEACHING ASSISTANTSHIPS

Teaching assistantships are part-time jobs, usually limited to fifteen to twenty hours per week, performed in exchange for a stipend or hourly wage and/or benefits, such as tuition waivers and health insurance. Teaching assistants (TAs) generally answer to and help one or more professors who lead one or more classes. Some TAs are responsible for an entire class as the instructor of record; in this case, they may alternatively be known as a graduate student instructor or teaching fellow. Duties may include helping with grading, proctoring exams, leading labs or discussion sections, managing a course website, answering student emails and handling communication with students, holding office hours, developing a syllabus, selecting readings, printing or preparing class materials, and preparing and giving lectures. If you lead class sessions, you may also design lecture slides and notes, create assessments, lead class activities, and evaluate and grade students.

Some people enjoy teaching—it can be a highlight of their graduate program. If you're considering a career as a teacher or professor, being a TA gives you valuable experience. You can learn a lot by teaching. But teaching (and all accompanying activities) can also gobble up your time. If, as a TA, you cannot complete the amount of expected work in the expected number of hours per week, it's exploitation. Check whether your university has a graduate student union. Student unions help protect student interests. (More on this in chapter 14.)

Some institutions have support for student teachers, such as classes on teaching methodologies or a student teaching office you can visit for help planning classes. However, many universities, especially underfunded public universities, throw TAs into teaching with no guidance at all. What do you do then? If you're teaching a lower-level introductory class, there may be example syllabi, slides, notes, assignments, exams, and other materials online, which you may be able to use outright, or use as models on which to base your own content. Sometimes, you can reuse materials from your adviser or other professors that you work for—ask permission. Many disciplines have teaching journals, websites, and Facebook groups where people share ideas about how to teach the subject. (See the resources.) You could also take matters into your own hands, and after gaining some teaching experience, organize a semester-long workshop for new teaching assistants yourself. Many department chairs would love for someone to take the initiative.

Take notes as you gain experience teaching. Document what worked well and what didn't so you can repeat or revise on the next go-around. Jessica Calarco recommends digitizing all your teaching materials so you can easily reference them later. Teaching experience is useful for academic careers—especially at teaching-heavy institutions such as smaller liberal arts colleges, community colleges, or regional campuses of state schools. If you discover that you dislike teaching, great—that's good information, so you can find a career that doesn't involve as much of it.

Effective Teaching

Effective and efficient teaching can take many forms. Common to all of them is treating your students with respect and aligning your teaching with the intended learning outcomes or learning objectives of the class. Set clear goals for what you want students to take away from the class as a whole, each class session, and each activity, then choose or design activities that help your students achieve those goals.[12] Set a range of learning objectives that build on each other—at the first level, student should remember/list/identify; the second level, understand/explain/describe; the third, apply; fourth, analyze; fifth, evaluate; sixth, create.[13]

When you plan activities, try active learning techniques rather than only lectures. Active learning engages students in the material through discussion, problem solving, review, and practice—it's hugely beneficial.[14] Formats can be small group discussions, break-out groups, in-class debates, or class-wide brainstorming. The book *The Surprising Power of Liberating Structures: Simple Rules to Unleash a Culture of Innovation*, by Henri Lipmanowicz and Keith McCandless, lists many discussion- and interaction-facilitation ideas.[15] Some of my favorite classes as a student had frequent open-ended large group discussions, for which students brainstormed questions and wrote reading responses ahead of time to get them thinking. Asking students to prepare for discussions as part of their homework can be especially helpful for introverted students, so they have time to think and are not put on the spot.

If you facilitate discussions, your job as teacher is to moderate, reiterate what students say, summarize and clarify long-winded answers, help validate what students have said and make sure no one is talked over, and call on people to invite them to talk if they look like they want to say something but can't seem to jump in fast enough.

If you will be teaching often, keep notes or a journal to track what worked and what didn't. Jessica Calarco recommends spending a few minutes taking notes after each lesson or class, especially if you know you'll be teaching that lesson or class again. For example, if one of the readings you selected didn't work well, find a new reading right away. If you wish you had explained something differently, work out a better way to explain it and write it down.

If you've read all this and thought, "But I just don't have *time* to develop learning objectives and carefully plan readings and design assessments!" Welcome to TA life! How do you teach well when you're overwhelmed?

Try alternative classroom formats and activities—lectures are "standard" but take more time and energy to prepare. Assign students to present on the readings each week, so all you have to do is add commentary. Invite guest lecturers to present on topics you're less familiar with. Add more discussion time, so the students do part of the work of engaging in the topic. Try a flipped classroom. Books such as *Teaching What You Don't Know* by Therese Huston and *Small Teaching: Everyday Lessons from the Science of Learning* by James Lang have good suggestions for minimizing your time.[16]

Inclusive Teaching

Put effort up front into inclusive teaching practices—that is, into creating an environment where all students can learn. Inclusivity starts before you step into the classroom, with course design and what's on the syllabus. For example, ensure that your class incorporates readings and highlights contributions from a range of people—especially minorities and women, not just the most prominent scholars in the field.

For assignments, state your expectations up front. Give detailed instructions and share a rubric outlining how you'll grade the assignment. This way, no matter what a student's background, they'll have all the information they need to do well in your class. Many times, problems arise when a student doesn't conform to "standard" academic expectations about how to complete certain assignments simply because they are unaware of the standard. Be inclusive when designing assignments and assessments. For instance, you could choose to avoid long, timed, in-class exams since these can be especially stressful or difficult for students with learning disabilities or ADHD. Use take-home exams, projects, papers, or portfolios instead.

Be mindful of how you interact with students and who you praise.[17] For example, it can be easy to only praise talkative students who contribute to discussions loudly and often; make sure you pay attention to your quieter students and give them opportunities to contribute and be acknowledged as well. Take attendance, so you can learn your students' names—and take notes on correct pronunciation!

Finally, the syllabus is the right place to list course policies, such as how you will handle absences for mental health, illness, and babies. Some inclusive syllabi include a "child policy" stating that it's perfectly fine for students to bring their baby or child to class with them if they don't have child care, so long as they do their best to minimize disruptions; some include diversity statements or wellness resources. Giving your students grace when needed and treating them with respect goes a long way.

RESEARCH ASSISTANTSHIPS

Research assistants (RAs) perform part-time research-related work, usually limited to twenty hours per week, for a professor, often their adviser but not necessarily. Like TAs, RAs are paid a stipend, hourly wage, and/or other benefits. The particulars of their work varies widely by field—organizing files, cleaning lab equipment, updating references, annotating bibliographies, conducting studies in the field, dealing with human subjects research such as surveys and interviews, writing software, bench work, analyzing data, writing papers. Generally, if you are an RA, you won't be required to teach. There may also be restrictions on other work you can take on. While I was at the MIT Media Lab, for example, we had an exclusivity clause—students were not allowed to take on outside work; all their mental energy was supposed to belong to the lab.

Be wary of anyone who asks you to work for free. Volunteering is only worthwhile if it allows you to learn something you're especially excited about. Professors may offer hands-on research training, the chance to help on a publication, or course credit; evaluate carefully, as you may get all of these *and* pay in other RA positions.

In STEM fields, where RAs frequently work in their adviser's lab, an RA's work may feed into their own independent research. This was the case for me: I was an RA for my adviser, received a stipend and benefits, and the research I helped with became the foundation for my dissertation. As Jessica Calarco mentions, you may be involved in the publication of the research as a coauthor, more often if you're receiving a stipend than if you're paid an hourly wage.

There's less to say about RAing than about teaching because it varies so much. You may find the tips on negotiation and managing your adviser useful (chapter 5), as well as the sections on managing research (chapter 7) and managing time and projects (chapter 8).

chapter 7
Research, Theses, and Dissertations

For months, I mulled over ideas, reviewed reading notes, and drew diagrams to connect concepts and questions that fascinated and delighted me. Seeking my dissertation topic felt like putting together a puzzle. Once I found the right arrangement of pieces, the topic would be perfect. I just had to find it.

I had recently stalled on writing my dissertation proposal because I didn't know where it was going. I had an outline; I had some background and a general topic; but I didn't have the *story*. I scheduled daily time to think, until finally, I worked out the specifics of the final project I would do to tie everything together.

How do you plan and execute research? The details will vary based on your discipline and particular graduate program, but the gist is the same: generate ideas, hypotheses, and questions; draft a research proposal; find and work with a committee; systematically gather data, document your process and findings, analyze and interpret your findings; and write about, present, and defend your work. This stuff is the meat of graduate school, especially in research-focused master's or PhD programs. Here's a rundown of the process.

EXAMS

If you're a doctoral student, you spend the first two or three years on required coursework. After that, you face a set of intensive written and/or oral examinations. If you pass, you advance in your program. The exams may be called general exams ("generals"), qualifying exams ("quals"), graduate oral exams ("orals"), comprehensive exams ("comps"), field exams, preliminary exams (prelims), cumulative exams ("cumes"), or some variation thereof. For the sake of simplicity, I'll refer to them as "exams" throughout the chapter.

These exams entail months of studying. They may cover material from your graduate coursework, exam-specific reading list, and/or thesis proposal. They are designed to demonstrate that you are an expert in your sub-domain and could teach and/or perform research on the subject. You are tested both on your knowledge and your ability to reason about the subject—can you explain the central theories and concepts? Do you know your sub-domain's history? Are you familiar with key scholars, methods, and data? Can you situate your work among everything happening in your field, in relation to any ongoing debates in your field? Can you synthesize and integrate work across your field and in your sub-domain, and not merely regurgitate summaries of what you've learned?

The exams also let you *act* as an expert in your field, as Jessica Calarco explains.[1] By completing the exams successfully, you show that you can share knowledge about your topic, like you would in a press interview. Amanda Seligman says exams can showcase a student's professional demeanor—for example, how they handle questions they don't know the answers to, and how well they can present a synthesis of their topic.[2]

The exams are an opportunity to deeply read, think, and learn about your field. They're practice for making good arguments supported by current literature. Exams are also an opportunity to work on project management skills, such as breaking down a huge amount of studying and reading into specific, doable steps (more on that in chapter 8).

Exam Format

Most students are examined by a committee of three to five faculty from their department. In some departments, you will have a say in who your examining committee is; in others, you won't. If you do get to help pick your exam committee, be sure to read the section later in this chapter about picking thesis and dissertation committee members—all that advice applies here as well.

Before your exams, you generally have to make a reading list, or even a research proposal. Your committee may have to approve it; you may have to revise it before they approve it. Then, you spend a lot of time reading and studying the material your exams will cover.

The exams are most often written or oral, with pass/fail grading. Most programs let you retake an exam once, perhaps twice. If you don't pass, you do not get to continue in the program.

Written exams can follow the conventional exam format—a bunch of problems to solve or questions to answer (e.g., as short essays) within some time limit, anywhere from hours to days. Sometimes they involve writing a paper or a literature review.

For oral exams, on exam day, you may have to give a talk about your proposed research or about the areas your reading covered—anywhere from ten or fifteen minutes up to an hour. Then, the faculty will ask questions (and sometimes they interrupt your talk with questions). Their questions can encompass whatever you agreed to study in your proposal or reading list, as well as questions related to your coursework and field more broadly. Their goal is to figure out where the limits of your knowledge are. Oral exams usually last between one and three hours. At the end of the exam, you'll be asked to step out of the room while your committee deliberates, and then they'll give you feedback right then and there: whether you passed (conditionally or unconditionally), whether you failed, and sometimes, how your performance was with details on what they liked and what you could improve.

Exam Examples

Here are two examples of different exam formats.

My department was highly interdisciplinary with a broad range of research groups (covering biology, art, robotics, and mechatronics, among others). There was no one-size-fits-all exam that all students could take that would be relevant to their discipline. Students selected their own three-person exam committees (with advice or suggestions from their primary adviser) and designed both their own reading lists and their exams. My exams had four parts: a two-hour pass/fail oral exam with the whole committee, and three written exams, one with each committee member. Two of my written exams were pass/fail short essay format; the third, covering my primary research area, involved drafting a paper.

Taylor, a student in cellular and molecular medicine, shared her exam format on her blog: a pass/fail hour oral exam with five faculty lasting one and a half hours.[3]

She had to submit a research proposal two weeks ahead of time and give a fifteen-minute talk on her proposed work at the start of the exam. The remainder of the time was spent being questioned on both her proposed work and on anything related to her coursework or anything brought up in her answers.

Preparing for Your Exams

First, find out exactly what the requirements and constraints are in *your* department. Ask more senior students: Is there a document laying out all the details? What topics are generally covered? How did *they* prepare? Students who have recently been through the process are your best resource. Try to get a sense of how much studying they did to prepare, what kind of knowledge you'll be expected to have, the types of questions students are asked, and common pitfalls. Find out who will be examining you—and if you can, what their personal quirks are when it comes to examining a student.

Prepare early. Start preparing earlier than you think you ought to, because reading and synthesizing takes time. Personally, because my exams were highly customized—I chose my own exam areas, created my own reading list, and picked an exam committee—I allotted a year for the whole process. You'll find my detailed timeline presented in the next chapter, where I cover project management, alongside strategies for handling procrastination. Many students worry about leaving too much studying to the last minute. For your exams, night-before cramming *won't* be your best friend.

If other students in your cohort are also preparing for exams, form a study group. Practice explaining concepts together, review topics, ask questions. If you're studying on your own, try to get friends together anyway, even if they're not in your field. Explaining concepts from your field to them can be good practice. Or ask more advanced students in your field if they're willing to sit through a practice talk (we often did this in my lab group).

THESES AND DISSERTATIONS

After exams, the next big milestone is your thesis or dissertation. In many PhD programs, you begin dissertation work after you have finished all courses and exams, usually several years in; but like everything, it varies by field. In the sciences, for instance, students generally begin working on research of some kind earlier than they might in the humanities, where students often have more classes first. Master's students are often required to complete a master's thesis or master's project in their second year, especially in terminal programs.

Regardless of whether you're working on a master's thesis or a PhD dissertation, the process is similar—it is simply condensed for the master's thesis. Here's the overview, which I'll expand on below. First, choose a committee. Then, write a proposal for the project or research you intend to do, which explains the key problem or question you're going to tackle, outlines how you plan to tackle it and what methods you will use, and what your timeline is for completing the work. Your committee approves the proposal—sometimes after requiring you to revise it, or after a proposal defense meeting during which they give you feedback. After approval, you do the work. You write about it. Your committee gives you feedback; often, you're required to do a public oral defense or presentation. Once you've made all required changes, your committee signs off on your dissertation and you're done.

Scale and Scope: Master's Thesis Versus PhD Dissertation

A master's thesis is an independent project that shows you can do the kind of research or creative work common in your field. It is smaller in scope, shorter in length, less ambitious, and less revolutionary than a PhD dissertation. Often, it takes the form of a long paper about research you've completed; in the arts, it may involve a performance, or creating a portfolio or piece of art. The average length is fifty to a hundred and fifty pages;[4] theses are longer in the humanities and shorter in sciences.

Take your master's thesis seriously—especially if you're doing it along the way to a doctoral degree. It's one of the first big research projects you'll do, and thus an important milestone. In STEM fields, it may even net you a peer-reviewed published paper (more on publishing in chapter 9). My master's thesis was a proof of concept for my eventual dissertation project, both in the technical details and in proving that I could complete a long-term field study.

Dissertations are more substantial in every sense. At the MIT Media Lab, my professors liked to say, "A master's thesis adds to the conversation in your field. A PhD thesis *changes* the conversation." A psychology professor once told me that a master's thesis is one experimental study, while a dissertation is three. In my case, my dissertation was even more than that, but the general takeaway is that dissertations in every field are a lot more work than master's theses. You have more time to complete it, you're more skilled in your field, and you're expected to scale up the scope of your research to reflect that. Your project has to be original. You'll be writing a substantial document.

In the humanities and social sciences, your dissertation will resemble a book: two to three hundred pages. In STEM fields, your dissertation will be shorter, one to two hundred pages, and may look more like a collection of articles, each of which you may have separately published and stitched together into a coherent whole for your dissertation. In arts or applied fields, your dissertation might consist of a performance report. Seek out theses and dissertations from your adviser's past students and from other students in your department. Skim them to get a sense for the document format and the kind and amount of work expected.

Exactly how independent you are expected to be during your research varies widely by discipline. You will always receive at least some advice and direction from your committee. Beyond that, on one end of the spectrum, you may work on a project designed by your adviser or highly influenced by or related to your adviser's research—more common in STEM fields. You may work with other students or professors. In the social sciences, you may use an existing data set to do an original analysis. In the humanities, you're generally expected to come up with your idea entirely on your own, unrelated to the work your adviser does. Your funding source may also influence your level of autonomy. Regardless of discipline, however, and regardless of where the idea comes from, you will be expected to do the majority of your project individually.

Format

A dissertation or thesis is a long document, divided into chapters, with sections and subsections within each chapter. You generally need to supply an abstract; acknowledgments; a table of contents; lists of illustrations, figures, and/or tables; glossaries; appendices; and a bibliography—but of course, it varies by discipline and institution. Your institution will have a set of formatting guidelines you will need to follow, which you can probably find somewhere on the institution's website—or ask a librarian where they are. The institution or previous students may provide Word or LaTeX templates you can use as well. If you want to see what's common at your institution, and, specifically, in your department, find copies of theses and dissertations from your adviser's past students and from other students in your department, either online or from your campus library.

Timeline

Be up front with your committee about any constraints on your timeline for completing your thesis. For example, perhaps you're hoping to go on the job market in the fall, or your funding is only guaranteed for three years. The school itself may have a deadline—some require students to finish in a certain number of years. Visas, family, children, a spouse or partner's work, medical issues, and all sorts of other things can add to the pressure you feel to complete your degree in a given time frame. If you tell your committee, they can work with you to ensure you scale your project appropriately and get the resources you need to finish. (More on timelines in chapter 8.)

Your Dissertation Committee

Your committee will consist of two to five faculty, usually including your adviser, who evaluate your research progress, give you advice and feedback, and decide when your dissertation or thesis is done enough for you to graduate. Some universities require all of the committee to be from your university, while some don't; some require an outside reader or external reviewer from another university or even from industry or practice. In my department, for instance, most students had a three-person committee: their adviser, one person from the department, and one from outside.

When choosing your committee, consider expertise, responsiveness, fit, and connections.

Expertise You want people who can support your research trajectory. First, you need someone who can help you design your research projects, choose appropriate methods, and follow through on your methodology—and then you'll know up front that they'll have signed off on your methodology. Jessica Calarco calls this "your methods person": someone who knows the *how* of research in your field, whether it's figuring out statistical models, working lab machines, getting access to archives or interviewees, crafting institutional review board proposals, and so forth. This could be your adviser, or it could be another committee member.

You also need someone with a deep knowledge of your field, your field's open questions, and the challenges you might face—the *what* and *why* of your research. To find out what expertise people have, check their websites and their CVs. See what work they've done. Ask your adviser about them. Ask other grad students about them. You also may already know from working with them in the past, taking their classes, or reading their papers.

Responsiveness Expertise is only useful if your committee members are responsive. They should give you advice in a timely manner and care about you graduating on schedule. They don't necessarily have to be local to your area, since you can communicate via email and video calls, but that can help. If there are two equally qualified people, pick the one who answers your emails promptly and seems like they'll be able to give you more support and feedback. During my general exams, my adviser gave me a suggestion for one committee member. I met with the guy, and he seemed great: useful knowledge, right field, all that. But then he never responded to another email I sent. So, after waiting a month or two, I gave up and looked for someone else. Err on the side of responsiveness. Timely support and feedback are invaluable.

Fit Pick people you like and who don't hate each other. If you pick two individuals with a professional grudge against each other and who commonly go in different directions on the same topic, they'll give you conflicting advice and their arguments will influence how they deal with you. Not a great position to be in. Similarly, if you don't get along with someone, even if they are the greatest expert ever on your topic, pick someone else.

Connections One of my mentors recommended being strategic: choosing committee members is an opportunity to connect with an expert in a field of interest who you might not otherwise come into contact with. If you're planning on the tenure track, look for someone at an institution you may want to work at someday, or who could provide a useful letter of recommendation. If you're considering industry, look for someone with great industry connections.

Your adviser may have suggestions for who to pick for your committee. Listen. Thank them. However, as discussed in chapter 5, your adviser's suggestions are not requirements—you don't have to *take* their suggestions. In the ideal case, your adviser will be able to introduce you to people who can support and further your research. If your adviser can't connect you to people who would make great committee members, you'll have to do more of the legwork. Ask other professors if they can connect you. If you can't get an introduction, you can also reach out to potential committee members directly.

How Do You Ask Someone to Be on Your Committee?   First, check with your primary adviser to see if they think the person would be a good fit. If so, send a short email asking them whether they would consider being on your committee, why you think they would be a good fit, and, if they *would* be interested, whether you could meet them in person (e.g., during their office hours) to discuss further. Be brief, be polite! If they turn you down, remember it's probably not about you. Professors have a ton of demands on their time and energy. Turning you down could simply mean they don't want to overextend themselves. Or, perhaps they don't see themselves as the best fit for your research.

For any potential committee member, ask questions that will help you set expectations and determine whether you'll work well together. Determine ahead of time what you actually want out of each committee member—say, feedback on your methods or study design. Are they prepared to give that? Do they prefer to see your work as you complete it, or once you have finished chapters? What initial feedback do they have on your dissertation ideas? How often can you meet with them? It's important to meet with each committee member at least once every semester, and with your primary adviser at least once a month. These meetings can be remote; after the COVID pandemic, most people are familiar with virtual ways of meeting and providing feedback. I'll talk more about keeping everyone in the loop later in this chapter.

DISSERTATION PROPOSALS

Once you have a committee, you craft a dissertation proposal (sometimes called a dissertation prospectus). The proposal outlines the question you will address or the problem you are tackling, as concisely and clearly as possible, using the active voice. Usually, it includes a literature review explaining why your topic is of interest, how other people have approached the topic, and why what you're doing is different and novel. Then, it describes the methods you plan to use, your plan for analyzing the data you collect, a timeline for completion, and sometimes, a chapter outline. Leonard Cassuto says a proposal is a provisional document, a statement of ideas and questions, "not a polished work of compressed scholarship that need only be inflated to become a dissertation."[5]

Some departments expect you to write the first few chapters of your dissertation (such as the introduction and a literature review); some expect preliminary or pilot data. Some may require a presentation instead of a written proposal.

Your proposal is an opportunity to get feedback on your topic, plan, and proposed methods from your committee, as well as from anyone else with whom you might share the proposal. Early feedback can help you discover fatal flaws prior to investing years in the work. Your committee can suggest improvements, or endorse what you have proposed, which can give you some confidence going forward.

Your institution will, no doubt, have its own special format you need to follow. Ask more advanced graduate students for copies of their proposals, if you can. My lab group kept a shared folder with everyone's proposals in it, which newer students could reference when crafting their own. Regardless of the format, be sure to talk with your committee during the process. Ask them questions as you plan and write about equipment, methods, ethics, safety, data collection, archive access, analyses, and so on.

FINDING RESEARCH IDEAS

A friend from grad school, Nick de Palma, said he thought of academia as a creative profession. He did not mean that doing research required some amount of creativity, though it does, but that research was *fundamentally* creative—creating knowledge, ideas, and theories. Because research is a creative profession, the advice you find aimed at other creative professions—such as for artists and writers—can be borrowed and applied to research. For example, many writers set aside special time for working and developing ideas; they allocate other time for administrative or business work (more on that in the next chapter). Many creatives keep journals or notebooks tracking all their ideas; in *Notebooks of the Mind*, Vera

Johnson-Steiner explains how these pieces of ideas can come together to form new, creative thoughts.[6]

In a doctoral program, you will be expected to have creative ideas and execute your own original research in the form of your dissertation. Yes, in some disciplines, especially lab sciences, your dissertation adviser may help you pick a topic that is closely related to the lab's general research direction. But you will need to make it your own.

How do you find your topic? You've read papers, taken classes, learned about open challenges and questions in your field. Somehow, you have to find a gap in what's already been done, an opportunity to make your mark, and do something original.

First, recognize that generating ideas is a process. You won't find your topic in a day. I spent a semester pondering ideas and connections before reaching the topic that formed the core of my dissertation. Adam Grant, in his book *Originals*, explains that procrastination can, counterintuitively, be useful for creative thought and idea generation.[7] Let your questions sit in the back of your mind while you do other things. This can enable you to come up with more creative, unusual, and divergent ideas than you might otherwise have generated. When a task is incomplete—such as choosing a dissertation topic—it may lodge more deeply in your memory and stay active in your mind.[8]

That said, Grant is careful to remind us that procrastination doesn't always fuel creativity, nor does it help with productivity. If you are not intrinsically motivated to find a dissertation topic and finish graduate school, then stalling will only set you behind. This is a good reason to start thinking about topics early—but make no early decisions. Let your topic ideas percolate. Let them mature. Let your mind work when you're busy on other projects.

The Foundation for Ideas

To support the process of generating ideas, besides time, you need fuel. Adam Grant explains how you need a wealth of material to draw on in order to remix it into your new, original idea. For example, when writing his famous "I Have a Dream" speech, Martin Luther King Jr. wrote draft after draft, revising up until the moment he started speaking. The final version was largely improvised, but he had given so many other speeches, gone through so many drafts, had collected so many quotes, Bible verses, anecdotes, lines from poems, and bits of sermons that he could craft something new and amazing. That's what you want to do with your dissertation idea.

You've already begun the process of building your foundation through classwork and reading. As you progress through graduate school, explicitly add to your foundation. Gain a sense of what's current and cutting-edge in your discipline by talking with other scholars in your field, attending seminars, and reading the latest journal or conference papers. Join or organize a regular academic reading group (the logistics of keeping one going can be tricky–my own success varied year to year). In mine, we took turns choosing papers to read, which meant I often read papers I wouldn't have read otherwise. Some were highly relevant; others, not so much. One question I always tried to ask was "How can I apply the ideas in this paper to my work?" That is, what can I learn from this paper? Having this question in mind helped me ground what I was reading in what I already knew.

Read the "future work" sections in papers you find interesting–common in STEM fields. These sections are full of researchers' ideas that didn't quite make it into the current project, ways to extend their work, and ways to improve it.

If you have time–even a little–read outside your field, especially nonfiction books. This can give you new perspectives on the topics in your discipline and introduce you to new areas that you might find interesting.

How Do I Learn About New Research in My Field?

Find papers using digital archives and indexes such as JSTOR, Google Scholar, PubMed, Web of Science, ResearchGate, and Scopus.[9] Most institutions have subscriptions to the digital versions of many journals; if your library doesn't have what you need, try interlibrary loans or search online (e.g., sometimes authors post pdfs on their websites).

Set up article alerts. With Google Scholar, for instance, you can set up keyword alerts to receive a weekly digest of the latest publications with specific keywords, and you can follow authors to get notifications when they publish new work. You can subscribe to journals' table of contents alerts, and read with a newsreader or RSS reader. In some STEM fields, the newest work shows up at conferences, so you may want to set up alerts for the proceedings (the collection of papers presented at the conference) when they are released (usually soon after the conference is held).

When searching, don't only focus on the most-cited research. Use keyword searches and look for recent research, including work by junior and minority scholars or from smaller, specialty journals. Ask your adviser and more advanced graduate students which journals or conferences in your field to keep tabs on. You can see who is citing relevant papers by clicking the "cited by" links on Google Scholar. Other indexes may have similar search tools. In some fields, the newest papers are posted on preprint servers (more on that in chapter 9). Research blogs in your field may do roundups or summaries.

Once you have a reading list, block off time to read—such as fifteen minutes a day, or a couple hours every Thursday afternoon.

Pulling Your Ideas Together

Keep a research journal as you read. This is common advice I've received from numerous professors. Begin early in graduate school if you can, not only when you need to start planning your dissertation. Write down ideas and questions you have—good or bad, don't judge them yet—and return to them later. Jot down thoughts on what you're reading and how concepts connect back to other things you've learned. Periodically—every month, every semester—review your notes. Are there themes? Do you see patterns in what draws your interest? Some of these ideas may be seeds for new projects or even your dissertation.

Set aside time for thinking, processing, summarizing, planning, and synthesizing. I do this on paper, in my research notebook, and while writing. The process of drafting coherent paragraphs on a topic means I'm clarifying and summarizing my understanding of the topic at the same time. I'm synthesizing information across sources. The important thing, however you do it, is to not only accumulate knowledge but also process what you've learned. Connecting ideas deepens your understanding of how different pieces of knowledge fit together. Connecting ideas in new ways is the basis of creativity.

Conversation with colleagues and friends can help you pull ideas together, summarize, and synthesize. In my lab group, for example, the students and postdocs took a daily walk downstairs to get tea or coffee from the third-floor kitchen. We'd troop back up to our lab space, steaming mugs in hand, and stand around throwing ideas off the wall for half an hour before getting back to work. We discussed serious stuff, like the ethics of child-robot interaction, and random stuff, like ceiling robots that could unobtrusively steal leftover food from other people's meetings. It is also beneficial to talk with people from outside your field. Hearing from people who see the world from a different perspective or who need you to explain your ideas in a different way can produce new insights and help you see your work in a fresh light.

You may find opportunities to explore ideas without committing to an entire dissertation via class projects and papers. Some professors in graduate courses are amenable to you tweaking topics or assignments to better fit your research interests, so long as you talk to them about it first. While most of my explorations in class projects were one-offs, a few became full-fledged parts of my dissertation.

Throughout all of your thinking, conversations, and writing, try to keep asking, "And then what?" If your hypotheses are supported, what next? If you're wrong about something, what are the implications? Where are the opportunities? What might happen *if*? How is your work related to other people's work, or other research areas? What are the implications of that? What could be changed or improved? And *then* what?

Finally, remember the scale and scope of your thesis or dissertation. How much time do you *really* have to complete the work? For a master's thesis in particular, which usually must be completed in a semester or a year, it is all too easy to dream up ideas that are too big for the time frame. Dream big, but be practical. Push back against committee members who urge you to do too much—so long as you know it is actually too much (some committee members push because they know you can accomplish more than you think). You can have bigger ideas and a grander vision than what you actually implement. You can write about your grand vision, explaining how what you actually did fits into that vision, as one step along the way.

Judging Your Ideas

How do you know which ideas are worth pursuing? Adam Grant says that if you have expertise in the area or field, then you can trust your intuition and gut feelings.[10] Brains are, after all, remarkable at pattern recognition when trained up sufficiently—that is, when you're an expert on the topic—so let your brain do its thing and see how you feel about the ideas. Run your ideas by your adviser and peers. Your adviser definitely has expertise, and peer evaluations frequently provide some of the best judgments of the potential success of an idea, especially when those peers are familiar with your field or domain.

Finding Your Path

Finding your thesis topic is a personal journey. You're exploring what you find meaningful. If you want to change your research focus, a good time can be during a transition period: from master's to PhD, after general exams, during your proposal. Pick an area you'll be happy working in for a couple years. After your dissertation, you can change areas again. Pick something interesting, run with it, see where it goes. It's okay if you go in a different direction later.

Critically, you need to tell a good story about how your past work led to where you are now. So long as you have a proper story, it doesn't matter if what you do *actually* directly follows what you did before. For example, early in my graduate career, all my research focused somewhat narrowly on social robots as language-learning companions for young children. I realized I could frame that work as a piece of a broader story and discuss it nonchronologically. The simple act of talking about my prior work in a different way freed me to create a more coherent dissertation story.

Passion Comes Later

A prospective student once asked me how I decided I wanted to pursue my particular dissertation topic. For some students, the answer is passion. They work on a burning question, a beloved topic, one thing that drives them like no other. Not me. I had many questions that could be pursued through the lens of my dissertation research, and many other questions and interests too, which arguably informed my work in unique ways. I thought my work was interesting and enjoyable. I could tell a compelling story connecting the work I did through my master's and PhD. And I graduated.

You don't need to have burning passion to succeed in graduate school. You need curiosity, dedication, and drive—but burning passion for your topic is optional. Burnett and Evans, in *Designing Your Life*, argued that the advice to "follow your passion" is extremely unhelpful, because in most cases, passion comes after mastery, not before: "Many people operate under the dysfunctional belief that they just need to find out what they are passionate about. Once they know their passion, everything else will somehow magically fall into place.... [But] the research shows that, for most people, passion comes after they try something, discover they like it, and develop mastery—not before."[11]

What If My Adviser Doesn't Like My Ideas?

Some advisers have an agenda of their own and may not be inclined to let you go any direction you wish with your dissertation. If this is the case for you, return to chapter 5 for negotiation strategies. Assess the trade-off between the effort and potential interpersonal strife of negotiating your favored topic, and being stuck working on something you don't care about. Neither is ideal. I'd argue the latter is worse, because if you're not interested in your topic, you won't have the motivation to finish your dissertation. That said, if the topic is sort of interesting, and keeping your adviser happy is worth a lot to you, you may be able to push through.

EXERCISE 11: IDEATION

Ideation is simply the act of producing ideas. At the first stage of ideation, the goal is to produce as many ideas as possible—judgment comes later.

1. Get a sheet of paper or a blank text document.
2. List themes that have occurred in your work. What topics or areas have you touched on so far? For example, when I was brainstorming, I came up with the following list: robotic learning companions, attention, emotion, longitudinal studies, memory, children modeling robots, personalization . . . Now, come up with some similarly broad categories.

3. List things you find interesting in your area. These don't have to be broad. They can be as specific as you want. What questions intrigue you? What is unanswered? What do you want to understand better? When you were reading papers, what sparked your interest? In your classes, which lectures, assignments, or readings excited you? These are all areas that could be good for diving into in your dissertation.
4. List current, cutting-edge issues in your field. You may have a sense of this from papers you've read, courses you've taken, or people you've talked to. If you're not sure, find a top journal in your field and look at the titles of recent papers to get an idea of what's being published right now (see chapter 9 for more on finding research in your field).
5. Now reflect. Make a list of five possible dissertation topics. For example, you can go deeper in any of the areas you've listed. You can go broader and tie everything together in an interesting way, or look at some underlying theory or framework. You can pick a small question that you can address in a big way, or even a small question that just pushes the edge of what's known. You can work at a different level of granularity—for example, physiology versus psychology (lower level versus higher level). Each level of granularity uses different methods and theories, and generates different insights.

DOING RESEARCH

Once your topic is approved, it's time to work like bees in spring. The next sections cover the groundwork; the next chapter lines up time management and timelines.

Research Methods

In deductive research, like most lab sciences, experimental research, and quantitative and survey research, you begin with a hypothesis. Then you test it and report whether or not your data supported the hypothesis. Inductive research, on the other hand, starts with a question. Then, you look for data that will help answer the question. Inductive research often uses qualitative and descriptive quantitative methods, such as ethnographic interviews, archival research, and text analysis, common in social sciences and humanities.

In your proposal, you may have explained the methods you intend to use to answer your research questions. You may already have an understanding of the basics of doing research in your field from courses taken as an undergraduate or graduate student—a research methods course, a statistics class, or lab classes. You may have research experience if you work as a research assistant. But no matter what kind of work you do—pipetting chemicals, running samples, designing interview guides, coding transcripts, running regressions, performing field studies, observing behavior, comparing commentaries—it's certain you don't know everything you need to know. You'll learn on the go, as you need it, just in time. Cultivate your learning mind-set (see chapter 4), and you'll be able to learn the methods you need.

Doing Quality Work

Regardless of your discipline, you should aim to produce quality work. Unfortunately, there is significant pressure in academia to produce constantly, in quantity, often at the sake of quality.[12] Decisions about funding, hiring, and career advancement use number of publications as a key metric. This "publish or perish" culture means the number of scholarly articles has skyrocketed—there are over thirty thousand academic journals, over two million articles published each year,[13] and over fifty million scholarly articles in total.[14] Big numbers aren't the problem per se; the problem is that the culture has shifted toward publishing excess mediocre work, rather than choice, impactful articles. Paired with this publishing issue is the replicability and reproducibility crisis: when scientists try to redo others' work following the methods laid out in their papers, they frequently fail.[15] Doing replications is disincentivized; replication studies are harder to publish and aren't seen as novel work advancing your own research agenda.

Resist the quantity-over-quality trend. Imitate researchers who are, instead, pushing for a rigorous, quality-first approach. Use appropriate methods to explore important questions in your field via thoughtful, ethical, carefully conducted projects or experiments. Use well-documented, precise, and easily explainable methods, with research and evidence that's presented in logical ways and employs appropriate analyses and argumentation. Some researchers will preregister their research questions, methods, and experiments by submitting their research plan to an online registry before they collect any data or make any observations, thus separating hypothesis generation from hypothesis testing, and making their science more rigorous.[16] Some journals will even agree to publish work based on the preregistration alone, regardless of the results. (Chapter 9 talks more about publication.) Preregistration is not always practical; it can be sufficient to keep detailed documentation about what you did and why.

How Much Data Do I Need?

The short answer: enough to answer your questions or test your hypotheses to a sufficient degree that your committee signs off on your dissertation. The longer answer: at some point, you need to switch from reading and collecting data to analyzing, thinking, and writing. When is that moment? Look back at your research proposal. Hopefully, you clearly stated up front the questions you wanted to answer or which hypotheses you wanted to test. You made a plan—you chose a methodology—for obtaining and analyzing data or information for answering your questions or testing your hypotheses. Follow your plan and ask your adviser. You don't want to cut corners even if you're behind schedule or over budget; you also don't want to take forever because you have *too* much data. That said, too much data is better than not enough. It's okay to use some of it for your dissertation and save some of it for later.

What Are My Options for Doing Statistics or Analyzing Data?

Options abound! Statistical software programs such as Stata and SPSS usually have shorter learning curves because they have a GUI (graphic user interface). Programming languages such as Python, Matlab, and R have libraries and shortcuts that make it easy to manipulate data and run complicated statistical analyses, but are more complex to learn, since you need to understand the language. Either avenue allows you to produce graphs and figures from your data. Ask your adviser and fellow graduate students what they use; it's not a bad idea to go with whatever your adviser uses so they can help you.

Should I Learn to Program?

If you're in a STEM field, or even the social sciences, the answer is probably yes. Knowing some programming can speed up otherwise tedious tasks like data cleaning, coding, and analysis. If you want to use programming to solve other problems, learning Python is a good place to start. Python is a higher-level language you can use to hack stuff together, and it's popular for data analysis and statistics.

If you're in the humanities, probably not, unless you do a lot of complex data analysis, or want to switch careers after graduating. (And if you want to switch careers, then why are you in grad school in the humanities?)

If you do learn to code, write unit/integration tests for your code. It will save you time in the long run. Also, document your code. I don't know whether anyone besides me read my documentation, but I sure did, and it saved me time figuring out what past me had been thinking.

Back Up Your Work

Back up everything, often—on more than one hard drive, and in the cloud (e.g., Google Drive, Dropbox, OneDrive, iCloud, etc.). You don't want to lose all your work if your computer dies.

Future Work

Repeat after me, "That's outside the scope of my project!" Every time I have a cool idea or an interesting question about a current research project that is out of scope and would take too much time, too much money, or too much energy to pursue, I add the idea to a notes file called "future work." Usually, I start this list before I've written anything else and before I've collected any data or analyzed anything. It's a way of acknowledging the limits of my current research without squashing the good ideas that could become the seeds of future research. Then, when I eventually write a paper about the research, I have my "future work" section already filled out, and I have baskets of ideas for what to tackle next.

Keeping Everyone in the Loop

Know your timeline and keep your adviser and your committee up to date on your progress toward your milestones—such as getting ethics approval, planning a study, accessing archives, collecting data or performing interviews, drafts of chapters, defense preparation, etc. (more on timelines in the next chapter). Regular check-ins give you the opportunity to explain any problems you're encountering, so your adviser and committee can ensure you get the help you need to finish your dissertation. Remember, they're on your side—they look good if you look good.

At a minimum, schedule a meeting with your primary adviser once a month. My graduate adviser scheduled weekly meetings with each student to check in. If I was out in the field collecting data, I might send a quick email update and follow up in more detail the following week. Meet with other committee members at least once every semester. You may need to meet with some more frequently during specific parts of your project. For instance, one of my committee members had expertise in developmental psychology and early childhood education, so I met with him more frequently when planning my final experimental study and developing assessments for the study, and when analyzing my data, but not often in between.

WRITING YOUR DISSERTATION

When Do I Start Writing?

At some point, you have to stop collecting data. Stop reading others' opinions. *Have your own* opinion. That's the point when you start writing.

Writing requires several weeks at a minimum, and often up to several years or more. Depending on your discipline, writing could be the majority of your work—in the humanities and social sciences, for instance, writing is as much a part of the research process as finding information in libraries or archives or performing a survey or interviews. Or, as is more common in STEM fields, you may spend a lot of time thinking and making notes about problems, performing experience experiments, or doing other data collection or analysis prior to writing it all up.

I'm a big proponent of starting early—earlier than you think you need to—and writing as you go, instead of writing everything at the end. For example, if you are running a study, write the design, hypotheses, methodology, and materials sections about the study as soon as you have them planned (or perhaps as part of the planning process). It is relieving to not have to write this stuff later, because after you have your data, you may forget details about why you chose to do things the way you did, or you may be way more excited about generating pretty graphs. I wrote my introduction and some background and literature review sections before I had even finished planning my final study. During study holdups, such as when I was waiting on feedback from committee members, I switched to writing. I wrote data analysis sections as I did the data analysis so I wouldn't forget details about what I did. I wrote results sections and generated the relevant figures and graphs as I was doing the analyses and getting results.

Writing as I went worked for me because of my constraints. As discussed in chapter 11, I was balancing caring for my one-year-old with finishing my dissertation. I knew I wouldn't be able to dedicate ten hours a day to writing, let alone four, and certainly not for weeks on end. I was fitting most of my writing in early in the morning, during naps, and after bedtime. But the format that worked for me doesn't work for everyone. Some people may prefer to schedule a block of several weeks to just work on writing, nothing else.

However you plan it, writing takes a long time. And even when you turn your attention to writing as your primary task, there will be plenty else to fill your time too: more reading, chasing down references, reanalyzing data or running models, creating figures, graphs, and illustrations. The next chapter will cover strategies for breaking up a big, amorphous project into manageable pieces, developing deep work habits, dealing with procrastination, and more.

What Should I Write First?

There are two main strategies for writing: (1) outline and plan, or (2) don't, also known as discovery writing, freewriting, or "pantsing" (i.e., writing by the seat of your pants).

If you outline, find out what dissertations in your department look like. Look at the dissertations of past students of your adviser. Examine the questions they tackled, the data used, their analyses, arguments, and structure. Look at the general length, number of chapters, and kind of content in each chapter. Then try to fit your topic into that structure. What chapters and sections will you need?

If you find outlines overwhelming or unhelpful, try writing down all the thoughts you have about your topic, the gaps in the literature, your interesting ideas related to your topic (or not related), citations that seem to be relevant and why they seem relevant. Then, patch it together. Flesh out the content. Determine your pieces, then connect them.

Writing Is Hard for Me! What Should I Do?

Writing can be difficult for many reasons. You've been told that a good thesis is a done thesis—but how do you get it done?

For some, writing is hard because they don't know what they should be writing. Possible solutions:

- Try making an outline if you don't have one yet. Plan out which chapters, sections, and subsections you'll need. Then tackle just one subsection.
- Set milestones in your writing sessions. For example, "Make a chapter outline" or "Write two paragraphs in this section." These are small goals you can achieve. Reward yourself for hitting these milestones.
- Make an argument map. Write down one main point you want your readers to understand. What do they need to know to understand it? Use a whiteboard or large piece of paper to map out what information needs to be included in your argument or discussion to support the point.
- Find the story in your work. What are the themes? What's the problem you were trying to solve, or question you were trying to answer? How does your work so far feed into that solution or answer? Start making notes and see where they lead you. (Also see chapter 9 for more on stories in writing.)

Sometimes writing is difficult because it's hard to sit down and start writing. Possible fixes:

- Schedule writing into your day, at your most productive time—for example, after breakfast or from eight to ten at night. Outside of your writing time, do whatever else you want—so long as you use your allotted time for writing. (See chapter 8 for more on schedules.)
- Set a timer for exactly five minutes. Write until the timer goes off. Sometimes, simply starting will get you in the rhythm, and you may find you continue.
- Write in a new place: coffee shops, outdoor spaces, pubs, libraries. Reward yourself with a change of scenery.
- Go on a mini-retreat—at home, in a cabin in the woods, anywhere. Set aside a couple weeks to focus on nothing but writing.
- Join a writing accountability group or sit with others to write together (some groups are virtual!). At the start of the session, everyone states their writing goals for the day. Then everyone works. At the end, everyone checks in to discuss their progress.

Sometimes writing is hard because you don't like writing.

- Focus on what you *do* enjoy about the experience—such as focusing intensely on one subject, making connections between disparate sources, delving into your interests, or learning new things.
- Try dictating instead of typing. Most phones and laptops have a voice-typing or dictation mode. Even if it doesn't correctly capture everything you say, it can be a way of getting down *some* words, which you can edit later.
- Reward yourself for attaining your writing milestones to help yourself get through it.

What About Revisions?

Some advisers prefer to see drafts of every chapter as you finish them, and to give you feedback along the way; others require the entire document before they provide feedback. Regardless, after reading your first draft, your committee and your adviser may require you to revise or rewrite portions of your dissertation. They may ask you to add information or new chapters before signing off on it. My committee, for instance, requested a new chapter synthesizing all the work I had done, which helped clarify my contributions. They asked for minor edits, such as clarifications of terminology and questions I should address in the text. They also asked me to reorganize a particular beast of a chapter, which I had expected. Fortunately, they gave me useful suggestions for *how* to do that reorganization, which was exactly the feedback I needed.

Clarify the final due date for revisions when the revisions are requested. Ask your committee whether they want to see the entire revised dissertation at the end or receive updates as you go. One of my committee members, for example, requested updates as I went, because she had her own deadlines around my revision due date and wanted to front-load the work.

Should I Hire an Editor?

The services editors can offer range from fixing sentence-level structure, punctuation, and grammar to improve readability, up through organizational and developmental help on the overall shape, structure, and content of an entire document. Editors are generally expensive; more so if they have expertise in your domain. Thus, as their usefulness increases, their price also increases. It's up to you. If you think professional help would save you significant time or headaches, and if you have the cash to spare, then it may be worthwhile. Sometimes, a campus writing center or a peer writing group can provide equally useful support. Some students take a middle road and opt for a proofreader or copy editor to make a final pass over their thesis before turning it in.

What Software Should I Use for Writing?

Your two main options are (1) a "what you see is what you get" word processor, such as Word, Pages, or LibreOffice, in which you see the words and their formatting all together, or (2) a "what you see is what you mean" program, such as LaTeX, in which you write text and formatting code, compile it, and see the output as a formatted pdf. LaTeX is more common in STEM, since one of its strong points is formatting formulas and equations; choose it if you are in STEM, as it will save you time in the long run. I used a mix of both, depending on whom I was collaborating with and what they preferred to use. If you submit papers to conferences, formatting templates are generally provided for Word and LaTeX.

What Do I Say When a Family Member or Friend Asks When I'll Graduate or Why It's Taking Me So Long to Write?

Tell them that grad school is a journey, not a destination. Tell them that it's none of their business. Tell them the truth and say you're working on it. You can share your anticipated graduation date, or you can explain that you're not sure because you haven't finished your coursework yet. If you're feeling gracious, Amanda Seligman suggests that you talk about your process.[17] Explain what it is you actually do—both the exciting and the tedious parts of your research process. Once your interlocutor understands what you actually *do*, then perhaps they'll understand why it's taking so long for you to do it.

DEFENSE

Most graduate schools require students to perform a public oral defense of their dissertations. Usually, this involves giving a presentation while your committee and other people watch and listen; then they ask you questions about it; then your committee deliberates by themselves; then they tell you the outcome. The outcome is similar to your exams: pass, fail, or conditional pass, pending some revisions or additional work. Your adviser should prevent you from defending until they know you will pass or conditionally pass. Students have been known to fail, often because they didn't talk to their committee sufficiently ahead of time and weren't actually ready; frequently, they are allowed to try again in a later semester.

Occasionally, a student won't be required to have a defense, and their committee will simply sign off on their dissertation. It varies by institution whether the public defense is scheduled before or after turning in the written dissertation. Ask your adviser or more advanced graduate students about the typical format in your department.

Schedule your defense when your committee agrees you're ready to defend. Since your committee likely consists of busy faculty members, give yourself ample time to negotiate a date that works for all of them; I scheduled mine months ahead of time, and I scheduled a backup date a couple weeks later just in case something came up that would necessitate postponement, like your adviser falling ill or having some other emergency. Ask your adviser how much time you'll need to schedule. In my case, I gave a forty-five-minute presentation, followed by about twenty minutes of Q&A. My committee deliberated for about fifteen minutes, then called me in to give feedback and request revisions.

What do you say during your defense talk? First and foremost, you want your audience to know what you did—what your contributions are. You're building a defensive narrative, telling a story, and you want to include only the most relevant information to support your story. You shouldn't be comprehensive about all the work you're building on (though you should know it and reference it); instead, focus on the questions you're answering or problems you're solving, and how you've made a unique contribution (however small) to your field. I prepared extra slides for my talk covering "future work" to show how my ideas would be extensible, such as how what I'd studied might apply to other fields, domains, and application areas, and what might have to change in the process. Do at least one practice presentation with an audience—peers, students, a crit group, your research group, your spouse, etc. (See chapter 9 for more on presentations.)

How else can you prepare? Take a long walk. Practice talking to yourself about your work. Prepare answers to questions about your argument, theory, methodology, sources, and where your work fits in the field. Consider the defense a teaching opportunity to share your work; you're the expert on your topic.

If your committee requests revisions, discuss the timeline up front. For instance, if there is an impending institutional dissertation submission deadline you'd like to meet, make sure you discuss how much time your committee might want to review your revisions and how much time you'll need to get your paperwork in order, and then make sure the time left between defending and sending revisions to your committee is sufficient for you to revise. You can push back against some requests to mitigate extra work. For example, reiterate your dissertation's primary contributions, and if your committee asks for something that doesn't strongly relate to one of those contributions, ask why they feel the revisions are necessary—perhaps they have good reason, but perhaps they don't.

If you're feeling confident, print signature pages to bring with you to the defense. If your committee approves without revisions, they can sign then and there. If you do need to make revisions, and one of your committee members is visiting from far away, or will be traveling a lot in the near future, they may be willing to sign their page and let your adviser hold on to it until you've completed the requested revisions (and thus decrease the amount of time you'll have to spend chasing down signatures later).

Finally, invite people to your defense! It's a big day and you'll appreciate friendly faces in the audience.

HOW DO I DO IT ALL?

Now that you have a handle on planning and executing graduate research, you may be wondering: How do I actually *do* all of that? Turn the page. The next chapter is all about time management and productivity.

chapter 8
Managing Projects and Managing Time

I'm going to tell Tega about the book!" said the five-year-old boy. He glanced at me, then turned back to Tega, the robot. The robot was the size of a large pumpkin and covered in bright red and blue fur, which other kids had described as "snuggable," "soft," and "like a rock star." The boy was playing a storytelling game with the robot as part of a research study I was conducting at a Boston kindergarten. I had all sorts of questions about the uses of technology in early language education; this study was just the latest in a series of projects exploring the topic.

I glanced at the clock on my laptop. Only 11:30 a.m. I could probably fit another two kids in with the robot before heading home for lunch. Then ... I listened to the boy explain a vocabulary word. I could squeeze in afternoon playtime with my toddler, data entry from today's kids, backing up all my data, writing more of the introduction for my dissertation, reading a paper that my adviser recommended I take a look at, dinner, more toddler time, and prepping all my materials for continuing the study at the school the next morning. Totally doable. Probably. At least I didn't have any meetings scheduled on campus until later in the week.

It was my final semester of dissertation data collection. I'd fallen into a new rhythm, visiting local schools with my robots in tow four days a week, plus the occasional afternoon. I watched kids learn words and play; I conducted interviews and assessments; I hoped I'd get interesting results. Every semester had its own rhythm. A different mix of projects, classes, meetings, writing, and research; different stages of personal life as I advanced through my graduate program.

This chapter is about creating *your* rhythm. It's about managing your tasks, your timeline, and your time: the *what*, the *when*, and the *how* of getting stuff done.

In grad school, you frequently work with little guidance. That means it's critical to estimate task time, set manageable timelines and goals, and structure your day.

WHAT WORK? TRACKING TASKS

The first beat in your rhythm is managing tasks. Task management can take many forms. The simplest: don't write down or track anything; hope you don't forget too much. That's not advisable. What is advisable comes down to personal preference. Some people prefer sticky notes, paper planners, or wall calendars. Some keep lists of tasks with software—for example, in a spreadsheet; a calendar app such as Google Calendar, Outlook, or iCal; or a task-managing app (see the resources chapter). Some use their email inbox as a task list, and tools such as Boomerang to have messages return to their inbox when relevant. Some set appointments and follow up events on their calendar. And these are just a few of the systems available.

The best system is the one you use and that works for you. If you don't have a system yet, try one for a month and see how it feels. If it seems to be working, stick with it. If you keep forgetting to check the list, miss deadlines, or hate every moment of using the system, change it up. Try a different system for a month. And repeat.

You don't have to use the same system all the time. I used to prefer a week-by-week paper planner. I went through phases where I kept paper lists on my desk. For longer projects, like my dissertation, or writing this book, I used a spreadsheet with columns for the task, the type (e.g., code, writing, paperwork), deadlines, and additional notes.

Calendars can be useful for seeing where your time is going. Block out hours spent on nonnegotiables, such as hours in class or meetings, doctor's appointments, picking up kids at certain times—anything you can't move around. If you have a lot of responsibilities—say, teaching, your personal life, and research activities—Jessica Calarco suggests color-coding everything in your calendar.[1] That way, you can see at a glance what types of activities will be taking up your time.

If to-do lists are overwhelming, try a tiered approach: list out things you definitely *will* do on a given day versus things you definitely *won't* do, so you know that you don't need to spend mental energy thinking about the things you won't do. You can also list things you *might* do in a given day, pending time and energy.

WORK WHEN? TIMELINES AND DEADLINES

Once you have a handle on *what* you need to do, plan *when* you'll do it. Start with the big picture, on the scale of years and degrees. Then zoom in and break every project or objective into specific, actionable, bite-size pieces that you can actually accomplish. Ayelet Fishbach recommends setting positive goals (i.e., "Do something!" not "Don't do something!") that are in a sweet spot between abstraction and concreteness—abstract enough to link back to your personal values; specific enough that you can easily evaluate your progress and tell when you've accomplished them. For instance, while writing this book, I gave myself writing goals, like, "Write 200 words a day" or "Revise for 20 minutes a day." It was easy to track my progress—the word count kept going up! I was finishing my revisions!—as I worked toward the overarching goal of "write a helpful book about thriving in graduate school."

Here's an exercise to get you started.

> ### EXERCISE 12: MAKE A DEGREE TIMELINE
>
> 1. Make a list: What are your degree requirements? What major tasks or milestones do you need to meet? Do you have formal deadlines—for your proposal, proposal defense, or defense? For example, my master's program required some classes, a master's proposal, and a master's thesis; students were given two years (plus maybe an extra summer). For my PhD, I had to plan and pass my general exams, write my dissertation proposal, actually do the research I proposed, and write and defend my dissertation.
> 2. Write down the semester you would like to graduate—say, spring 2014. (It's okay to revise this later.) My master's program followed a strict two-year-year schedule; in the PhD program, the ideal time to degree was four years, but many students went longer.
> 3. List each semester from now until your ideal graduation date: fall 2012, spring 2013, fall 2013, spring 2014.
> 4. Now, map the first list of milestones onto these semesters. In my master's program, my timeline looked like this:
>   - Fall 2012: classes
>   - Spring 2012: classes, think about thesis topic

- Fall 2013: classes, thesis proposal
- Spring 2014: do thesis project, write and submit thesis

My initial PhD timeline looked like this, though in the first year this plan was derailed and delayed:

- Year 1: plan, propose, and do general exams
- Year 2: plan and submit dissertation proposal
- Year 3: do proposed research
- Year 4: wrap up research, write and defend dissertation

5. This high-level timeline starts breaking a very big goal ("graduate") into smaller milestones (exams, proposal, etc.). Next, pick one milestone (perhaps the next one coming up). Break it into even smaller milestones, some of which may be actionable, and some of which may need to be broken down further. Here's my high-level general exam timeline (as discussed in chapter 7, your exams may follow a different format):

    - January-March:
        i. Think about exam topic areas (main, contextual, technical), narrow it down to what's most interesting
        ii. Talk to adviser and other advisers/professors about plans

    - April-May:
        i. Contact potential committee members
        ii. Start drafting exam proposal with "main question" for each exam area
        iii. Start collecting papers for reading list for any exam areas that are finalized

    - June:
        i. Consolidate reading lists, make them into a coherent story
        ii. Finalize a "main question" for each exam area for proposal
        iii. Finalize committee
        iv. Send first draft of proposal to committee
        v. Start reading any papers I know aren't going to be taken off the reading list

- July:
    i. Incorporate committee feedback on proposal and reading list, send to committee again
    ii. Get approval and signatures from committee
    iii. Read papers (at least one a day)
- August:
    i. Submit exam proposal to department
    ii. Get department approval, make any changes they require
    iii. Get serious about reading papers (two to three a day)
- September:
    i. Schedule contextual exam
    ii. Do contextual exam
    iii. Schedule technical exam
- October:
    i. Schedule oral exam
    ii. Do technical exam
- November:
    i. Do oral exam
- December:
    i. Main area paper
- January:
    i. Finish up anything remaining—for example, if the paper takes a while

I began reading and studying before my exam proposal was approved. I knew some material would stay on the reading list no matter what, and I erred on the side of preparing early because last-minute work stresses me out. Then, based on the length of my reading list, I set a schedule for how much to read each day to get through everything by my expected exam date. If you're primarily studying content you learned in classes, rather than reading new papers, you may want to allot a certain amount of time per day to study (e.g., two to four hours a day) instead. My exams had both oral and written components, so I blocked out an approximate time frame for them, based on my overarching goal of completing the exams within a year.

You probably won't stick to your ideal timeline. That's okay; I didn't either. But I knew *what* I needed to accomplish, and approximately *when* I needed to accomplish each task—so if I had to shift the whole timeline by a semester because I was having a baby, well, I could do that. The timeline helped me make consistent progress.

Writing a timeline for your degree milestones will also help you plan a project of appropriate scope and size, and help you identify issues in your timeline. You may learn, for instance, that your project requires an extra semester, or two—and so you need to request extra time, find additional funding, or else reduce the size of your project. Perhaps your fieldwork can only be performed during a certain season, which is a constraint on your timeline—but perhaps there are other milestones you can work toward in parallel, so you don't have downtime while waiting for fieldwork season. Identifying issues early will help you deal with them early, before they become enormous problems.

How Do I Estimate Task Time?

When making timelines, setting milestones, and breaking up big milestones into manageable pieces, you'll need to realistically estimate how long it will take you to accomplish each task. Realistically. That's the hard part! Most people underestimate how much time and effort tasks will take. This is called the *planning fallacy*. We also tend to assume we won't encounter many (or any) delays... This is *optimism bias*. We need to account for both when estimating time.

The simplest way to combat the planning fallacy and optimism bias is to overestimate how much time completing a task will take you. Take your best estimate and double it. Or triple it. However, this only gets you as far as your best estimate... which may not be very good, not for lack of trying. For example, nearly everyone underestimates how long writing software takes because they only estimate how long the initial writing takes—not the additional time required to test and fix bugs in the code. If you're in a technical field, I recommend reading *The Mythical Man Month*, which, while somewhat dated, is a practical book about managing software projects.[2]

Improve your best estimate by estimating the best-case scenario, the worst-case scenario, and the most realistic scenario you can imagine. Use mental contrasting: think of all the obstacles you might face on the way to your milestone, and consider specifically how you might overcome each obstacle.[3] As a bonus, this technique can also improve your discipline in achieving your goal. Imagine how long someone else would take to finish the task—sometimes people estimate time more accurately for other people. Estimate a range for how long a task might take—for example, four to eight hours, two to three weeks.

You can develop a keener sense of how long tasks take you by tracking how long they actually take you. Use time-tracking software for a few weeks or months (search the app store). Make notes about the setbacks you encounter. Periodically, review how you've used your time—this can help you see how long it takes to write, program, read, analyze, etc.

Many graduate school milestones depend on other people. Pad your timeline whenever you need something from someone else. For instance, if you work with animals or humans, you may need ethics approval for your studies or experiments. Allow weeks, or even months, to submit your experimental protocol to your institution's ethics board and get approval (often called an IRB, or institutional review board, an ERB, ethical review board, or REB, research ethics board). Maybe you need to allot time to perform fieldwork, travel to research locations, libraries, or archives, or schedule time on a telescope or other special lab equipment. Maybe you need to include preliminary or pilot data in your proposal. Allot extra time for scheduling important events, such as your exams or your defense. Faculty are notoriously busy; there's a lot of back and forth when finding a date that works for your entire committee. Allot time for your committee to read your proposal or dissertation and give you feedback, and time for you to respond to their feedback.

Fishbach writes that many people who face harder, more difficult tasks set earlier deadlines to motivate themselves. Time estimation is only part of the story, however. Later in this chapter, I'll talk about motivation, procrastination, and hitting milestones. But first, what do you do when you can't keep to your timeline?

Setbacks, Failure, Rejections, and Perseverance

During my dissertation, I relied on a couple undergraduates to help me with data collection. These undergrads scheduled children to come to our lab, observed the kids playing with the robot, performed assessments, and reported back to me. During one study, they messed up some data collection. I had to spend weeks collecting additional data. Frustrating, yes. Manageable? I gritted my teeth and tried to remember that the experience was helping me grow as a researcher and as a manager of undergrads.

While you can't predict precisely *what* setbacks you'll encounter, you can assume that *something* will delay you. Whether it's experiments that don't work, data to re-collect, rejected papers, mental health challenges, relationship drama, adviser drama, funding drama... *something* will happen. It takes a tough cookie to succeed in the failure- and rejection-rich oven of academia.

Plan for setbacks by building breathing room into your timeline. Then, learn from your failures as well as your successes. Ayelet Fishbach acknowledges that learning from success is easier: you just have to repeat whatever it was that made you successful the first time.[4] Learning from failure is harder because you have to figure out what *else* to do that wasn't what you just did. However, negative outcomes can provide unique information you can use to determine how to succeed.

To better learn from negative experiences and negative feedback, Fishbach has four suggestions. First, ask whether you feel you've made progress. If you feel confident about your commitment to achieving the goal in spite of the setback, recognizing your progress can help you move forward. Second, remember your learning mind-set. Feedback helps you grow and learn. Third, distance yourself from the failure. Imagine it happened to a stranger—and imagine what that stranger may have learned from the experience or how they might resolve the issue. Increasing our psychological distance can increase our emotional distance and give an event less power.[5] Fourth, give advice to someone who has a similar issue, which can increase your motivation to deal with your own issue.

Talk with peers or your adviser about similar issues they've faced, and how they've dealt with them.[6] Be compassionate toward yourself. Sometimes, setbacks make you feel like you don't belong and can affect your mental health. See chapter 4 on imposter syndrome; see chapter 10 on mental health and finding support.

Finally, be aware that your adviser, committee, department, or graduate school could take action against you if you fail to complete your program in their desired time frame. Some universities have residency requirements that mean you have to be on campus for a certain amount of time, usually while you're enrolled in courses. Some programs have time limits within which you must complete your degree—for example, five years for a master's or ten years for a PhD. If you think you may fall behind in your degree timeline, have conversations with everyone early. Find out their expectations, the possible consequences, and what remedies may be available.

WORK HOW? TIME MANAGEMENT AND WORK HABITS

Next, find a rhythm for day-to-day work as you move toward your milestones. Graduate school is akin to a seesaw. Sometimes, you find yourself trying to squash classes, lab time, picking up kids from school, and everything else into a hectic, heavily structured schedule. Other times, you're floundering in vast stretches of unstructured time with vague goals like "study for exams" or "finish dissertation." Breaking those vague goals into discrete, manageable chunks certainly helps. But even with doable tasks, how do you structure your days to actually accomplish everything?

> **EXERCISE 13: FINDING YOUR RHYTHM**
>
> 1. Keep a "good time journal" for a few weeks.* For every activity you do each day, jot down notes about how you felt about it: Were you engaged or disengaged? Focused, in flow, or distracted and tired? Energized or not? What were you working on? Where? Who with?
> 2. After you have a couple weeks of data, review your notes. Your goal is to discover which activities energize you and which ones drain you. What patterns do you see? When do you feel most energized to work? Do you like to start early? Are you a night owl? You may not like working during typical nine-to-five hours, so perhaps you should save your important tasks (like writing your dissertation) for the times you *do* like working. What work energizes you most? Later in the chapter, I list motivation strategies for completing all the tasks you need to do—including tasks that bore you. Where are you when you get good work done? Who are you with?
>
> * Bill Burnett and Dave Evans, *Designing Your Life: How to Build a Well-Lived, Joyful Life* (New York: Knopf, 2016).

Your goal is to find a system that works for you. Knowing when you do your best work can help you set aside that time for being productive, and, ultimately, help you better integrate work into your life. Here are some strategies.

Deep Work

Cal Newport, author of *Deep Work*, says all work can be divided into two broad buckets: shallow work and deep work. Shallow work is emails, filling spreadsheets, printing out copies of all those papers you want to read, organizing a binder of notes, fixing the formatting of references in a paper, "noncognitively demanding, logistical-style tasks, often performed while distracted," that are easy to replicate and don't create much value.[7] Deep work, on the other hand, requires intense focus and distraction-free concentration. During deep work, you're creating value or improving your skills, and it's hard for someone else to replicate the results: planning experiments, thinking through hard problems, understanding a theory, or writing your dissertation.

To earn your degree, you need time for deep work. Newport recommends *time block planning*—that is, scheduling your tasks for the day in time blocks.[8] Then, only work on tasks during their scheduled times. He advocates for this method because task switching drains your attention. Switching frequently means some of your attention is still on the previous task. Set aside extended blocks for deep work during your most productive hours. Schedule your shallow work in between (e.g., twenty minutes for checking emails). Give yourself time limits, small goals, and deadlines to increase productivity. However, you don't have to stick to the schedule like glue. If you're in a deep work session and being amazingly productive, or if you finish a task early, just update your schedule when you have time.

Newport also advises using in-between times—such as time spent in waiting rooms or on commutes—to do high-level planning, think about concepts, solve problems, or even squeeze in some reading. I commuted to campus by train and always brought along a paper or book.

I was a big fan of Newport's time block planning, up until I had a baby. After that point, it became untenable due to the unpredictability of my schedule. Which time block would be "baby nap time/work on dissertation?" Would my son wake up early, or have two short naps instead of one long one? The distinction between deep versus shallow work remains useful, but I had to adopt a more flexible approach to my time. What I adopted was similar to what's called the Pomodoro Technique.

The Pomodoro Technique

The Pomodoro technique, developed by Francesco Cirillo, is a method of blocking out distraction-free time for work that can jibe with a Newport-style schedule.[9] In brief, set a timer for twenty-five minutes (Cirillo originally used a tomato-shaped kitchen timer, which is how his system got the name Pomodoro, Italian for tomato). Focus on one task—say, writing the next section of your dissertation—until the timer goes off. Take a five-minute break, and repeat. After four pomodoros, take a longer break. Group smaller tasks together to fill up the whole time. Break big tasks into smaller pieces so you can accomplish them. If something interrupts you mid-session, take note of it and return to it later. If you absolutely must attend to it, take a five-minute break and restart the session.

With a baby, I treated naps as my sacred work times (and sometimes early mornings before my son woke up, or evenings after he was asleep). During the day, as soon as he fell asleep, I began a work session on one specific task, and I worked until he woke up—essentially, he was my timer. Because this quiet, focused time was limited, I saved it for deep work and shifted shallow work to other times.

Changing It Up

Sidney D'Mello once advised me to have research projects in all stages: some projects you're planning, some you're collecting or analyzing data for, some you're writing up or otherwise have in the publication pipeline. That way, when one project stalls, you can jump to the others. If you're not in the mood to face words, you can code, organize data, or generate graphs for a paper.

To generalize: Be flexible and switch tasks as needed. Procrastinate on one task by working on a different one that still moves you toward your goals. Sometimes I had time available at night, when I was sleepy and certainly not at my cognitive peak. I'd shift drudge tasks there: emails, cataloging which data files were missing, updating the publications list on my website. If I had morning time, I'd ignore important emails in favor of energetically pounding out the introduction to a paper. Sometimes, if you're finding one task especially difficult, working on something else for a while can give you renewed energy when you try again later.

Eisenhower Matrix

What if you're not sure how to prioritize your work, and find important tasks falling through the cracks? One of my advisers suggested the Eisenhower Matrix. Categorize your tasks into a two-by-two grid labeled "Urgent, Not Urgent x Important, Not Important" (see table 8.1.) Then, spend time in all the boxes. Important, urgent things with imminent deadlines need your attention. Schedule the important but not urgent things so you don't lose track of them. Don't waste too much time on the urgent but ultimately not important things—do them fast or delegate if you can. Try to remove as many not important, not urgent things from your task list as you can—say no to them!

There are numerous adaptations of this matrix. For instance, Newport favors the 4 Disciplines of Execution: First, focus most of your effort on a small number of wildly important, essential, urgent goals. Second, act on *lead* measures, not *lag* measures. Lead measures describe time spent in a state of deep work and lead you toward your goal, such as counting words written per day toward the goal of writing a dissertation or a book, or hours spent on data analysis for a paper. Lag measures describe output, such as finishing three classes this semester or publishing one paper this year—they don't help you figure out what to do today. Third, keep a visible scoreboard, such as tally marks on a piece of paper for every half hour spent on deep work toward your goal. Finally, keep a cadence of accountability—review your progress regularly to see how much you've accomplished, and make a plan for future work.[10]

TABLE 8.1 Eisenhower Matrix

	Urgent	Not Urgent
Important	Important, urgent things	Important, not urgent things
Not Important	Not important, urgent things	Not important, not urgent things

Streamline Meetings

A writer I knew always scheduled meetings and administrative minutia for one day of the week, keeping the other days available for long deep work sessions. It's not a bad plan when you can swing it—another way of minimizing transition times and task switching.

Make meetings as efficient as possible by creating an agenda that covers what you need from the meeting, with clear tasks or questions to address. By meeting's end, you should have clear action items or next steps planned. Give meetings time limits and don't let them run over—and don't allot more time than you need. In my lab group, for instance, we held one-hour group meetings each week. We assigned one person as timekeeper. That person solicited agenda items before we gathered, kept the meeting moving to ensure we covered all items in the allotted hour, and cut people off if they rambled too much.

How Do I Manage Email Overload?

Everyone gets too much email. Start by unsubscribing from everything you possibly can. Only stay subscribed to stuff you *actually* read—don't even keep the stuff you aspire to read. Then turn off email notifications on your phone. Don't let it go "ping!" every time you get an email. You can choose when during your day to deal with email; you don't have to be on email constantly. Some advisers may expect you to check your email frequently. It's okay if "frequently" is on your schedule, in between bouts of deeper work.

Next, write better emails yourself.[11] In the subject line, summarize rather than describe. For example, bad: "Paper draft." Better: "Paper camera ready—approve changes before deadline Oct. 12?" In the body, remind your reader what you're responding to (so they don't have to scroll through layers of email lasagna to figure out what's going on). If your email is addressed to multiple people, explicitly call out why you're including all of them and what they each need to do in response to your email. Make clear action requests. Be as brief as you can while still being polite.

Cal Newport recommends process-centric email—that is, spend more time up front identifying the goal so that you can craft emails that get you to that goal while minimizing future emails.[12] If you're asking for a meeting, for example, add a couple meeting days/times that work for you up front in your first email.

MAKING THE MOST OF YOUR TIME

Tracking Progress

How do you track progress? Newport advises measuring progress in time, not milestones.[13] Sometimes, if you didn't solve anything big or finish anything major, all you can say is, "I put time in on the problem today!" You can also break up milestones into little milestones, like finishing a section of a paper rather than submitting a paper. When writing my dissertation, for instance, I made a list of all the sections I had to write, and every day, worked on one for at least two hours. At the end of that deep work session, I could either check off a section as written or check off that I'd at least worked on it for two hours.

If you don't have deadlines for milestones in your research or your dissertation, try setting some. It may feel arbitrary and silly at first, but it gives you direction—something to track progress toward. You can ask a friend or even your adviser to hold you accountable for hitting those deadlines.

Procrastination, Motivation, and Self-Control

We often procrastinate when we're feeling negative emotions about a task: insecurity, shame, self-doubt, frustration, confusion, a sense of being overwhelmed. We prioritize feeling better now and voluntarily delay the task to do something else that's more fun, despite knowing that our future self will suffer the consequences. But hey—maybe our future self will have more energy to deal with the task! (Or maybe not, but that's also our future self's problem.)

Contrary to popular belief, procrastination isn't a time-management problem—it's a motivation problem.[14] Motivation for any given activity is the combination of four things: (1) *value*: how fun or pleasurable the activity is; (2) *expectancy*: how likely you are to succeed; (3) *impulsiveness*: your general impulsiveness and self-control; and (4) *delay*: when you get the payout or reward.[15] People like to work toward pleasurable things that they are likely to achieve and that will reward them now, not later. If this equation doesn't tip in favor of a task, then we delay it and do something else—which is to say, we procrastinate.

When choosing an activity, we weigh those tasks we ought to do against temptations. Temptations are pleasurable activities that reward us immediately (and have delayed costs), which, if we give in, means we *won't* be doing our ought-to-dos. Detect temptations with self-awareness. What behaviors are undermining your ability to achieve your goals, or undermining how you see yourself? Imagine yourself in ten years—how will you feel about what you're doing now? What will future you wish you'd done differently? Thinking about the future puts you in a broad decision frame. Being in a broad decision frame helps you detect conflicts with your goals more easily.

Battling temptations is a matter of increasing your motivation for your ought-to-dos and decreasing your motivation for the temptation. Since there are four components to motivation, there are four levers you can pull.[16]

Value
- Increase immediate enjoyment of the activity: notice any fun or enjoyment you might already be having, since there may be some if you look for it! On the flip side, remind yourself why a temptation might *not* be as fun as it sounds.
- Use temptation bundling: associate doing something you *don't* like with something you *do* like, such as watching your favorite TV show while working out, or listening to your favorite music while formatting references.[17]
- Work when you have high energy. As Piers Steel argues in his book *The Procrastination Equation*, when we're tired we make poorer decisions, have a harder time maintaining interest in our work, and experience greater difficulty following through with tasks.[18]
- Create habits around work. For instance, pick a "power song," an energizing song that help get you into "work mode." In college, I listened to a couple Goo Goo Dolls albums on repeat when writing papers. I got a motivational kick: "This is working music," I thought, "so if I'm listening to it, I should be working." Some students start the day with tea or coffee; use a mug emblazoned with a favorite inspirational quote to nudge you into work mode.
- Enter the task expecting it to be boring and difficult. Fishbach explains that if you're expecting something hard, you're more likely to persist, because you're ready to do so. Expectations are critical.
- Take a break, perhaps over the summer or for a semester. Take a leave, get off campus, do something different. This can either remind you what

you valued about working on your dissertation, or help you realize that finishing isn't even worth it.

Expectancy
- Be compassionate toward yourself and forgive yourself for procrastinating. This can decrease your negative feelings and may decrease how much you procrastinate in the future.[19]
- Use mindfulness to identify negative emotions and the root issues underlying your procrastination. Procrastination is negatively associated with mindfulness.[20]
- Make the goal small and achievable. Assign yourself one bite-size task that leads to your goal—say, washing one dish, working on a paper for exactly five minutes, reading just two pages of a book—and do it right now. Sometimes all you need is to show yourself that you *can* accomplish one little piece. Once you start, it may be easier to continue.
- If your commitment to a goal is relatively low, Fishbach says, you can look back and appreciate how much you've done to reach it already. This can make you more enthusiastic about what work is left to do. If you're already highly committed to a goal, try looking forward to see what tasks are yet to be accomplished. This can motivate you to make more progress.
- Goals can be all-or-nothing, such as a reward program at a café to get a free drink or finishing your PhD, or cumulative, such as working out or reading twenty books this year. Making progress on all-or-nothing goals makes every bit of additional progress feel like it has more impact. Progress on cumulative goals increases your commitment to the goal. In both cases, seeing that you've made progress can increase your motivation.[21]
- Make it harder to do the temptation using precommitment strategies. Eliminate the temptation before you are tempted. For example, remove unhealthy foods from your house when you're on a diet. Use an app to block social media during work time. Remove yourself from the space where the procrastination activity is available, such as working in the library so you can't watch shows online.
- Satisfy your needs in a safe way before they're too big of an issue—say, by scheduling leisure time before starting work.

- Declutter your environment—remove triggers that tempt you; add triggers that remind you to work. For example, delete distracting apps from your phone. Put your phone in a drawer while working.
- Give yourself penalties for giving into temptation. For instance, there's a platform that makes a monetary donation on your behalf to an organization you don't like when you succumb to the temptation, such as sleeping in too long, checking Facebook when you should be writing, or not exercising that day.

Impulsiveness
- Increase your psychological distance from the activity. Imagine, for instance, that the situation is happening to someone else in the distant future. Would they make the same decision you are making? Would a health-conscious person or a hard worker make the same decision? We assess situations differently when we increase our mental distance from them.[22] You could also try helping a friend with their work or talking over a research problem, as this can move you into a different headspace and change your perspective on your own projects.
- Practice mindfulness: notice your desires, give them space, reject your first impulse to act on them, and let them go. This builds self-discipline.[23]
- Practicing self-control might improve self-control.[24] For instance, try self-denial or discomfort training; both involve noticing that you want something to be different about your situation—you want more dessert, you want to scratch an itch, you want to be warmer or colder—and then deliberately *not* acting to change your situation. Instead, you persist through the discomfort, building discipline as a side effect.
- Psychologist Peter Gray argues that we develop self-discipline through play—through activities that bring us into flow, from opting in to activities with systems of rules, and from practicing imposing rules on ourselves for the sake of continuing the activity.[25] What activities bring you into a state of flow? These can build your self-discipline for other activities too.

Delay
- Remind yourself why accomplishing the task moves you toward your goals. Make the reward feel more tangible and closer. Psychologists

Edward Deci and Richard Ryan argue that people are intrinsically motivated to pursue three psychological needs: competence (mastery of activities), autonomy (doing things by one's own choice), and relatedness (social connection with others).[26] Connect the task and your goals with one of these three needs.

- Reframe "shoulds" into "wants."[27] What's the connection between whatever you think you *should* do (waking up earlier, writing more, exercising regularly) and your long-term goals? Reframe "this is a thing I should do" to "this is a thing *I want to do* to achieve my goal." Remind yourself why the action matters. What are the consequences of doing it, or of not doing it? Do you actually care about the outcome? Maybe you don't—and recognizing that you don't frees you up to do things that further your goals.

- Avoid the long middle. Fishbach warns that on long projects—like a PhD—the middle is the most dangerous. People are most enthusiastic at the beginning and end of pursuing a goal; motivation dips in the middle. Break large projects into weekly assignments so you don't lose steam. Frame work as being at the beginning of the next milestone or at the end of the current one, rather than just "in the middle somewhere."

- Celebrate reaching milestones along the way to your goal to decrease the time to reward. The rewards can be small: a nice cup of coffee, a walk with a friend after a tough exam, dinner at a favorite restaurant for completing a paper draft. Of course, incentives can backfire, but it depends on the type of work and type of reward. Daniel Pink, author of *Drive*, loosely categorizes work as either algorithmic or heuristic.[28] Algorithmic work is directed and includes routine tasks, following a script over and over—stuff that can eventually be outsourced or automated, like most shallow work. Heuristic work is nonroutine and often self-directed, involving experimentation, developing novel solutions, creative thought, empathy, and knowledge—like deep work. Extrinsic rewards can be useful for algorithmic work, since people have little or no intrinsic motivation for those tasks already. But heuristic work requires more intrinsic motivation, and is more often hampered by extrinsic rewards.[29]

- Increase your intrinsic motivation by considering what you're achieving via the activity and what you enjoy about it. This can reduce the delay to reward, since the reward is, in part, the activity itself.

Delegate? Undergraduate Students

Some graduate students have the opportunity to mentor undergraduates during semesters or over the summers; this is more often the case in STEM fields. My institution, for example, had a program for undergrads to work in labs on campus for class credit or pay.

If you or your adviser can get undergrads, great! Treat it like a mentor-mentee opportunity. You're there to help the undergrad learn about doing research in your field. Your main goal is for the undergrad to come out the other end feeling like their time with you was well spent. Your secondary goal is for *you* to feel like their time was well spent. Not everyone agrees with me on this, but people do better work when they like what they're doing. If work is tedious, it can be tolerated if it's in service to a meaningful goal that they believe in.

Undergrads generally don't have a lot of experience. Don't expect them to produce great stuff off the bat. Find small but interesting places where they can contribute. If you only assign drudge work, they may opt to stop working for you. Instead, balance it out, and make sure you explain why such drudgery is crucial to the project. I had the best success when placing a team of three undergrads on a project tangential to my main research—still related, not critical. They worked together and took ownership of the project. It had boring components, like behavior coding—that is, sitting at a computer for hours watching recorded videos of children playing with robots while marking what the children were looking at. But, since my undergrads had been involved from the beginning, they knew that eye gaze was an important metric, they had collected the data themselves, and they got through it.

Be careful when assigning work that is on your critical path to completing your degree. Undergrads have different concerns than you (remember, they are busy with college classes and college life!). They are not as invested in your project as you are—so they may not treat your deadlines with the urgency you require. What is your plan if they fail or bail in a crisis? Are you willing to find out?

Managing undergrads can help you develop mentoring skills. You can practice leading efficient meetings. Meet with your student at least once a week, or every other week if they're very independent. If you have a student full-time over the summer, meet more frequently. Explain why questions or problems in your research matter. Identify methods for addressing those questions or problems, and help the students working under you understand why you chose those methods. Emulate mentors and advisers you think did a good job; copy what you liked best. But at the same time, recognize that people are different. The kind of mentoring style that has helped you may not work for the undergrad under your tutelage. Communication is key here, like in everything else. Be kind. Be encouraging. Nominate your students for awards if appropriate.

ADHD and Other Challenges

What if you've tried all the strategies above, but none seem to work? Some brains work differently. Individuals with ADHD (attention deficit hyperactivity disorder), for instance, think about time differently, and many classic time-management techniques just don't cut it.[30] Individuals with ADHD are commonly more absorbed in the present, and have greater difficulty both ignoring external stimuli and doing tasks whose payoffs are deferred to the future. Some people with ADHD find that using easily visible clocks and writing tasks into a scheduling system (including blocks devoted to transition, prep, and travel) can help them manage the passage of time. Post deadlines where you can see them. Try to vividly imagine the consequences of delaying tasks, and remember how you felt last time you procrastinated. Besides ADHD, undiagnosed dyslexia, learning disabilities, and anxiety or depression, among others, can make grad-student life difficult.

If you're wondering whether one of those labels might apply to you, talk to a psychologist, psychiatrist, other mental health professional, or even your primary care provider about getting tested. Sometimes, a diagnosis changes everything and can help you get the support you need to succeed. Most institutions have a campus center or office that supports neurodivergent students—usually with a name like student support services, educational support office, or student affairs office.

Managing Your Whole Life

The need to manage projects and time continues outside academic hours, in housework, meal preparation, and managing children and family. There are many systems that can help you fit these projects in too; see the chapter on resources. Try them and iterate until you land on a system that works for you. (And see chapters 10-12 for more on life balance.)

9

Your Work and the World

For two years of my PhD, I was partially funded by a fellowship that, among other things, required each fellow to write a public-facing blog post about their research. Many researchers are shy about sharing their work with the wider, nonacademic world—or perhaps they're simply too busy to bother. But, as Leonard Cassuto writes in his book *The Graduate School Mess*, part of the point of scholarship—of research and knowledge production—is to communicate that knowledge to others so they can do something with it.[1]

I vaulted into the blogging exercise with ballistic energy. My first post was over two thousand words long, a veritable epic expounding on my research journey up to that point. Perhaps some would look at this and say, "Wow, what an overachiever. Why put so much effort into a blog post?" But the effort paid off. I could link to the article when people asked me, "Wait, so you did *what* with robots?" I got a consulting gig. Media folks contacted me as an expert on child-robot interaction. On top of that, from the writing and revision process for that post and several that followed, I learned how to succinctly distill the core questions, methodologies, and results of my work. I developed a clearer vision of my research trajectory. When drafting my dissertation, it was easier to see and summarize my contributions to the field.

RESEARCH DISSEMINATION

Disseminating research simply means telling other people about your work. It's an important step in the research process. We do research to contribute to larger conversations in the field and the world at large.

Research dissemination can take many forms: papers published in traditional academic journals; papers, posters, and talks delivered at academic conferences; blog posts written for the general public; op-eds or magazine or newspaper articles; social media threads and stories; podcast and radio interviews; TEDx talks; press releases. In the arts, you may aim for exhibition, acquisition, or performance. Which mode of dissemination you use depends on numerous factors, including your field, your adviser's preferences, your comfort level with different media, who you want to reach, and your long-term career goals. If you want to be taken seriously in academia, for instance, you'll need to publish in peer-reviewed academic journals, attend conferences, and maybe even write a book. But if academia is not your long-term goal, other forms of dissemination may be preferable. You use different media to reach policymakers, practitioners, or the general public than you would if your audience is predominantly other scholars.

Unfortunately, there is significant bias in higher education toward "academic" dissemination at the expense of everything else. As Leonard Cassuto observes, academia tends to look inward, but it ought to look outward. Higher education ought to engage more with the public than it does now. If the people in academia are indeed in the business of knowledge production, then they also need to be in the business of communicating this knowledge to others in a useful form, whether written, via public speaking, or through teaching. Scholarship should not only be produced for the sake of scholarship, or for the sake of conversation among a very narrow set of people in your particular discipline. Cassuto further argues that reaching multiple audiences enables you to create more broadly. This broader, outward focus enables you to tie your work to a wider range of topics and fields, in multidisciplinary and interdisciplinary ways, which can be as valuable as a water bottle in a desert.

Next, I'll describe different dissemination routes, starting with academic publishing. My aim is to give you familiarity with why you might publish in different places, not to provide a step-by-step guide on how to publish an academic article. (Such guides exist; see the resources chapter for some of them.) After talking about venues, I'll get into the mechanics of crafting stories for different media.

In the next few sections, I say less about the arts because their format is substantially different than other disciplines; while you may write about your artistic work, the gold standard for success is being selected for exhibition or acquisition at a gallery or museum, or having your work performed at a prestigious venue by you or a professional company, not publishing an article about it.

ACADEMIC PUBLISHING

Academic publishing includes papers published in academic journals (original research, book reviews, commentaries, data papers); papers, posters, and talks given at academic conferences; and academic books. The prestige of each varies by field. To find out what's normal in yours, ask a more advanced grad student or your adviser. Look at your adviser's CV to see what and where they've published.

Common to most academic publishing—especially any prestigious academic publishing—is the fact that these publications are peer reviewed.

What Is Peer Review?

Peer review is a process aimed at ensuring rigor in scholarly work. Written reports about research, in any of the forms mentioned above, are sent to other researchers in your field ("peers") for assessment. The reviews you get back include what the reviewers liked and didn't like, and their comments, recommendations, and suggestions for improvement. It's a way for others in your field to comment on the significance, rigor, and methodological soundness of your work prior to publication. Often, you're given an opportunity to respond to the reviews and revise your work accordingly (called an R&R: revise and resubmit—more on this below when we talk about getting feedback on your writing). An editor may use the reviews to decide to publish the work. Funding agencies and academic publishers also use reviews in making decisions about funding grant proposals and fellowships, or going ahead with a book project.

Peer-reviewed publications are seen as "better" because other experts in your field have, in a sense, vetted the work. That said, peer review has its issues. For example, reviewers are usually anonymous, which can lead to less-than-constructive feedback and more vehement comments; reviewers aren't paid, so it can be difficult to find appropriate reviewers in a timely manner; and, the big one, reviewers often contradict each other and sometimes miss big issues in others' work.[2] But, regardless of its effectiveness, peer review is extremely common in academic publishing.

The Economics of Academic Publishing

Most of the writing that you do in graduate school will not be for money. You generally don't get paid for the work you publish in academia—not for journal papers, not for conference papers, not for book chapters. If you go on to publish a book later, you may get a small amount in the form of royalties. If you happen to write magazine or newspaper articles, you can be paid per article (anywhere from fifty to five hundred dollars and up, depending on venue and length). The real reason to engage in academic writing is to share your work with the world. If you're interested in a research career, especially in higher education, you'll need published work listed on your CV.

Why don't academics get paid for articles? Once upon a time, academic publishers printed hard copies of journal articles and conference proceedings and mailed them out, and were paid for this service. Now, in the era of the Internet, the economics make little sense. Academic publishers are still well paid, but they provide relatively little service; they keep online-only articles paywalled because they can. Many researchers are rightly outraged at the system.[3] Some journals have responded by creating open-access options, wherein the author pays an "open-access fee" up front, and in return, the article isn't paywalled. Sometimes universities have funds available for covering open-access fees for their employees. Some researchers have started their own open-access journals with low or no author fees.[4]

When you decide to publish, beware of scams. Many illegitimate and "pay-for-play" journals will publish anything if you give them enough money. When in doubt, ask your adviser or a more advanced graduate student about the venue. Look online; there are lists of which journals or conferences are reputable and which are not.

Books

Books are one of the highest-prestige publications, especially in the humanities. Academic books are primarily published by university presses. They take the longest and are the most work. However, you probably won't write a book as a student. Even if your dissertation is book-style—common in the humanities and social sciences—there's a ton of work involved in converting a dissertation into a book. So, don't worry too much about books while you're a student.

Book Chapters

Sometimes, a scholar or group of scholars will create an "edited volume." These scholars, called volume editors, will invite other people from different institutions to contribute chapters on a topic or theme, which then editors compile, edit, and submit as a book to a publishing company (usually a university press, such as Columbia University Press—the publisher of this book). As a graduate student, you may have the opportunity to contribute a book chapter. The prestige afforded to this type of publication varies widely; some disciplines see book chapters as less important than journal articles, while some rank them the same or better. It may depend also on the book itself, the publisher, and whether the book was peer reviewed (some are, some aren't).

Journal Articles

Academic journals are run by scholarly organizations, universities, and nonprofit foundations. Originally created as actual printed publications, many still publish an issue every couple months or a volume once a year containing articles written by different researchers that have passed a lengthy peer-review and editorial process. Journal articles are generally longer, higher in prestige, and, after books, require the most work in academic publishing. However, some journals also publish shorter articles, such as commentaries and book reviews. In the humanities, one way to get started publishing is by writing book reviews.

How do you know which journals to submit to? Ask your adviser or more advanced graduates in your program. Look at their CVs: Where they have published work? Check where research you've been assigned in classes has been published. You'll start to get a sense of which venues are considered high impact in your field. Most fields have a couple of top journals, which tend to publish the most novel and impactful work, such as the *Annual Review of Psychology* and the *Psychological Bulletin* in psychology. Then there are more specialized journals that focus on different subfields or topics, such as the *Journal of Child Psychology and Psychiatry* or the *International Journal of Child-Computer Interaction*. When submitting an article, if you aren't in a hurry to be published, you can submit to a higher-impact journal first (there are usually rules about submitting to one venue at a time). If the article is rejected, try again at a midrange journal or more specialist publication. You never know if the higher-status journal will work out or not—there's a lot of subjectivity in the peer-review process.

Conferences, Workshops, and Symposia

Conferences, workshops, and symposia are run by scholarly organizations. The goal is to bring researchers interested in the same field or subfield together to discuss their latest work, share ideas and feedback, and move the whole field forward. The peer-review process is generally shorter than for a journal, with only one or two rounds of review; work is accepted to the conference by the program committee based on its quality and relevance. In some disciplines, researchers submit work in progress to conferences and the work is considered an unreviewed preprint; in others, completed work is submitted and the resulting publication is treated much like a short journal paper.

At the conference, researchers present their papers, usually in a panel, roundtable, or in individual presentations one after another, grouped loosely by topic. Some papers may be presented as posters during a poster session—an event where some researchers display large posters they've made describing their work, and everyone else walks around and talks to them about their work. Conferences frequently include keynote talks by notable scholars in the field. Some also include workshop sessions, which are smaller gatherings of researchers focused on a specific topic who share ideas and works in progress. Workshops are usually more hands-on and involve more discussion sessions, while conferences are mostly lecture or presentation format. Symposia are much like conferences but smaller, though it varies by discipline.

The main considerations when submitting to conferences are the cost of attending in order to present your paper, as mentioned in chapter 3, and whether the conference would be worth your time. The latter question is difficult to answer—ask your adviser and more advanced students. At a conference, you get the publication. You can attend sessions to hear about new research and methods in your field. In between sessions, there are coffee hours, book or industry exhibits to explore, and time to socialize; receptions fill the evenings to provide more networking opportunities. Conferences range in attendance from a couple hundred people to thousands, depending on the discipline. Some people set up meetings in advance with students they're friends with on social media, professors they haven't seen in a long time, or people they want research advice from. Some conferences have mentoring programs that pair grad students with more senior scholars in the field, so the students get more out of the conference.

What Do I Wear to a Conference? Whatever is common in your field. Many professors wear whatever they wear when they are teaching. Wear what you find comfortable. Layering works great. Consider wearing comfortable shoes because you often walk a lot. Same with bags; often a backpack is better for carrying your laptop and everything else. One conference I went to, I actually wore hiking boots the entire time, because I had a week of travel planned post-conference and didn't want to pack too many shoes.

Getting Scooped and Preprint Servers

In some fields, such as physics and biology, papers are frequently posted on a preprint server such as ArXiv.org or bioRxiv.org prior to being reviewed and published in a journal. The point is to get the work out sooner, claim authorship quicker, get feedback faster, and let others build on your work as soon as possible. It can prevent you from being "scooped"—when someone else beats you to print with a similar experiment or results. Ask your adviser if preprints are common in your field. They weren't common in mine (education, psychology, human-robot interaction), and being scooped wasn't something I worried about either; we published when we had a result that was ready to publish, full stop.

NONACADEMIC PUBLISHING

If you have nonacademic aspirations, or want to reach policymakers, practitioners, or the general public, write for nonacademic venues. I wrote blog posts about my work, which helped me land consulting jobs years after graduate school. Your credentials as a researcher make you someone to listen to.

Some venues are informal, such as many social media sites. Research reports, policy briefs, and press releases are more formal but don't require external review before publication. Magazines, newspapers, and guest posts for blogs frequently require you to submit a pitch explaining what you will write, the general argument, why it's important, and how it would make a good fit for that venue. If the editor accepts your pitch, you write your piece, go through one or more rounds of revision, and then it gets published. Sometimes, you are expected to submit the entire article (writing "on spec"), not just a pitch. Sometimes, you get paid—check the website Who Pays Writers? to see common rates.[5]

COMMUNICATING IDEAS

When you share your work, you tell a story. Compelling stories mean something to your audience. They engage audience curiosity and explain why the reader should care. Fortunately, all research begins with curiosity: questions and problems. Begin your story—whatever format it will ultimately be in, journal paper or blog post or beyond—in the same place: with curiosity. Start big. Situate your work in the larger context. Find a big, important thing people care about, tell them how that thing impacts their lives, then explain how your work is related to that thing. The question you need to answer is not "What are you researching?" but "Why should the reader care?" Ask yourself about the implications of your work and the broader impact on theory or in the world. Do you challenge assumptions, develop a new concept or theory, extend existing ideas in new ways, inform policy, or highlight the effectiveness or ineffectiveness of practices in the field? This stage-setting section doesn't have to be long. Anywhere from a sentence up to a couple paragraphs will suffice. Once you've broadly opened up a question or problem, narrow in on your specific slice of the problem pie. The rest of the story is an argument or narrative explaining what you did, why you did it, and what you learned.

Here's an example. I researched and developed robotic language-learning companions for preschool children. Why should anyone care? As it turns out, language and literacy are important for everything humans do. It's the primary means of human knowledge transfer! Language is *super important*. Plus, there's research showing that if children *don't* get enough language exposure early on (i.e., between the ages of three and five), it's harder to catch up in school later. Oh no! Language skills are important for academic and life success! But not everyone has those skills. Enter robot. This robot is a tool we can use to help young kids develop language skills at a critical time, thus saving them from a life of misery—or, you know, something less dramatic, like reduced academic success. Situate your work inside a larger problem. Then dive in and explain how what you're doing fits into the larger problem, even if it's just a tiny little piece of that larger problem.

As an aside, discussing the broader frame and merit of your research is good practice if you ever intend to write grants or apply for fellowships and other funding, since many applications require you to explain the broader impacts and intellectual merit of your work.

HOW DO I MAKE OR FIND GOOD FIGURES FOR PAPERS AND PRESENTATIONS?

You can generate basic graphs and figures using tools such as Excel and PowerPoint. You can make more complex figures with statistical programs and software such as SPSS, SAS, Python, R, and Matlab. If you are in the life sciences, Biorender.com provides icons and graphics you can combine into complex figures. Make sure to label all important information in the figure or graph with a sufficiently large font—especially axes, tick marks, and values. Learn about the types of figures or graphs commonly used to present data in your field from other graduate students, your adviser, and recent papers.

WRITING

Starting a New Draft

You're faced with an empty screen, cursor blinking. What words do you type first? As discussed in chapter 7, on writing dissertations, you can take one of two routes: make an outline to follow, or start collecting relevant thoughts and arrange them later.

When writing shorter work—anything that's not a book or a dissertation—you should know up front where you're planning to submit the work and what format it will take. This gives a first stab at structure. You'll know if you have to fit your story into a six-page conference paper or a journal article of twelve thousand words. You can look at previous work published in that venue to see how other people have organized their ideas.

Peter J. Feibelman, author of *A PhD Is Not Enough! A Guide to Survival in Science*,[6] suggests imagining that you are speaking with a friend in your field whom you haven't spoken to in a long time. The friend asks what you've been working on. You launch into a description of the project you're writing about—and write it down (or dictate it). This puts something on paper. Then you can revise.

What Do I Do If Writing Is Hard?

Flip back to the section on writing dissertations in chapter 7. Most of that advice applies to any writing you do.

What Does Good Writing Look Like?

Recognizing good writing is easier than writing well. It's engaging and easy to follow. The argumentation is clear. It's accurate, precise, and concise. It doesn't bury essential points—it gets to the point. Here are some tricks to improve your writing:

- Use shorter sentences with simpler sentence structures. Complex sentence structures require more cognitive effort to understand, leaving fewer resources for parsing the content of the sentence.[7] When in doubt, end the sentence and start a new one.
- Never use a complex word or phrase when a short one will do.
- Define all terms that could be considered jargon.
- Use topic sentences in your paragraphs. After you've written a paragraph, check whether the last sentence could actually be moved to the beginning of the paragraph to act as the topic sentence. People have a tendency to hide the most important information at the end.
- Include all relevant details—especially in methodology sections. Methods can be technically detailed and should read like a recipe. The target audience is composed of experts in your field. Include everything they would need to know in order to reproduce the exact work you did.
- Be concise. Nearly everything you write will have a word or page limit, and you need to fit your message into the available space. One tactic championed by author Stephen King: after writing a draft, cut at least 10 percent of the words.[8] Go through sentence by sentence. Find shorter

ways to say what you said. When cutting entire paragraphs or sections to get a manuscript down to size, go back to your main story. Remove or summarize anything that's not critical to your central storyline.
- Find people who write well and follow their structure and style. Look for papers or books you found particularly engaging. What did the writer do that seemed to work?

Writing Well for General Audiences   When communicating with general audiences, being concise is doubly important. Christopher Caterine, in *Leaving Academia*, points out that the academic world is filled with people who can examine any problem or question from every possible angle, and delve into every bit of theory that might possibly be relevant.[9] The rest of the world doesn't care about those problems and questions *nearly* as much. People in your field already have something at stake; general audiences have far more competing for their attention. They want information for a purpose, probably to make a decision in a limited amount of time, so you must answer the question "Why does this matter?" early and well.

Writing as Practice

Many students see writing as a chore. It's the thing they have to do after they finish the fun stuff—reading, collecting data, having insights, and making amazing discoveries. Maybe writing feels like a chore because it's difficult: the struggle to explain your ideas coherently and concisely; a never-ending battle with proper English grammar; an hour agonizing over a single paragraph. But repeat after me: writing is not a chore.

Writing is practice. Writing is a key means of communication everywhere. Learning to write well will never hurt you, and in fact it will only help. Writing is planning, thinking, synthesizing, and ideation (see chapter 7.) Writing can add rigor to your thinking. Writing to communicate can help you see flaws in your arguments, realize new connections between ideas, and generally help you organize your thoughts. Writing introductions and discussion sections are especially useful in this regard, since these are the parts of a paper where you connect your work and your ideas to everyone else's.

Revisions and Feedback

One of my first academic papers was rejected from several journals and went through over thirty revisions (I lost count of the exact number) before I gave up on it. Then, two years later, on the suggestion of the professor who had worked with me on the paper, I returned to it. After more revisions and another year (but who's counting?), it was finally published.[10] The process was neither easy nor fun—but the paper that came out the other end was decent. The revisions and feedback along the way improved it significantly.

You may feel like your paper is never good enough to submit. That doesn't necessarily mean you're a perfectionist—it just means you recognize a truth about writing: writing improves with revision.

Writing isn't a onetime action. It's not like baking a cake—mix the ingredients, pop it in the oven, and it's done. Writing is a process. Editing is part of that process. The road to publication includes space for receiving feedback, editing your work, and improving it. Of course, you want the work to be as good as possible *before* submitting so it has a better chance of receiving a favorable peer review, but you can't make your work the best it can be without revision and without feedback.

How Do I Get Feedback? You can request writing feedback on any kind of writing: papers, grant proposals, fellowship applications, research designs, course materials, statements, blog posts, essays. First, ask peers and friends. You can ask informally, or you could form a peer writing group or a crit group with other students in your program, as suggested in chapter 6, "Labs, Classes, and Teaching." That way, it's a reciprocal relationship wherein you all give and receive writing feedback, and you won't feel like you're asking too much. You can get feedback from your adviser, other professors, the writing center at your institution, and (after you submit) reviewers and/or editors. Feedback from knowledgeable people in your field can help ensure your paper follows the conventions and expectations of your discipline. Feedback from people outside your field is useful because you learn whether your writing is understandable to those unfamiliar with your work. It's easy, for instance, to skip over explaining concepts or procedures that seem straightforward to you because you're already familiar with them.

Don't be afraid to ask for feedback, even if everyone seems busy. It's part of writing. Just be respectful of people's time. Send feedback requests early—not at the last minute, certainly not hours before your deadline—so people have time to read what you wrote and to offer substantive comments, and you have time to revise after that. Attach the document you want feedback on. Be specific about the kind of feedback you're looking for. For example, if it's an early draft, you may be looking for higher-level structural feedback rather than detailed line edits. Do you want someone to check your background and literature review? Are you leaving out relevant citations? Is your argument clear? Can the reader follow how you got your results, and what those results mean? Do you need another figure to illustrate your data? Seek feedback from different people at different stages of producing a paper, so that you can incrementally improve the end result.

You'll notice that throughout this chapter I've spent very little time on spelling and grammar. Spell-check programs catch most spelling errors. Grammar rules are arbitrary, especially in English, and many writers do not follow the rules and yet are considered great. So long as your writing is clear, you don't have to follow any particular style guide with regards to grammar rules. If you're worried, find someone to read your writing with an eye toward odd grammar and typos.

What Do I Do with Feedback?   When you receive a critique or review, first, briefly skim it. The format of critiques and reviews varies widely in length, tone, and helpfulness. There's no standard, even among journals and conferences. The suggestions will involve things to edit, cut, and add; they may point out flaws and give supportive tips for improvement; they may critique without offering any concrete fixes. Sometimes people are unhelpful and their comments don't make sense. While you're reading, remember that feedback is aimed at making the writing better. Your reviewer is trying to help you express your ideas more clearly and coherently. This doesn't make them definitively *right*, it just means you should read the reviews generously.

Feedback is useful for discovering *where* writing needs work. If a reviewer was confused or concerned, other people probably will be too. However, you don't have to take all the suggestions given. Many people can spot problems in writing, but unless they are truly excellent editors, they are rarely as good at knowing how to *fix* those problems. (Most will happily supply suggestions nonetheless.) As Tracy Kidder and Richard Todd write in *Good Prose: The Art of Nonfiction*, most writing problems are best fixed by the author. Use your best judgment and ignore suggestions as needed.[11] People encounter ideas from where they're at. They may need different amounts of detail or supporting information to understand your words. And that's okay. Learning to judge your audience is a skill that takes practice too.

When revising, begin with major revisions, such as big changes to the document structure or major reframing of entire sections. Kidder and Todd say that most problems in writing are structural, whether at the level of the entire paper, the level of paragraphs, or even within a single sentence. After the big changes, dive in: typos, confusing phrasing, clarifications, citations to add, and so on.

Keep all your drafts. There's no downside in the age of unlimited storage space. That way, you can go back, if you ever feel you need to. (I've only rarely looked at old drafts. But having them in existence makes me feel more comfortable about getting out my proverbial red pen.) Have a system for titling your draft files—ideally, use sequential numbers or the current date in the file name, both of which make it easy to track which draft is the most recent.

Find the Right Words Thanks to Twitter, around the time I got the email about returning to that abandoned paper, I found myself reading the blog of science fiction and fantasy author Kameron Hurley. In one post, Hurley wrote about her experiences as a professional copywriter. She wrote words for other people for a living. She talked about a manager trying to "gently" give her feedback from a client. Her reply: Don't mince words. Give it to me. If the words were wrong, she needed to write them until they were the right words. It was literally her job to make the words right for that client. She needed the client's hard-hitting feedback to revise.

I loved her attitude. She reminds us that we are not the words on the page. They're just one attempt at communicating an idea through the imperfect and difficult medium of language. If that communication attempt fails, we are given the opportunity to try again. As Hurley puts it, "You write until the words are the right ones."[12]

If we care about communicating our ideas, then the revision process can be a conversation. The goal is to make the writing better. The goal is to improve the presentation of ideas. The goal is to make the words right.

Put another way, the goal of the first draft is to exist. The goal of each subsequent draft is to be a bit clearer, more concise, better than the previous draft. That's all. At some point, it will be good enough, at which point it can get published.

Editing Your Own Work   When editing your own work, try to read it anew, with fresh eyes. Set it aside for a while (days, weeks, months), then come back. Use a text-to-speech feature or read it aloud to yourself. Change the font and size. Print it out and edit the hard copy.

Peer Review and Harsh Feedback   Most academic work goes through peer review, during which the reviewers make one of four recommendations:

1. Accept the work as is (very rare)
2. Accept it after minor revisions (reasonably common)
3. Require major revisions and resubmission (very common)
4. Reject it entirely (most common if the work isn't a good fit for the venue)

Anything that's not rejection is a *good* outcome. You are being given the opportunity to improve your paper—making it clearer and stronger—before resubmission.

When you resubmit a paper, you also submit a letter explaining what you fixed. An easy way to do this is copy all the reviews into a new document. Highlight all the things you need to fix. When you fix something, un-highlight it and write a sentence or two in boldface just below it politely justifying your revisions, answering the reviewers' concerns, and explaining what you fixed or why you think they're wrong (and what you did instead). Ask to see examples of past cover letters and response letters that other students, postdocs, or your adviser have written. This can help you learn how to craft your responses.

In peer review, you may get extremely harsh feedback. Most peer review is blind, meaning the reviewers' identities are hidden from the authors, or double-blind, meaning that both parties' identities are hidden. An unfortunate side effect of this is that some people feel the anonymity gives them license to be mean.

Harsh reviews can be hard to read. You can ask a friend to read the reviews for you and share the highlights. Take a step back. Set the reviews aside. Get a cup of tea. In a little while, after reminding yourself that reviews are intended to improve the writing, go back to them. Tackle them head-on and revise your paper. Remember that, since people are busy, the comments they write on your drafts may be terse. Revise your paper anyway. Even the harshest feedback has *something* you can glean from it that will help you improve your work. So revise your paper just to spite them.

Ask for help from your adviser, a postdoc, or another professor you trust. They've seen harsh reviews before and can help you determine which comments you need to address and what you can safely ignore.

Giving Feedback and Writing Reviews   As a graduate student, you may have the opportunity to review papers for peers, colleagues, and conferences and journals, especially in STEM fields. This can be a great learning exercise. Critiquing other people's writing helps you see what is, and is not, good writing. It helps you realize that when you get feedback, the person offering the critique is trying to point out stuff you might've missed the first time around.

As Steven R. Shaw explains, reviews cover two parts: internal and external.[13] The internal part is about the research itself: whether the rationale for the research has been sufficiently established, whether the research questions or hypotheses are clearly stated, whether the methods used are appropriate for answering the questions, whether the results logically flow from the methods, and whether the conclusions stated are consistent with the results. The external part is about how the research connects to the wider world, the "So what?" question.

When you write reviews, give the kind of feedback you'd like to get. Be friendly, helpful, detailed, and critical. The goal is to improve the work. Try to provide not only a list of issues you see, but also suggestions for how to fix those issues, which can help the author determine the best solutions. Mention positive qualities when you notice them, such as a well-worded argument or an especially clear methodology section.

Writing with Coauthors

Many students write manuscripts with other people. The process of coauthoring varies with the authors. I've written the entire first draft of a coauthored paper before passing it on to my collaborators for comments. Another time, my adviser had written a grant with two other professors to fund a series of experiments. Two students and I were heavily involved in planning the first experiment, and we had boots on the ground executing the work. I wrote the first draft of the methods, data, and results sections, plus part of the introduction. The professor most familiar with the field took the next stab, adding literature and theory to the introduction and discussion. Then we passed the paper to everyone else for comments and additions. Another paper was far more collaborative from the outset. We had regular phone calls to discuss structure and content, created an outline together in a shared Google Doc, assigned sections throughout the paper to different authors, and left comments throughout about clarifications, citations, examples, phrasing, and other changes.

Whatever method you use, discuss it up front so you have some idea of who's going to be writing what, how often you're going to meet about it, and even what software you will be using to collaboratively write (such as LaTeX, Overleaf, or Word) and how you'll manage citations (see more on citation managers and writing software in chapter 7).

What's the Deal with Author Order?

Outside of the humanities, many academic papers and books describe collaborative work by multiple authors. The order in which authors are listed says something about the importance or relative responsibility each person had in contributing to the published work.

The most prestigious position of authorship is awarded to the person who was the lead on the research, had the original idea, performed the most experiments, wrote up the paper, or headed the lab. Sometimes they're listed first; sometimes last. Occasionally author names are arranged alphabetically. Sometimes a footnote will list how each author contributed, and whether any contributed equally. It varies by discipline. Ask a more advanced student or your adviser what's common in yours.

When writing with coauthors, have a conversation early about how author order will be determined, as it can be a source of significant conflict.

EXERCISE 14: THE POINT OF THE FIRST DRAFT IS TO EXIST

1. Pick a project you need to work on, such as a paper or dissertation chapter. Spend a couple minutes looking over what you already have written (if anything), or at your notes, outline, or the assignment.
2. Find a timer. Set it for ten minutes.

3. Start writing. Write whatever comes to mind. Write about the topic, relevant literature, and anything remotely related to the project.
4. If, when the timer rings, you have additional thoughts to add or want to fix up what you've written so far, do it.

SPEAKING

The most common speaking engagements for a budding researcher are class presentations, department workshops and brown bag sessions (usually a less formal talk, often within a department, during a lunchtime talk series or similar event), and academic conferences or symposia. Near the end of your degree, you may also give job talks, guest lectures, interviews on podcasts or radio, or even a TEDx talk. Regardless of the venue, the way to ace a talk or presentation is to prepare and practice.

Preparing for a Talk

The two secrets of chair-gripping talks are story and stagecraft. As Peter J. Fiebelman puts it, "As the speaker, you are putting on a one person show. Your listeners are investing an hour of their valuable time. Of course they want to learn something from you, but like theater goers, they expect to hear a good story, with a beginning, and middle, and an end."[14]

Plan and rehearse your talk in advance. Project an air of confidence—even if you feel like a puddle of knotted spaghetti—and speak with volume and energy. As my dad liked to say, "Act like you're supposed to be there, and no one will question you!" If you want to deliberately hone your speaking skills, take a theater or speaking class or join an improv club. Watch comedians—they're masters at using the range of their voices and using silence to punctuate speech. Always talk slower than you think you should. Everyone has a tendency to speed up in front of an audience. Look at the audience and make direct eye contact with individual people. It's fine to have notes or a script, but make sure to look up from your notes now and then, and practice enough that it doesn't *sound* like you're reading off your notes. Talk loud. Project! Especially if you are not given a microphone.

Practice alone and practice with an audience. Everyone in my lab group was expected to give at least one practice talk to the group before their big day. Some also gave practice talks to friends or spouses. Your audience can give you feedback: Was the message clear? Did you communicate your results well? If you have slides (more on those next), did they help? Could the design be improved?

When you're giving a talk about your research, begin like you would a paper, with the "So what?" Establish the theme and context, explain your research goals or hypotheses, give an overview of techniques or methods, then launch into your main message. Spend the most time talking about what you found and what it means. You don't have to fill up time on background—just toss in a few key citations so your audience knows you know what you're talking about. Remember, if audience members want the details, they can read the associated paper. If you're going to include technical details, don't gloss over them using unexplained technical terminology to "give the flavor," because all the audience learns is that they don't know the jargon.

One more secret to a successful talk is staying within the time limit. No one minds a talk that's a few minutes short. Say you're given fifteen minutes—you can safely cut it at twelve. Half an hour? Twenty-five. An hour? Fifty. This leaves more time for questions and discussion, and can help make up for all the people who will inevitably ignore the clock.

I generally wrote out my talks before giving them, especially for shorter ones, so I wouldn't accidentally forget to mention important details. I timed myself talking to get a general sense of how many words per minute I ought to speak (slower than conversational speech is good), then scripted a talk of the right length. If you're going to script a talk, only use phrases you would actually say. Nix every sentence that sounds extra-academic just for the sake of sounding academic. Then, practice enough that you sound natural—you don't want to sound like you're reading aloud. Some students prefer to prepare a set of slides or notes to talk to, and then practice enough that they develop a general sense of what they're saying and how to keep within their time limit.

Presentations and Slide Decks

Visual aids accompany many academic talks, especially in STEM and the social sciences. Whether you make slides with PowerPoint, Keynote, or some alternative (see the resources chapter for options), it's imperative to learn to use those slides for good.

First, remember that the slides are support, not the focus. An unfortunate consequence of the pervasiveness of slide decks is that the slides themselves are assumed to be the lion leaping through the flaming ring at the circus, while they should be the guy holding up the flaming ring. I once sat through a presentation in which the speaker used a gimmick of little cartoon fishies with whom she "conversed" and who "helped explain" her topic. Multiple times, she announced, "I'll let my fish friends explain!" then stood quietly by as a garbled, bubbling audio track played. The audience was expected to awkwardly sit and read her slides.

Don't do that. If I can't understand the talk because I'm not reading along, you're doing it wrong. Besides leaving fish in the ocean, how do you make your slides clean, memorable, and valuable? Here are ten suggestions:

1. Use large text. People at the back of the room shouldn't have to squint. The defaults in presentation software are too small; try for a minimum of font size 28.
2. Reduce the amount of text. No paragraphs and no sentences, unless there is an extremely important quote you are reading aloud.
3. Corollary: your notes can have paragraphs, and your notes should not be on your slides.
4. Ditch the outline slide for short talks. Outlines are great for your own use; the audience doesn't need to see them. That said, it can be helpful to drop some sort of proverbial bread crumb to show where you are in a longer talk, especially if you keep returning to it as the talk progresses.
5. Proofread your slides.
6. Pay attention to color contrast. For example, never use yellow text on a white background. Make sure your slide content is actually readable!
7. Label the axes on all your graphs and charts.
8. Use images wisely. Only include images that add to your message—don't fill space with images just for the sake of filling space. I like making my own graphics instead of using clip art, but if you're not artistically inclined, there are plenty of Creative Commons-licensed images that you can pull from. I also use pictures from my studies depicting the robots and materials to illustrate my points.

9. On your first slide, list the title of your talk, your name, the names of your collaborators, and put anyone else that you want to thank. Sometimes, for work involving many people, I will include a separate acknowledgments slide at the end of the talk.
10. The last slide (which is often left on screen during the Q&A) should be a repeat of the first one with your contact details added. That way, if someone wants to follow up with you, they can snap a quick picture of your slide and have all the information they need.

Accessibility

When giving presentations, pay attention to accessibility. Present essential information in more than one format; for example, have the bullet points on your slide when you're going over them. If there's a microphone, use it. Ask for a mobile mic and laser pointer, so you won't be rooted to a podium, flailing ineffectively toward your slides. Speak slowly. Caption all of your video and audio. Use big fonts—at least size 28. Use contrasting colors. Don't move too fast through your slides. A good rule of thumb is to spend at least one minute per slide, unless it's a building slide that adds more information on top as you talk. Optionally, provide printed copies of the slides, especially if you have important text on them.

Handling Q&A

Most talks terminate in a question-and-answer, or Q&A, session. Honestly, I think this is the most stressful part of giving a talk, because I don't know what I'll be asked and can't prepare eloquent turns of phrase ahead of time. Some preparation is possible. You can try to prompt questions, such as alluding to some analyses or data that you've left out of the talk but are in your paper. I knew some people who would create extra slides at the end of their talk with extra figures or data just in case they got asked questions about those topics. Common questions will be about the details of your methodology that you didn't cover at length, implications of your work, alternative explanations of your data, limits of your data, and how your research might affect the questioner's favorite topic area. You may also get the unfortunate "This is more of a comment than a question . . ." lead-in, in which someone, usually an established academic, rambles about something vaguely related that interests them more than you.

Respond to all questions courteously. Restate the question when you begin, since this can give you time to think and clarify what you're responding to; it's also useful for accessibility, since many times, the presenter has a mic but questioners don't, and some people in the audience may not have heard the question.

But Public Speaking Is Scary!

Most people are afraid of public speaking (one estimate: 77 percent).[15] Careful preparation and practice can go a long way toward helping you feel comfortable. Sit like a stone before your talk, breathe, and remind yourself to speak slowly and enunciate. Ask a friend to sit up front so you can see a friendly face. Visit the venue ahead of time so the unfamiliarity doesn't add to your anxiety. Reflect on what the worst scenarios would be, and directly challenge your worries with alternative, positive outcomes. Focus on the fact that your talk is a teaching moment for the audience—they're here to hear *you*. If you lose your place mid-presentation, take a few deep breaths; a moment of silence is perfectly fine, and can even help your audience catch up.

Finally, don't tell yourself to be calm—it won't work because you're not feeling calm. You can, however, reframe your nerves and anxiety as excitement, a trick that has helped numerous people perform better.[16] Tell yourself that the brick of butterflies in your stomach is really an exhilarated cloud of monarchs waiting to burst free on stage.

What About Technology?

If you have slides, bring your own laptop if you have one, along with any cables for connecting to projectors, as well as a backup of your presentation on a flash drive in case you need to borrow someone else's machine to present. You can't bet on the venue providing the adapters you need. That said, I generally got away with borrowing Mac adapters from other presenters. Your mileage may vary.

POSTERS

Poster sessions are an invitation to start a conversation about your research. The presenters set up posters in a big room, and then other people can walk by to read and discuss the research. You're not glued to the poster—you can wander and learn too—but you should spend a good chunk of the session nearby to explain and answer questions about your work.

Good poster design is like good slide design: less words, more pictures, bigger fonts. Posters are an invitation. They should include the same basic elements of talks and papers: titles, authors, the "So what?" of your research, your questions or hypotheses, what you did, basic findings or discussion. When printing your poster, double-check the recommended size. Consider printing on fabric instead of paper if you have to travel (carrying a poster tube on an airplane gets old fast). The resources include pointers to good poster design, with examples.

SHARE YOUR WORK

After you publish, let people know! Send emails to colleagues. Post on social media, including a brief summary of the work. Many researchers don't have article alerts set up and are happy to hear about new work from you directly. It can help engage others in your work and build community in your field.

If you engage with public audiences or conduct interviews with major news outlets, the public can engage right back. You may get public criticism of you or your work, especially if your research runs counter to mainstream cultural narratives. Determine first whether the negative press is worth responding to—sometimes staying silent or continuing as you have, without responding directly, can be the best course of action. If you do respond, be tactful and polite; review and edit before responding. If you know your facts and know you're right, hold true to yourself and your work.

Online

If you have a website or public social media accounts (the benefits of which are mentioned in chapter 2, "Career Plans"), keep them current. Every time you get a paper accepted, travel to a conference, win an award, finish a major project, or do an outreach activity, post an announcement, add a news item, or, at a minimum, update your publications list. While you're at it, add your accomplishments to a master CV draft, so when you need a current CV or resume, you won't be stuck panning for your golden achievements in a morass of forgetfulness.

Keeping your web presence up-to-date is more important for future you than present you, so be nice to your future self and make sure the information that potential employers and colleagues may find about you is correct!

Connecting with Other Researchers

Follow other scholars on social media: scholars you know, scholars in your field, scholars working on interesting research. You can also follow professional organizations, journals, publishers, and academic hashtags (see the resources). Some platforms have affinity groups you can join (e.g., academic mothers, teaching assistants, first-gen students).

Be intentional in who you follow. Follow people with diverse backgrounds and viewpoints. If you are in an insular bubble, you won't see the full breadth of conversations that are happening. Being willing to listen to other people can help you build empathy and tolerance toward people who are different from you, whether different politically, ethnically, racially, or any other demographic you care about.

While the point of social media is to be social, you do not have to engage constantly. For example, I found Twitter useful as a tool for getting the lay of the academic land, a place where I could taste the sampler platter of conversations happening in my various disciplines and in academia more broadly. You can eavesdrop for a while to get a sense of norms in different spaces before posting. When you do post, be constructive and friendly; don't exclusively talk about yourself; if you misstep and come off as hateful, mean, or uninformed, apologize and move on.

Use social media to build connections. For instance, if someone in your field shares their latest research paper and you read it, reach out with questions. Sharing research online is an invitation to engage, so engage! Ask follow-up questions in the thread or in the comments, send a direct message, send an email. Many scholars use online connections to build in-person connections (e.g., meeting up at conferences later). You can request a video chat or face-to-face meeting if you feel you have a lot to discuss.

PART III

The Rest of Your Life

chapter 10
It's Just Grad School

A quiet sip of tea. Warmth and sweetness. Tang of raspberries. Familiar *scrape*, *chink* of ceramic mug lifted, returned to the tabletop. A reminder to pause. I will absorb *this* moment, *this* breath, *this* sip of tea. A reminder to take time.

Your work may be your life, but your life is more than just your work. Sometimes, in the midst of paper revisions, running studies, benchwork, writing code, homework, exams, it's easy to forget. But your life is more than your research. It's more than your art, your hobbies, your second job, your sports, your relationships. Your life is *all* of these. You *will* have to take time away from one facet to tend to another. And that's okay.

When I was fifteen, I spent a lot of time at the local fencing club. One of the programs I attended was called "junior team"—twice-weekly practices for all the kids who wanted to be serious about fencing. The kids who thought they might like to compete in local or national tournaments, who wanted to train hard, and learn the sport inside out. Of course, being kids, sometimes we'd goof off and stand around chatting instead of fencing. That was a cue for our coach, George Platt, to call all of us sweaty kids into a circle to divulge some of his hard-won life wisdom—usually in the guise of stories of past students or tournaments from years gone by. Some kids would stand gulping water from plastic bottles, others would plop down on the floor, fanning their faces. The room always felt warm; no AC, just a couple of big fans pulling hot air from outside.

One talk was ostensibly about commitment. George would remind us that we were all at junior team practices by choice. We were there to train hard, fence hard, work hard. So he expected us all to do that. Come to practice. Care about the sport. Then he'd say, "But in the end, it's just fencing." *It's just fencing.* The lesson was, treat this sport as really important—but don't forget that the rest of your life matters too. At the end of the day, it's only one piece of your life, even if it's a really important one right now. Sometimes, other stuff takes precedence. That always holds true. Sometimes, other stuff takes precedence.

It has been two decades since I first heard George say, "It's just fencing," and I can't count how many times that phrase has popped up in my head to remind me that *the rest of my life matters too*. Whatever I'm working on, whatever I'm doing: it's just fencing. My whole life matters, not just that one thing. Spend time on what's important. Stay balanced.

Granted, sometimes it's hard to know what *should* take precedence, now or in the long term. Sometimes it's hard to take time when you need it—and to not just take time once, but to continue taking time. You're more yourself when you take time for hobbies and relationships. You're more energetic and productive when work is not the only thing you do all day, every day. Sometimes you feel you *can't* take time, because there is no time: it's all coursework and outside work and paying rent and job applications.

I used little things to remind myself to take time. A mug of tea became a reminder to stay present. I took that moment to pause, relax, refocus. My daily commute on the Boston subway became a reminder to take time for things I enjoy, like reading books as I waited for the train.

A walk across campus became a reminder to spend more time outdoors. I remembered to relish the mile walk from my apartment to the subway every day—a walk I could easily dread, especially in January, when the snow was falling and the wind was biting. But it was a reminder to see the world—sunbright forsythia in the spring, leaves carpeting the sidewalk in the fall, icicles gripping the eaves in the winter. In walking through the city every day, I saw its small changes. Sometimes, I used the walk as time to call family or keep in touch with friends. A reminder that relationships matter. The twice-daily walk was a good transition time and helped me maintain balance between my school life and my home life. (And in the midst of hectic deadlines, the walk was a welcome break between working in the lab and continuing to work from my laptop at home. Those days happened too.)

Find small moments to take time. Be present in your life. We all know how easy it would be to spend all day and all night in our labs and offices . . . but sometimes, other stuff takes precedence. Other stuff matters too. Grad school is only one piece of your life. It may be a really big piece. It may be the biggest piece. But it's only one piece, and it won't last forever. Don't put the rest of your life on hold while you're in school. Find time for hobbies, other interests, family, and friends. Find a school-life balance that works for you.

BALANCE AND HEALTH

Your grad school-life balance, or your work-life balance, is dividing your time between "work" activities and "nonwork" activities, such that you're happy with how much time you spend on each. "Work," for a grad student, may include all your school-related obligations, such as classes, homework, lab work, research time, grading papers, etc., as well as any work you're doing for an outside job, and work at home (like chores and caregiving). "Nonwork" is everything else you do, but especially the things that recharge you: hobbies, time with your family or friends, relaxing, exercising, sleeping, and so on. There's no magic formula that can tell you what the right balance is, because the balance will be a little different for everyone. Some people argue that work-life balance is a myth because work can't be separated from the rest of life—too many hours are filled with work for it to *really* be separate—but that feels like semantics to me. The distinction between work and nonwork is useful because of how we often mentally divide our time and energy between the two. Work-life balance is balancing the time you give to all the different things you value, in a way that makes you happy with your balance.

The reason finding a balance matters is because doing so will enable you to protect your health. In *Designing Your Life*, Bill Burnett and Dave Evans divide life into a four-slice pie: health, work, love, and play. Health undergirds everything else. Mental health, emotional health, physical health, spiritual health. You need health to work (study, get a degree, earn extra income to pay rent, etc.), love (friends, family, relationships), and play (hobbies). Most of this book has been about work; this chapter and the next two are about health, play, and love.

Graduate school is stressful. Between failed experiments, rejected papers, tough exams, critical supervisors, absent friends, the daily grad-school grind can get tough and lonely. Systemic issues in academia, such as sexism, racism, power abuses, workaholism, and mental health stigma, can be crushing—not to mention precarious employment and the difficulty of finding work relevant to your degree, especially in the humanities. Depression, anxiety, and other issues can make you feel unable to get or unworthy of getting help. And of course, mental health issues may be unrelated to grad school, developed as a result of other life events. A 2019 *Nature* survey of over six thousand grad students around the world found that 36 percent had sought help for depression or anxiety.[1] However, many students don't seek help, so the number of students suffering is almost certainly much higher. Graduate study, Amanda Seligman writes, can exaggerate insecurities and the feeling of imposter syndrome (discussed in chapter 4); grudges at school can become excuses to ignore other issues in your life; there's always a way to use graduate study as a reason to put off confronting issues—after all, that work won't do itself.[2]

But you can't work constantly. If work is the whole shebang, then sooner or later, even if you enjoy your work most of the time, you'll suffer from burnout. Burnout is a combination of emotional, physical, and mental exhaustion caused by prolonged stress. Symptoms include feeling overwhelmed; a sense of dread about your work; feeling emotionally drained; a lack of energy; difficulty concentrating; feelings of irritability, cynicism, and/or anger; and being unable to keep up with the demands of life or work. Even if you don't get to the point of burnout, if your life balance isn't optimal, you'll see declines in your mental and physical health, in the health of your relationships, and in the quality of the work you do. The sedentary nature of much graduate school research can have a significant effect on your physical health.[3] Graduate student culture tends toward late nights, odd hours, straining your eyes, and too much caffeine—so much so that my labmates were bewildered when, unlike the rest of them, I did not develop an addiction to coffee. (My secret was that I don't actually like coffee; I drank tea instead.)

The chronic stress that graduate school can cause is the silent killer.[4] Our bodies' stress response evolved for short-term, physical threats. Out on the savannah, you spot a lion and your fight-flight-or-freeze system kicks in full gear. Adrenaline floods your blood, your blood vessels constrict, your heart rate increases, your blood glucose rises. You'd escape the lion—by running away, hiding, or fighting back—then your body would go into recovery mode, and you'd go back to normal savannah life. The problem is, this stress response isn't a good fit for modernity. Public speaking, deadlines, exams—these stressors don't warrant your body preparing for battling lions. But your body reacts that way anyway. When chronically stressed, your body's attempts to recover overshoot and lead to all kinds of negative outcomes (and, eventually, burnout). Look: The national median for the time spent in graduate school for a PhD is 7.7 years.[5] In STEM fields, you may get away with 6.7 years; in the humanities, the median is 9.3. That is a *lot* of years to be chronically stressed.

Yes, grad school is supposed to be hard. It's supposed to challenge you. But it's not supposed to break you. It shouldn't feel impossible. It shouldn't send you into a spiral of depression or anxiety. Fortunately, and contrary to what some disgruntled graduate students might tell you, balance *is* possible for most of us. You aren't doomed to suffer. Despite the many stressors, many students make it through grad school with their mental health relatively intact (that was certainly my experience). The key? Prioritizing mental health and life balance. To students dealing with precarity, being under-resourced, and the crushing uncertainty of the job market, that answer may seem trite. Bear with me.

THE THREE-STEP PROCESS FOR FINDING BALANCE

Finding your balance is a simple, three-step process: (1) Try out some allotment of your time into work and nonwork activities. (2) Observe whether you're happy with that allotment. (3) If not, make iterative adjustments. "Simple" does not necessarily mean "easy." For some people, the hard part is convincing themselves that they *should* be taking time away from work. For others, it's committing to reenergizing activities, or figuring out what activities to do. And for some, it's *finding* time in between other, nonnegotiable commitments—especially for students who work or care for family while in school. Here are some strategies that may help.

Finding and Taking Time

- Set your expectations. Having free time for other stuff—reading, exploring, exercising, etc.—should be *normal*. I spent the year prior to entering graduate school working as a research intern (like a graduate research assistant, but with set hours and fewer responsibilities). During that year, I became accustomed to having time for my other projects. I brought this expectation with me into graduate school.

- Take little bits of time, if those are all you have. Can you use your commute for reading or listening to a favorite podcast? Can you sneak in your exercise by changing how you commute—for example, by walking or biking?
- Boost your productivity and waste less time during work hours using strategies from chapter 8, "Managing Projects and Managing Time," so you don't feel as strong a need to bring work home with you.
- If you find yourself thinking about work even when you'd rather not be, create a worry jar. Write down your worries or concerns on small pieces of paper or sticky notes. Put them in the jar. Once they're in the jar, they're the jar's problem, not yours. Let go.
- Revisit chapter 4's section on dealing with imposter syndrome.
- Find more resources or reduce stressors—more on that later in this chapter.

Committing

- Put the activities on your calendar. For instance, schedule a fifteen-minute block each week that you can use to meet yourself for coffee, practice meditation, engage in some fun reading, or anything else that relaxes you. I know people who add blocks of "free time" to their calendars in the evening. Just make sure not to stand yourself up! (See chapter 8 for more about scheduling.)
- Make a commitment and use other people or structures to hold yourself accountable. One semester, I decided I needed to get back to doing art. But I kept not doing art, because I had too much other stuff to do. So I signed up for an on-campus ceramics class. Once I was signed up, class paid for, I felt the usual obligation of, "Oh, I said I'd do a thing, I guess I better do the thing" settle in. I had a commitment. I went to class. I spun nice clay bowls on the pottery wheel. I glazed them, took them home, and admired them. I even set aside time outside of the scheduled class periods to work in the studio, since I wouldn't have had time to finish all the bowls otherwise. It was peaceful and relaxing. But to get there, I needed the nudge of outside commitment.

- Make it a routine. For example, exercise each morning before teaching, or Friday date nights. When building a routine, start with a small, manageable regular activity—say, reading for fun ten minutes a day. You want to build the habit first, then increase the amount—for example, by five minutes every week until you hit your goal of reading forty minutes for fun a day.
- Set boundaries. As Cal Newport argues in his book *Deep Work*, when we don't have strict boundaries, work often slides into the rest of our day.[6] You can use physical cues as boundaries, such as the physical separation between working on campus and being at home. I lived off campus; I used my commute to divide my day and give myself clear start and end points for school work hours versus other hours. Or it can be smaller, especially when your schedule is more fluid (like when you have a baby): Clean off your desk. Close your laptop. Go for a short walk outside. Listen to a favorite song. Something that helps you switch out of work mode and into nonwork mode.

What Activities to Do?

What activities make you feel like yourself? What reenergizes you? Think back to the exercises in chapter 1, "What's Next," about why you're in school and what you value most. What are your life goals? What do you want to learn? Who do you want to be with? If you looked back at your graduate school years a few decades from now, what would you wish you had done more of?

- Exercise. Regular exercise is linked to improved mental and physical well-being. Exercise gives you energy. I had a daily yoga routine and enjoyed walking with my husband. I knew a student who was an avid CrossFitter; she spent an hour (or more) at the gym every day. A student in my lab was president of the campus kickboxing club. I knew students who biked to campus, loved running, or hiked on the weekends. Others were involved in the intramural soccer league or joined campus clubs for different sports. There are lots of options. The key is finding exercise outlets that work for *you*.

- Go outside. Nature energizes, relaxes, and inspires.[7] Perhaps your favored method of exercise can happen outdoors. I knew a PhD student whose dog was her reason to get up in the morning for a while, because no matter how bad she felt, her dog still needed to go for a walk. One way to bring a little nature to you is to grow a plant. Once I realized I had a sunny windowsill in my apartment, I bought pots and dirt and grew herbs. Fresh basil, oregano, and cilantro! The flavors made me happy (cooking is another one of my hobbies). Growing a plant gives you something to cultivate, something low-stakes to invest in—plants and seeds are relatively cheap. You give it water, let it have sunshine, and see it produce tasty leaves or pretty flowers. What a reward!
- Get involved on campus. One of my friends was active in the campus trivia group. I ran the weekly discussion group for the campus secular society for nearly four years. Every university has extracurricular clubs and classes, from arts to sports to academics. You can also get involved in student governance, campus committees, and other, more "professional" activities, depending on your personal interests (see chapter 13, "Making Changes to Your School").
- Invest in your community. Volunteer for local nonprofits, such as groups offering tutoring to low-income students. You can find meaning by helping others in a sincere, direct way through volunteer work, like with a church group.
- Schedule time for family—in person if they're nearby, or time for phone or video calls if they're distant. When my son was a year old, my husband and I scheduled more family excursions to local parks and zoos.
- Check in on your friends. Schedule outings and coffee dates. Helping others can make us feel better ourselves.
- Eat lunch. Food is fuel. Food gives you energy. In my lab, students got in the habit of eating lunch together (instead of having working lunches), so we would all remember to take that time to enjoy a break, chat, eat, recharge. If cooking or baking brings you joy, make sure to set aside time for those too—leftovers make fantastic lunches.
- Remember what things in life give you joy. Listen to your favorite music. Read for fun. Watch movies. Knit, paint, carve wood, bake, decorate your apartment—whatever it is that brings you joy.

> **EXERCISE 15: A DATE WITH YOU**
>
> Find your trusty paper (or text doc, voice recording app, etc.). This exercise is about your hobbies and taking time for yourself.
>
> 1. Write a list of things you enjoy doing that aren't part of your graduate school work. If you have trouble thinking of things, look back through the previous section for ideas: hobbies, sports, art, etc.
> 2. Now, look at your calendar for the next two weeks. Find a thirty-minute slot each week and schedule in a date with yourself.
> 3. Pick one of the things from your list and do it during your scheduled time.

BUILD HEALTH

Try Treating Grad School Like a Job

A friend who started her PhD a year before me recommended treating grad school like a job. You don't owe any job every hour of every day—a truth that is fairly obvious.[8] Maybe you put in some overtime for special deadlines, but not every week. Many grad students don't realize that they can treat grad school the same way. You don't owe graduate school every hour of every day. Depending on your situation, you don't even owe grad school consecutive hours in your day (having kids, for example, can require you splitting up your work time, and may involve doing email on your phone during playtime). Some professors or students may argue otherwise, and they are emphatically wrong. If someone says, "But I suffered in grad school, and spent all my waking hours in the lab, and I turned out fine!" then you have my permission to question whether they did, in fact, turn out fine—because there they are, wishing suffering upon you simply because *they* suffered.

The advice to treat grad school like a job shaped my initial approach to graduate work. For my first several years, I went to the lab each weekday morning. I did work for my research assistantship, I attended classes, I did homework, I read up on possible thesis topics, I drank tea with my new labmates. Then I went home.

Once I had a baby, my schedule became a bit muddled and my work-home separation blurred. I had to find new ways to harmonize my work and home life (more on balancing family in chapter 11, "Relationships and Family").

While you can sometimes treat graduate school like a job, it's not, in fact, a full-time job. Sometimes it's more. Amanda Seligman explains that the amount of time required to succeed in graduate school varies drastically by program—anywhere from forty to eighty hours a week![9] Another key difference concerns the amount of oversight and structure you have, and where you work. There's more formlessness than a nine-to-five job. You may have constraints on when you can work, such as when your children are in school, when certain archives are open, or whether you need to keep yeast cells alive by feeding them in the middle of the night.

Reduce Stressors

In addition to actively pursuing revitalizing activities, you should also take steps to reduce stressors. First and foremost, take care of your physical health. Exercise, sleep, eating well: these can all reduce stress and improve mood. Personally, I rarely sacrifice sleep for anything; I know too well that I function poorly on low sleep. Caffeine and other stimulants aren't a substitute for the energy you get from being well rested. Practice meditation or learn relaxation techniques, which can help you develop awareness, focus your attention, and produce your body's natural relaxation response.

Take care of your social health. The people around you are one of the biggest factors that can help, or hinder, your mental health. First, find supportive friends. They may be in your cohort, in your lab, in your department, in clubs or other activities, in support groups, in your church, or in your wider community. They may be friends from before grad school. Talk to them. Isolation and a lack of community or support, especially as a nontraditional student or a minority student, can be a major issue. Align yourself with a healthy and supportive adviser and other mentors—as discussed in chapter 5, "Advisers." Also see chapters 11 and 12 for more on finding friends and community.

See a therapist. Many people find therapy to be extremely helpful. Sometimes, the terms of your health insurance (if you have it) can make it tricky to afford a worthwhile therapist in a reasonable time frame. You may need to switch therapists a couple times before finding someone who jibes with you and truly helps. You can also check whether your campus health center has any relevant support groups—for people dealing with grief, perhaps, or for new mothers with postpartum depression.

Advocate for yourself. Practice speaking up. Say no, as discussed in chapter 4, "Making Grad School Work for You." Some people feel guilty for saying no, or even for having hobbies outside of work. But hobbies keep you balanced. Saying no can give you the time you need to take care of yourself and your other obligations, such as your family or other work. These are critical, not optional—don't feel guilty. If you still feel you don't have time to not work, decrease your workload if you can. Can you back out of something you'd initially agreed to that is eating up time and isn't strictly necessary? Can you delay or slow down a project that doesn't have to be *this minute*, spending a little less time on it every day, so you can get other, more important stuff done now?

Deal with daily stressors intelligently—and grad school has many stressors. Some students are stressed by the lack of structure in their work time. It can be hard to know whether you've had a productive day. Time management plays a role here, as you may find that many tasks will take longer than you expected, throwing off your sense of having accomplished anything. You may need to revise your time-estimate strategies. You may want to work on structuring your own day and setting manageable tasks and goals, which are key skills for being able to work with relatively little guidance—revisit chapter 8, "Managing Projects and Managing Time."

If you face unclear expectations, feel a lack of mentorship or supervision, little feedback, or poor communication from your adviser or collaborators, try the communication strategies listed in chapter 5. Ask for a meeting with your adviser to plan out clear milestones and talk over goals. Escalate if your adviser isn't responsive. Also consider whether there are other ways of gaining the feedback you need—for example, if you want feedback on your writing, you could form a writing group with other students to give each other feedback, or check whether your campus has a writing center that can help you. If a project is not a critical step on your path (to graduation), can you put less effort into it (especially if your collaborators are dropping the ball), and focus your energy on your own projects?

Alternatively, you may feel that you can't get work done because there are too many meetings and too much unnecessary communication. You know that joke about the meeting that could have been an email? If you're obligated to attend the meetings, can you help streamline them, as discussed in chapter 8? If you're not strictly obligated, can you say no? Decline meetings, or postpone them, or combine them. Schedule time for your own work and make sure you get done what you need to get done.

You may feel stressed by a sense of imposter syndrome, or self-initiated feelings of obligation or perfectionism. It can be hard to shake the belief that you need to be working all the time, and handling your many obligations to the utmost of your ability. But remember, *not working constantly* is what this whole chapter is about. You won't produce your best if you work constantly. You are a whole person, not simply a worker bot. You need to dedicate some of your time to the other parts of you too, not just the worker-researcher parts. You deserve your research career *even if* you don't work constantly! You are enough. Your job is to *be you*, not the perfect you that you imagine if you only work hard enough, not the you you'd be if you were the student in the lab next door who just won a grant and published two papers in top journals, not the you who you are *not*. Set realistic goals, and remember that the goal isn't actually to be *perfect*, judged according to some set of external criteria—it's to attain a standard of which you yourself can feel proud. As some people put it, the best dissertation is a done dissertation. Sometimes all you should do is turn the assignment in or submit the paper, perfect or not, because that's *good enough* for now. Strive for excellence without sacrificing yourself.

Maybe you have piles of unread papers and books stalking you, or maybe you have several hundred unread browser tabs. As it turns out, it's okay to close all those tabs without reading them. I've done it. (If you haven't read them by now, will you *really*? Who will know you didn't, besides you?) Set aside five minutes a day to scan the abstracts of two papers in your "to read" pile. Are they *actually* relevant to what you are working on today? If not, discard them. Schedule some reading time—perhaps fifteen minutes a day—and start working through the most relevant papers. Setting a time limit may make it feel more manageable. You don't have to finish a whole paper a day, just read for your allotted fifteen minutes.

Maybe money is stressing you. Go back to Chapter 3, "Money and Logistics." Take control of your budget and evaluate strategies for fixing your revenue stream.

Maybe you're plagued by the uncertainty of grad school: Will your research project succeed? Will you get good results? Will your paper be accepted? Will you get funding? Will the academic job market have any jobs? Will you be able to get *any* job relevant to your degree by the time you graduate? Academia is full of uncertainty. But so is life. Do a web search for "embracing uncertainty" and you'll find hundreds of self-help articles claiming to reveal the secrets of taming the winds of change. I don't have fantastic advice here, because the truth is, some career and life paths have more uncertainty built into them than others. Academia is one such path. Academic jobs are particularly precarious, and I would revisit chapter 2, "Career Plans," if that precarity is particularly stressful for you. Keep in mind that a paper that is not accepted in one journal will be accepted by another, eventually. Revision and resubmission are part of the process. An experiment that fails may still teach you something useful, even if it's not what you wanted or expected. If uncertainty is extremely stressful to you, can you build a life that minimizes the uncertainty of your job? That way, you have surplus energy for handling all the *other* uncertainties life shoves at you.

Find help if you can. Many departments have resources and flexibility to help students, such as moving a deadline or giving an extension. Ask a coauthor to take on more of the work. Find campus or off-campus groups to support you—chapter 3 covers money issues, and chapter 12 discusses finding community.

When Stress Can't Be Solved by Balance

For some students, especially in the humanities and social sciences, the prospect of finishing a master's or PhD and not being able to find a job relevant to their degree can be overwhelming. The daily grind of coursework and outside work, with the added stress of applying for jobs and planning your life, gulps up all your available energy. The suggestions to "take time for yourself" and "reduce stress" feel impossible, because you're churning away, barely treading water as it is.

I get it. I wasn't that student, but I knew that student, and that very tired, very broke student had some rough decisions to make. That student had to take a hard look at grad school, the job market, their own mental health, their values, and decide whether sticking it out was worth it. Because that student had two options: plod on, or not. If you've decided, based on your evaluation in chapter 1, "What's Next," that grad school is definitely what you want to be doing, then there's your motivation to stick it out. Is it possible? Can you make the finances work? It will be stressful, yes. But knowing that you've evaluated your other options, that you've looked at the opportunity cost, and that you've decided that grad school is *still worth it*, means you have the will to figure out a way. I'm a firm believer in your agency.

If grad school or academia isn't worth it, then bail. Sometimes staying isn't worth the cost in time, money, or health. Sometimes you are forced to choose between things that are mutually exclusive and mutually desirable. You can mourn the decision and the loss of what you wanted, personally or professionally, while also acknowledging the rightness of the choice to change your trajectory. Acceptance of your decisions is a process. You may be angry and frustrated; you may grieve; you may be excited and feel free—all at the same time. We are complex emotional creatures. Acceptance isn't always straightforward. Life is messy, and so is grad school.

Should I Take a Leave of Absence?

Most universities have a policy around leaves of absence—certainly for maternity leave and medical leave, some for mental health and other reasons too. Taking a leave of absence can give you time to recover, rejuvenate, and reconsider whether graduate school is what you want to be doing. It can give you much-needed space.

If you're contemplating taking a leave, find out all the details up front: exactly what the requirements are, exactly how much time is allowed, how it affects your timeline, whether you're responsible for paying any fees, how to manage your return, and so forth. Check any student loans you may have; some may be deferred while you are actively a student, but being on leave could change your status. Once you have all the facts, you can weigh whether taking a leave is the best decision for you.

EXERCISE 16: KEEP TABS ON YOURSELF

Keep a record of how much time you devote to work versus nonwork so you can see where your time is going, and where you might want to make changes.

1. Track time for a couple of weeks. For example, use a clock-in/clock-out list for when you start and stop certain activities; this

will allow you to estimate how many hours you spent on them. You can make a spreadsheet or use of the many time-tracking apps (just search the app store) that enable you to count every minute of every day, divided up into as many categories of activities as you want (e.g., eating, reading, exercise, class, lab work, email, playing with kids, watching shows, etc.).

2. Evaluate. Schedule a date with yourself if you have to. What you're evaluating is whether you're happy with your balance—which can be tricky, because how happy do you need to be? How do you know if you could be happier? "Happy" can mean satisfied and content, not necessarily "jumping with joy." Are you able to do all the work you need to do? Are you able to keep up with your relationships and friendships? Do you have time for yourself? Do you feel like you have enough energy? Or do you feel like you're falling behind? Are you feeling any of those symptoms of burnout that I listed earlier? Any burnout symptoms are a red flag that *something* needs to change, ASAP. If you're generally feeling energized, happy about waking up in the morning (or happy after a cup of coffee—different strokes for different folks), able to keep up and keep going... your balance might be fine.

3. Iterate. Look at your work/nonwork record. How can you shift your time around? Usually, grad students err on the side of working too much. If, however, you're not working enough, revisit the section on motivation and procrastination in chapter 8. Think about whether you're making progress toward your milestones.

Personally, I made changes many times during grad school as I underwent various life transitions. Initially, I wanted to be involved on campus. I attended lectures, participated in campus clubs, took extracurricular pottery and ballroom dance classes. Later, especially after I had a baby, any time on campus was for work, full stop. I worked from home more often then too. I didn't always get my treasured morning hours in; instead, I tried to learn to use whatever time I got (e.g., during naptimes) to the best of my ability. My focus was on my family and on the PhD finish line. Remember the four-slice pie of health, work, love, and play? My slice of "play" got small for a while; my "love" slice shrank to include my family and just a few friends (perhaps a bad decision, but I made it through).

As you progress through your graduate school journey, you may find that the four-way split will need to change. That's normal. It'll be different in different seasons of your life.

KEEPING YOUR BALANCE

Finding your balance is like tending a garden. It's a continual process of self-maintenance. I used little things to remind myself to take time: a mug of tea, a book to read on the train, a walk outside. Find little things to help you remind yourself to take time for the activities and people you care about, and remember, it's just grad school. Sometimes, other stuff takes precedence—such as your family and relationships, which are the subject of the next chapter.

chapter 11
Relationships and Family

"If you want to be the top of your class, *don't fall in love*." Duy-Loan T. Le, the first and only senior fellow at Texas Instruments, paused to give the audience time to absorb her advice. I was enthralled. The petite Vietnamese woman held herself like a full harvest moon glowing above a prairie. Her keynote talk at the 2010 Grace Hopper Celebration of Women in Computing was a master class in oration—no PowerPoint, just her and a mic commanding a breathless crowd.

That one line is what I remember most from the conference. Duy-Loan T. Le's words are completely true. Well, sort of. Yes, time is finite. You cannot simultaneously pour all your energy into your relationships *and* into climbing the next step on the career staircase. That said, Duy-Loan T. Le's underlying assumption is wrong. Ignoring relationships and your personal life will not necessarily make you more productive or successful at school and work. For some people, maybe. But the strategy can also backfire, leaving you adrift with no friends.

In this and the following two chapters, I'm planting seeds for a balance garden. Cut some flowers and make yourself an integrated life bouquet: work, family, friends, hobbies, and everything else. The same bouquet won't please everyone. And that's fine.

"HAVING IT ALL"

If I have a key message in this chapter, it's this: Don't put your life on hold for your degree or career if you don't want to. If you want to get married or have a kid (or three), do it. If you already have kids and want a degree, do it. It is, in fact, possible to simultaneously plan a wedding and finish a master's thesis (I did). You can have a baby while writing your dissertation proposal (been there). Or drop your kid off at kindergarten then work in the lab all day (my friend). Or schedule meetings around your kids' school plays (my adviser). It will probably be harder. It may take you longer to finish your degree. You will make some sacrifices. But it *is* possible.

In my first year, my department invited an alumna back to speak about her career. She was a tenured professor at a good university, running her own lab group, getting nice grants, doing all the stuff that signals "successful academic." She told us one key to her success was prioritizing her family. During her job search, she had applied for and been offered jobs in two different departments at the same university (she worked in an interdisciplinary field, so multiple departments were a good fit). The Computer Science Department offered a high salary. But the offices were mostly full of old dudes who worked long hours and expected their colleagues to do the same. The Child Development Department offered a lower salary, but "the faculty all left at 3:00 p.m. to pick up their kids from school." The schedule, culture, and environment of that department were friendlier and more family-oriented. That's the department she chose—despite the lower salary.

When balancing your work with the rest of your life, you'll have to compromise. You know that "having it all" myth, where we—women in particular—are sold the idea that we can have incredible careers, phenomenal families, extraordinary everything? Time's finite. If being top of your field means working overtime and missing your kid's baseball game, is that worth it? That's a question you'll have to ask yourself. Review your values. We're necessarily limited in what we can accomplish. You will not, however, necessarily be limited in how *content* you are with your life and your choices.

The daily balance will vary. Some days you'll need to put work before all else. Other days, you'll need to prioritize your partner or family. That's normal. You may feel that dividing your time between work and, well, *anything* makes you feel inadequate as a scholar. Let me reassure you: taking time for you, your life, and your relationships makes you a *better* scholar. You may feel like a failure in one aspect of your life if you have to prioritize another part for a while, but you are not a failure; you're normal. You're doing your best—which is all we can ever do!

> **EXERCISE 17: LIFE GOALS**
>
> 1. Revisit your life values and goals from exercises 2, 3, and 5 in chapters 1 and 2. What do you want to accomplish? What do you want to learn? Who do you want to be with? What matters in your life? The answers to these questions will most certainly *not* be the same for everyone—nor should they be. What *you* want to accomplish, who *you* want to be—that's what matters here.
> 2. Spend half an hour this week working toward a life goal that's not related to grad school.

RELATIONSHIPS

My husband, Randy, was instrumental in me finishing grad school. Between shared childcare, helping debug code, bouncing ideas, baking fresh bread (great hobby for a spouse, by the way), and so much more, the paragraph he got in my dissertation's acknowledgments section didn't do him justice. When I turned in my master's thesis, Randy made cupcakes with little toothpick flags declaring, "Happy Thesis!"

Many scholars flourish in academia because of a supportive partner. Having loving, stable relationships with people who believe in us, in what we're doing, and in why we're doing it can mean the difference between getting a degree (and being happy while getting a degree), or not. Whether spouse, partner, significant other, family, friends: you need people who delight in your successes, who hoist you onto your feet when you fall down—champions who will always have your back.

Take time for the people who matter. (If you ignore people enough, they go away, and it's sad.) Get together regularly with local friends and family. Stay in touch with those distant via phone calls, video chats, shared photo albums, and social media. Romantic relationships can be especially stressed by graduate school—how do you date, or maintain a marriage?[1] What about kids? Read on.

Making Friends

Anywhere there are people, you have potential friends. Theoretically. For introverts like me, the easiest way to meet people is through shared activities, such as classes and clubs; extroverts may also have luck at lectures, campus-wide events, local off-campus venues, and everywhere else. Be friendly. Strike up a conversation even if it feels awkward. An offer to study together can be a good excuse to get to know someone better.

In grad school, there often isn't a line between professional contacts and friends, at least where fellow students, coworkers, postdocs, and labmates are concerned. They can be your friends, and often will be; being friends with the people you work with most closely can help you integrate your work with your life. That said, if most of your time is spent in a research group bubble, make a point of popping the bubble. Knowing a variety of people can give you perspective, ideas, and maybe even a spouse or a job.

DATING IN GRAD SCHOOL

Some people enter grad school with significant others. Some don't. If you're a single student (and don't want to be single) you'll need to figure out the grad school dating scene.

Fortunately, you're in luck: you're an adult. The grad school dating scene is pretty much like the dating scene anywhere else, with the caveat that many of the people you interact with on a daily basis are off limits. Date ethically: Avoid the power imbalances of relationships with people who have significant influence over your academics, eventual graduation, or career (e.g., postdocs, your supervisor, professors—by university rules, professors are often forbidden to date or have intimate relationships with their students or anyone else's students) or over whom you have significant influence (e.g., students in classes you TA, undergraduates). If you're highly interested in one of these people, wait until the power structure is no longer in play. For example, one of my labmates wanted to date one of his undergrad research assistants, and so waited until she graduated before asking her out.

Dating students in your cohort or research group can be on the table *if* you're both mature enough to deal with how awkward classes or lab meetings could be if you break up. Be reasonable, evaluate potential long-term relationships before leaping in, and decide whether the potential benefits are worth the risk. That said, other students can be good partners during the long haul, since they have firsthand knowledge of what it's like to go through grad school and can be highly sympathetic. They can be study partners. They may have endless things to talk about since you likely share interests and goals.

But shared interests and goals alone aren't enough to make a relationship work. In any relationship, you need to share values and vision. I'm assuming you're dating because you're looking for a long-term partner, someone with whom to share the ups and downs of life. That means you need to find someone who shares your long-term approach to life, not just short-term interests or career goals. So, when dating, discuss your relationship and potential life together—talk about your expectations up front. Key conversation topics include:

- Career and family plans. For example, if you're looking for a full-time career and kids, is your potential mate interested in being either a stay-at-home parent or building a dual-career family? Feelings on this subject can change once you actually *have* a baby.
- Life values. Revisit the list from chapter 1. Ideally, you and your partner will share several key values, if not more. If you align in how you view and approach the world, even if you come at those values from completely opposite directions, you can make a life together work.
- Your grad school schedule. For example, you may have unpredictable hours around key deadlines, or may work odd hours if you're in the life sciences and need to keep cell culture or lab animals alive. How does that play into the time you spend together?
- Your daily stresses. If the person you're dating has little or no experience with the stresses of grad school, take some time to explain how it works and what to expect.

ENDING RELATIONSHIPS

Keeping relationships going in academia can be tough—as many stories show.[2] Give yourself time if an intimate relationship ends, whether you ended it or they did. Be sad. Be angry. Spend time with other friends, immerse yourself in work, go on date nights with yourself and spend more time on looking after yourself.

If you are leaving an abusive or aggressive partner, Tina Lasisi recommends finding support from people outside your university, such as local domestic violence shelters, whose staff are trained to advocate for you when you deal with police, hospitals, or even your university.[3]

KEEP YOUR MARRIAGE ON TRACK

If you start grad school with a long-term partner or spouse, or if you get married along the way (as I did), you need to keep your marriage running like a river. Grad school is stressful; anything stressful in life stresses a marriage. Prioritize the two of you—plan for the long-term and don't put your relationship on the back burner while you study.

Take time for just the two of you, and use most of it for talking. First, use the topics listed above in the "Dating in Grad School" section as conversation starters. Marriage is a partnership; you need shared vision and goals. Then, talk about your day; discuss your plans for the week; talk about your one-year and five-year plans for your family. The most common mistake in marriage is failing to communicate consistently and constantly. Talking is a big part of what keeps you together. Make sure you talk about money too—money is one of the top two reasons people divorce, usually because they don't talk about money enough.[4] Consider joint finances and shared budgeting so you can reach your family goals together.

If you have kids, schedule date nights with your spouse and also activities as a family. For example, my husband and I went to see movies. We took the occasional weekend trip to the mountains to hike and explore. When we had a toddler, we made regular visits to the nearby zoo. Some people like exploring local restaurants, going to paint-and-sip events, visiting the farmers market, stargazing, or even just Netflix and chill. Occasionally, do something exciting together. Take a vacation, explore somewhere new—it doesn't have to be big and expensive, so long as it's different from your everyday existence.

Do the mundane together. My husband and I went for frequent walks around our neighborhood. We ate dinner together most nights and spent time sharing stories about our respective days. We did chores together. We checked in nearly every day to harmonize our schedule, daily activities, and longer-term goals. Part of sharing mundane activities is ensuring you have time together to *talk*. Share experiences, share emotions, share the ups and downs of life.

Show your spouse you appreciate them and their support. Send them cards, love notes, or silly texts during the day. Start the day with a hug—and end it with one too. Physical affection can lower stress-related hormones and boost feel-good, connecting ones. Snuggle while you watch a movie. Hold hands when you go walking.

Find a community of people who support you as a married person. Make friends with other couples. For example, if one of your friends is married too, have them and their spouse over for dinner. If you have or want kids, make friends with other families. Having kids in grad school is, unfortunately, often seen as a weird decision, met with questions like, "But why aren't you waiting until you have tenure?" (As if an academic career is all that matters!) Finding people who share your relationship or family values makes a huge difference. This community may include your extended family, fellow students, and off-campus friends. My husband and I met other young families through his church. It was comforting to know that other people our age had kids, and that they, too, were struggling to balance everything. We could all commiserate over dinner or while our kids eyed flamingos at the zoo.

Prioritizing your marriage through the activities I've listed will go a long way toward maintaining and building your relationship. If you're having difficulties you're not sure you can solve, consider marriage counseling. Talk with friends and family. See the resources chapter.

The Two-Body Problem

The two-body problem: You and your partner are both investing in your respective careers. You're both location-dependent and need to be physically present where you work (not remote or independent). How do you balance both careers?

In the ideal case, you both attend school and find jobs in the same place. Sometimes a college or university will work with you to make a spousal hire, or help a spouse find work in the area. Sometimes they are no help at all.

In reality, though, you'll likely have to compromise somehow. Do you compromise one of your careers, or compromise living together? Talk about this decision *a lot*. You may decide that you'll live apart for months or years (e.g., if you attend different schools), with visits on weekends or between semesters. One of you may graduate sooner and begin a new job elsewhere. You may both go on the academic job market at the same time, but tenure-track job seekers can't be picky about location. Or you may decide staying together is more important. One of you forgoes an opportunity, opts for a less magical job, or leaves a degree program early. Only you and your partner can decide what's best for your family.

If you do find yourself in a long-distance relationship, make sure to attend to the following:

- Talk every day, on the phone or with video calls.
- Send each other texts or use other messaging services.
- Email.
- Talk about normal things that happen during your day. Don't work when you're together, unless you've also spent time not working. If you both want to read academic papers before you fall asleep at night, that's your prerogative. But ensure you have time together where you just talk about everything going on in your lives.
- The key to holding your relationship together is talking: about the mundane, the big stuff, what's going on in your research, problems you're facing, your plans together—everything.

EXERCISE 18: BUILD YOUR RELATIONSHIPS

1. Set a timer for ten minutes.
2. Write down what you love and appreciate about your partner. If you're not in a long-term relationship, choose a close friend or family member. Think back to the activities shared when you first met or were first dating. What initially drew you to them? What do you continue to love about them? How have they helped and supported you?
3. When the timer rings, review what you wrote and ask yourself the following question: Have you shown this person your appreciation recently?
4. Do something nice for them: send a thank-you note, a letter, or a card with compliments and genuine, heartfelt thanks for something they've done recently. Show your support and appreciation. I suspect this activity will make you feel as good as it does them!

PARENTING IN GRADUATE SCHOOL

For many students, graduate school coincides with prime baby-making and child-rearing years—estimates are at 10 percent or more.[5] A survey of University of California graduate students found that 12 percent were parents, and they were also more likely to be in an underrepresented group.[6] Women are most fertile in their early twenties; fertility begins to decline around age thirty, and drops even more after thirty-five. While men's fertility doesn't peak and decline as dramatically, age can still be a concern when planning children. With the average age of graduate students hovering around thirty-three, I'm honestly surprised that children aren't a more common topic among graduate students.[7]

Pregnancy and parenthood affect academic fathers and mothers differently, from the time they are students throughout their careers.[8] Here's an illustrative anecdote: A pair of married grad students I knew had a baby. The mother spent her maternity leave recovering from growing and birthing a human, while attempting to sleep occasionally. Her husband used his paternity leave to write a couple papers and catch up on work.

The data tell the same story: gender-neutral family leave policies can actually harm women, because men and women use their leaves so differently.[9] Men publish more than women, mostly because of mothers' short-term decrease in productivity from parenthood.[10] Women face the "motherhood penalty" and must deal with the frequently negative perception of working mothers.[11] Teaching evaluations penalize pregnant faculty.[12] Mothers of young children are 35 percent less likely to get tenure-track jobs compared to fathers of young children;[13] they're perceived as being less competent and given lower recommended starting salaries.[14] None of this is fair, but it never will be because mothering a child is not a gender-neutral event—babies need their mothers; mothers are the ones who go through the grueling experiences of pregnancy and childbirth. The best we can do is create policies that help families and support mothers (more on this in chapter 13, "Making Changes to Your School").

I had my first child in my fourth year of graduate school. Here's what I wish I'd known—and what I wish all graduate departments knew.

Pregnancy Symptoms

Being pregnant is no joke. Fatigue, aches, pains, nausea, high blood pressure, dizziness, heartburn, food sensitivities, gestational diabetes, and other unpleasant realities are on the table. Sure, you may get lucky and experience few symptoms, as I did, but you won't know which you'll get or how bad they'll be until you're pregnant. If you're planning your pregnancy, assume at a minimum that you'll be exhausted and nauseated during the first trimester, tired during the second, and fatigued and uncomfortable during the third.

If you do fieldwork or travel for conferences, plan for little or no travel in the last two months (in fact, your doctor may tell you not to travel, and some airlines won't allow it). The third trimester can wreak havoc on your back; standing for long periods of time can be mightily uncomfortable, which can be an issue if you teach. Many women try to plan for less work in month nine or rearrange their workload to put "easier" work (writing, data analysis, stuff that involves sitting) at the end of their pregnancy.

Prenatal Care

Prenatal health care is linked to better outcomes for both mama and baby. Your prenatal care may be covered by your usual health-care plan. If not, many states in the United States provide prenatal care as part of Medicaid, which you may qualify for as a poor, pregnant grad student. Under Title IX in the United States, all medically necessary absences related to pregnancy must be excused.[15]

Who you see for prenatal care and where you deliver your baby, while undoubtedly a personal choice, is, unfortunately, heavily influenced by what your health insurance will cover. If you are high risk—say, over thirty-five, under- or overweight, pregnant with twins, experiencing high blood pressure, or have a history of preterm births—you may be limited to obstetrician gynecologists (ob-gyns) at a local hospital. In some places, if you are low risk, you may be able to see a midwife; they may or may not be affiliated with a hospital, and some deliver at birth centers or will attend home births. You will likely have frequent checkups—from once a month early on, to biweekly or every week in the third trimester. Time at the doctor's office adds up fast—bring a book (or some of the papers on your reading list) to make the most of the waiting time.

When to Share the News

When do you tell people you're pregnant? The glib answer is, "Whenever you want." But practically speaking, you'll want to tell your department and adviser with enough advance notice to plan for your maternity leave and any other changes that may need to be made to your research or teaching schedule. For example, you will likely need to seek accommodations if you are in a bio lab or chem lab, since there are some chemicals and organisms you may need to avoid for your and your baby's safety. In these cases, sharing your status earlier rather than later is important.

Personally, I told my lab group near the end of my first trimester. I focused on finishing data collection for one of my field studies with children and robots, so I would be able to do data analysis and paper writing post-baby. I was working on my dissertation proposal; my plan was to submit it to my committee before taking maternity leave and hold the proposal-review meeting shortly after returning. In short, I was queuing up reading and writing work while limiting active fieldwork, at least for the first semester back.

Preparing for Leave

You should get some amount of paid and/or unpaid parental leave. (If you don't, see chapter 13, "Making Changes to Your School"). The length of your leave may be six weeks, two months, or more, based on a combination of federal, state, university, and departmental policies. While you are on leave, you are not obligated to work. Some advisers may try to convince you that you must be working, or at least on email and calling in to important meetings. You're welcome to do so. But I'd recommend using the time to do *other* things—like recover physically and bond with your new baby.

Many women find it helpful to make a formal return plan for after leave: plan out childcare; morning and/or evening routines with the baby; if, when, and where you'll pump breast milk; what projects you'll dive back into on your return; exactly what day you'll officially start work again, and so on. Some women like doing a trial run near the end of their leave, where they go through the morning routine and see how they do. Some women schedule a day to go in for a little while, with baby in tow, for a little baby meet and greet—which can also help them get caught up on what's been going on in the lab in their absence. See if you can schedule some work-from-home days for the first stretch back. Also look for support from other parents—for example, is there a campus mom's group you can join?

Research health insurance up front. Can you add your infant to your plan? How much will switching to a family plan cost? Are there other options, such as Medicaid?

Miscarriage and Complex Fertility Journeys

Sometimes you want a baby with all your heart, and it just doesn't happen. For some women, being on birth control for years sabotages their hormones and, when coming off the pill later, makes conceiving difficult. Other women wait to have children until near the end of their fertile years, when conceiving is far less likely already, and miscarriage more common (e.g., see Nandini Pandey's story about her experience with infertility and miscarriage).[16] Unfortunately, infertility treatments can be time-consuming and expensive, likely more so than the normal checkups you have during a pregnancy. But if you're in this boat, you're not alone—according to the Centers for Disease Control and Prevention, 12.2 percent of women between the ages of fifteen and forty-nine have used infertility services.[17] Find out what your health insurance covers. Find other parents who have gone through the process, and who can support you.

Among women who know they're pregnant, 10–15 percent of pregnancies will end in miscarriage.[18] If you have a miscarriage, don't expect to be back to normal quickly. It's not easy. Honestly, it shouldn't be: your baby died. You *should* grieve. You *will* need time for your heart and body to adjust—emotionally, mentally, hormonally, physically. If you are religious, follow your religion's funeral traditions for your baby, or have a service or mass dedicated to your child. Take time off if you can. In the United States, you should be entitled to medical leave under Title IX guidelines.

After Birth

When tiny, babies mostly do four things: eat, sleep, poop, and cry. Newborns usually eat every one to three hours. They sleep fourteen to eighteen hours in a twenty-four-hour period, but probably not consolidated into useful chunks. They cry whenever they aren't happy, which can be but hopefully isn't the entire time they are awake. Helping your baby sleep can be as easy as holding them or wearing them in a baby carrier, or as hard as pacing in the hall singing lullabies for hours and hours. You won't know ahead of time what your baby will be like. Plan for the worst; hope for the best.

Feeding   You have two feeding options: breast milk or formula (or a combination). If you choose the former, you either stay near your baby, or pump milk on a regular schedule, so another caregiver can help feed your baby. Pumping takes just as much time, if not more, than nursing, but does allow you to be away from your baby for longer periods of time.

Put baby feedings or pumping times on your schedule. This time is sacred (you are nourishing a new little human, after all!) and cannot be sacrificed. You may feel like you are inconveniencing others you work with by having such a strict schedule, being unavailable at times you used to be free, or needing to cut other meetings short to attend to your infant or your aching breasts (yup). Remind yourself this time is *nonnegotiable*.

Don't expect that you'll be able to multitask when nursing or pumping. Some women can. Many can't. Perhaps your baby is squirmy or a messy eater; or achieving letdown while pumping requires you feeling relaxed or looking at pictures of your baby; or perhaps you'd simply rather not try to have a conference call or write emails while snuggling your precious child.

Sleeping   If this is your first baby, people may share advice like "sleep when the baby sleeps" (no, I worked when the baby slept) or "oh, just let them cry, they'll learn to self-sooth!" (not when they're that tiny, they can't!). Listen to whatever parts of the advice you want; ignore the rest. I found that getting enough sleep wasn't my issue—it was getting used to the fact that I was now regularly awake at odd hours to feed a newborn, and those breaks in my sleep meant I had to allot more total time to my night to still get enough rest.

Prioritize sleep as much as you can. As discussed in chapter 10, "It's Just Grad School," the energy you get from being well rested can't be substituted by caffeine or other stimulants. When you have multiple kids, sleep can become more challenging, since everyone's sleep schedules may not line up.

Childcare

You have three options: (1) stay home full-time yourself (not usually feasible for academics or working parents, but sometimes necessary during global pandemics); (2) have your children stay with your partner or other family member while you work; or (3) put your children in a nursery or day care while you work, or, when they're older, in school. Personally, I did a mix of options 1 and 2. My husband and I split childcare duties. I cut back my hours and spent nearly all my nonwork hours with my son. My husband's work was flexible, and he loves being a father, so he took the rest. (I've listed essays I've written about being an academic parent in the resources.)

Many women choose option 3: outsourced childcare. With a baby, the adjustment period can be difficult, given all the biological imperatives keeping you and your baby together. Give yourself time and see if you can gradually introduce the baby to the nursery for increasingly longer periods so your baby has the chance to form attachments to these new caregivers. Check whether there is a nursery close to your workplace/school so you can stop in during the day. For instance, I had a friend who was able to place her son in an on-campus nursery, so she could feed and snuggle him between classes. If you can't do that, can you break up the hours you work, so you have time in the middle of the day to visit your child? Can you work remotely some of the time? Can you get help during the evenings or weekends with housework so you can spend that time with your child instead?

When your children are older, they can attend a school. But you may need to work before drop-off or after pickup times. And what about when school's out? Some schools have after-school programs and summer camps to help fill in gaps. You will need to find additional help for times between programs—for example, from relatives, babysitters, or nannies. You may also need help when children fall ill. Check whether your school or state has childcare vouchers to help cover costs.

Working with Children

Because of your child's feeding, sleeping, and snuggling demands, your work schedule will change, as will your work habits. The biggest change with an infant: I no longer had six plus hours of uninterrupted time to work deeply on a paper or code because of frequent baby feeding. Instead, I had to manage my time competently and work more efficiently. Here are some tips for how to make this transition:

- Never look at social media during work time. As discussed in chapter 8, "Managing Projects and Managing Time," switching tasks comes at a cost, draining your attention and slowing your work.
- Make the most of the time you have. Use the strategies from chapter 8 to match your work with your energy level, the work's urgency, and the time you have available.
- Write shorter emails. I stopped agonizing over wording and realized why so many professors wrote terse (though still polite) emails. I also used in-between times for emails if I didn't know what else to do. For example, sometimes, if I was awake at 3:00 a.m. with the baby, I went through a few.
- Write notes to yourself to make it easier to slip back into context faster. I knew my work would be interrupted; leaving comments in my own papers about what I was thinking, or why I was restructuring a section, or what I ought to work on next made it easier to get back into the right headspace later on.

Conference Calls   You may have to manage conference calls or remote meetings while simultaneously caring for your baby or other children. Older children are more able to quietly play or watch a video in another space or in the background. Babies require special preparation. Some tips:

- Schedule flexible/approximate meeting times when you can. This can make a huge difference in having a good meeting—babies don't care about "industrial time"; they're on "baby time" and want what they want when they want it.
- Keep meetings short. Half an hour or less is ideal; never go longer than an hour.
- If you breastfeed, wear a shirt that's easy to nurse in. Wearing headphones with volume/mute controls can make the call easier—or harder, if your baby likes to yank them off your head. Have a backup plan if headphones don't pan out.

- Tell people at the start of the meeting that you have a baby (or other children) and are balancing the call with childcare. After the COVID-19 pandemic, everyone is more used to people balancing parental and work duties. This is great and works in your favor. Being on mute is often assumed, so you can tell them that if you don't unmute to respond to a question, you'll reply as soon as you can or follow up via email, depending on the baby's situation.
- If your baby is asleep and doesn't wake up during the call, great! If your baby is awake, happily playing in the room, use mute liberally, so you can listen, participate, and occasionally unmute to talk. If your baby is hungry or grumpy, mute, listen, contribute when you can. If your baby is inconsolable, leave the call. The baby is more important.

Traveling Some graduate students travel multiple times a year for fieldwork or academic conferences. Travel is tricky with children. You have three options: (1) bring children along (not usually an option for fieldwork); (2) leave them behind; or (3) don't attend.

If you have older children, bringing them with you to a conference could be a fun learning experience; they could attend some or all of the proceedings with you. However, in most cases, you will need to arrange childcare at the conference, or bring a spouse or friend to care for them while you're busy. This will likely be on your own dime, and it can be expensive. The younger, sleepier, and less mobile a baby is, the easier travel with them is likely to be. In some fields, conferences regularly include childcare accommodations, but most don't, or the accommodations won't suit your specific needs. Leaving a baby or young child with new, unknown caregivers often goes poorly, simply because the baby hasn't established a relationship with the new caregiver.

Leaving children at home requires someone who can do all the childcare, such as a spouse, relative, or friend. This is trickier with a baby, as it may mean pumping extra breast milk for weeks prior to the conference and pumping while away. If the conference or event is longer than a few days, you and your children will miss each other; factor that in when choosing how long to be away.

In my son's first two years, I attended one conference workshop because it was at my university; I brought my husband for childcare support. I skipped all other conferences and work travel opportunities.

All Kinds of Parenting

One of the worst feelings is a gnawing sense that you're failing your children as well as your education. Every graduate parent, at some point, wonders whether they're prioritizing their lives correctly, whether they ought to be spending more time with their children or on their research, whether they've made the right choices. You can second-guess yourself forever. Don't. You're doing the best you can with what you have. Sacrifice and compromise key aspects of parenthood.

Ensure you spend one-on-one time with each of your children, and, as mentioned earlier, plan activities with your entire family. Explain your research to your children and why it's important, so they can learn with you and be proud of you when you accomplish your goals.

No matter what your family looks like, whether you are step-parenting, single parenting, adoptive parenting, or long-distance parenting, there are other people like you who have succeeded in graduate school. I've addressed some of the issues graduate student parents face, but this is just one chapter on a subject that has filled entire books. (See the resources for a list of some of these.)

chapter 12
Maintaining Your Sense of Self

REMINDERS

"PERSISTENCE," blazoned the carrot-orange letters I'd cut from construction paper and taped to my dorm room wall. The word was a reminder that hard work and endurance were my college goals. Below it hung other words, quotes, lines from novels, and song lyrics, all in florid color. Each was a delicacy of wisdom, a signpost to be heeded, a mechanism for keeping my values and goals present. Every time my gaze meandered beyond my textbook or my laptop screen, I would see them.

"It's a matter of balance," read another set of blue letters: an admonishment to take time for recreation, friends, and family as well as schoolwork and athletics. Beside it hung wisdom from a calculus professor: "Life is not always an integer. (Holly Kresch)." Mixed in were other reminders, like this: "To grow, you must be willing to let your present and future be totally unlike your past. Your history is not your destiny. (Alan Cohen)."

What are your reminders? Maintaining balance in graduate school is not only a matter of heeding both life and career goals, as discussed in chapters 1 and 2, or taking time for hobbies, friends, and family, as covered in chapters 10 and 11. Maintaining balance also requires finding harmony in yourself and identifying your place in the world. Maintaining your sense of self is important for your life satisfaction and long-term well-being.

Graduate school will challenge you. As Amanda Seligman writes, "graduate school can have a transformative effect on students.... [It] has the capacity to change how students see and act in the world, at the level of changing their values. That is normal, and is a sign that the student is paying attention."[1] Graduate study turns you inward. You're challenged academically, intellectually, and personally. You learn about yourself as well as about your discipline. Your view of the world may change as a result of your study of the world. What if you have a crisis of faith? What if you have a crisis of identity? How do you ensure that you stay *you*?

EXERCISE 19: WHO ARE YOU?

1. Brainstorming time: find a piece of paper and a pen.
2. Write down everything you can think of in answer to the following questions: What makes you *you*? List words, feelings, phrases, ideas, mantras, goals, identities. What reminds you of who you are and of who you want to be? Include music, quotes, books, role models, objects, keepsakes, places, actions, activities, foods, and people.
3. Spend at least ten minutes today with one (or more) of those reminders.

LIVING COHERENTLY

Living coherently, with increased connections between your values and your actions, leads to greater meaning, more satisfaction, and an increased sense of self (first discussed in chapter 1, "What's Next").[2] To be who you are is the ultimate goal. As Ralph Waldo Emerson once said, "Make the most of yourself, for that is all there is of you."

Check in with yourself periodically to make sure you're still on track—sometimes your actions veer or your values shift. Set a date with yourself, perhaps once a year, to work through the values exercise in chapter 1 again and reevaluate whether your path through graduate school aligns with your intended future. A good time for this is when you're less busy and feeling rested, perhaps during a holiday break or just after a semester ends, not in the middle of a hectic grading week or when studying for exams.

You'll find that you *will* grow and change. You *should*. Adapt your actions to continue being coherent with your values; as you move forward, keep your mission in mind (see chapter 4). Remember why you are in grad school. Remember what your goals and values are. Remember what else matters to you and why. This is especially important as you work through the hardest, darkest parts of your degree. Ensure that *you* are satisfied with who you are and who you become, through mud and clear water, through the mountains and valleys of graduate school and life beyond. After all, you have to live with yourself.

MAINTENANCE ACTIVITIES

Maintenance activities build your fortress of self-sustenance. These activities are the stones in your castle wall. They ground you and help remind you of your values and goals. Some were mentioned in earlier chapters (see, e.g., the "Keep Your Mission in Mind" section in chapter 4). You may also decide to make time to talk to the people who matter, who prop up your sense of self: a weekly phone call home, a chat with your grandmother, tea with your best friend. Look at what you brainstormed in exercise 19—use these ideas as the springboard for planning your maintenance. Let's expand.

> ### EXERCISE 20: REVISIT YOUR REMINDERS
>
> - When you did exercise 19, did you list any books, movies, music, art, or other media? If not, brainstorm some now: What art helped shape your view of the world and your sense of self? Are there any poems, a particular passage from the Bible, a book or song or painting, that used to be immensely important to you?
> - Think (or write) about why. What is it about that piece of art that spoke to you?
> - Revisit some of this art. For example, read a little of one of the books each week—it doesn't have to be a lot, and you don't have to finish the book quickly, since you're a busy student with lots of other reading to do. Make a playlist of the songs and listen to some while you are working or walking. Spend an evening each month watching one of those movies. Revisit the art, and you'll get back in touch with the you that you were when that art first spoke to you. You may gain something completely new.

BUILDING YOUR COMMUNITY

The ivory tower is often an insular ideological echo chamber. If your personal beliefs, values, faith, or politics don't line up with the mainstream, it's a short road to feeling isolated. Same story if you're an underrepresented minority, disabled in our ableist culture, a woman in a department full of men, a man in a department full of women, or in any number of other categories. Plus, the further you get in your program, as you switch from coursework with classmates to independent research, the more potential for isolation.

To fight isolation, find community. You have many sources of support on campus (see chapter 6); you have friends and/or family (see chapter 11). Here are more ideas.

Religion

Among adults with postgraduate degrees (all of whom were graduate students at one point), 75 percent were affiliated with a religion; 70 percent said religion was either somewhat or very important to them.[3] Religion often provides certainty and answers regarding one's place in the universe and the meaning and purpose of one's life. People who regularly participate in religious practices are frequently happier and less stressed: belief can positively affect physical and mental health; faith can be a motivator; and especially beneficial are the community, social support, and sense of belonging that frequently accompany participation in religious worship.[4] In addition, religion can also serve as a reminder that grad school is just one phase of your life, one thing you're doing that will end eventually, and when you're through, you'll still have your faith—whether or not you finish your degree, whether or not you continue in academia, no matter where your life takes you.

If you are religious, find ways to keep up your faith. Many universities have campus clubs or centers for students of different faiths. Some of these groups may have regular services, Bible studies, events, discussions, or rituals held at a campus chapel, or led by campus chaplains. Most towns and cities have a range of churches and places of worship—the bigger the city, the wider the range.

If your faith is especially important to you, research where you'll practice your faith *before* you commit to a graduate school. That way, you'll be sure of an adequate and supportive community. This is more important if you practice a minority religion that may not be represented in every city, are considering a school in a small town that is not particularly diverse, or have strict rules to abide by (e.g., an Orthodox Jew may want to ensure there's a nearby synagogue).

If you're not religiously affiliated, explore ways of finding community anyway. Many universities have a secular, atheist/agnostic, or humanist student group, which can be a source of interesting conversation and friends. For a few years I led the weekly discussion group for MIT's Secular Society; I enjoyed engaging in deep, worthwhile conversations with students from across the institute about the big questions in life—those touching on morality, the nature of happiness, and what makes life worth living. I also believe that regularly considering issues bigger than my narrow slice of research helped me place my work in context in the wider world.

Your beliefs may be challenged in graduate school. Your faith, or lack thereof, may be tested. Some students will conclude that they were wrong about their long-held beliefs—leaving their faith, converting to a new faith, finding faith for the first time. Leaving a religious community can be exceedingly difficult; it is not uncommon to lose the friends and support that came with it. If you experience a crisis of faith, seek friends, a new community, other campus clubs and activities—in short, people who will support who you are and what you believe.

LGBTQIA+

Feeling like you can be yourself and be accepted for who you are can go a long way toward increasing your positivity and energy in all areas of your life. On the flip side, feeling that others don't accept you or don't understand who you are can be an elephantine anchor dragging down your energy levels and emotional ability to deal with the rest of your life.

What do you do about it? Find others like you. Many institutions have a club or social group dedicated to the LGBTQIA+ community; if there's not one on campus, there may be a group in the local off-campus community. Search online platforms like Facebook and Meetup.com for events. Find remote support—there are online support groups on most social media platforms. Be yourself as much as you can.

If you are currently applying to graduate schools, research the programs ahead of time—online and during interviews and visits, as discussed in chapter 5. Try to get a sense of what kind of program support there is, whether any faculty or students publicly identify as LGBTQIA+, whether they appear to be treated with the same respect and courtesy as others in the department, and whether there is any ongoing research in the department focused on diversity issues. This can help you determine what support you are likely to find.

Underrepresented Minorities

There are many groups that are underrepresented in graduate school—racial and ethnic minorities; certain genders; individuals with disabilities or neurodivergencies; the list goes on. For instance, in 2016, 15 percent of doctorates were earned by African Americans, Hispanics, and Native Americans, but combined these groups make up more than 33 percent of the US population. Exactly which groups are minorities in the university can vary by discipline.[5] For instance, many STEM fields lean heavily toward men, while men are underrepresented in education and nursing.[6] Furthermore, the representation among the faculty in your program may be very different than among students, given pipeline issues and the rates of students who opt to leave academia compared to those who become professors (discussed further in chapter 2, "Career Plans," and chapter 11, "Relationships and Family").

If you belong to an underrepresented minority, focus on what unites you with your peers, not what separates you, as Nancy Padilla-Coreano suggests.[7] This can make you feel like you're part of a community, even if you're from a different cultural background. For instance, you probably share a sense of curiosity, a love of research, and similar fears and worries about coursework and dissertation proposals. Then, share your unique differences with each other; this can help you understand where you're each coming from and help you connect.

Speak up. Respectfully give feedback when others do or say things that make you uncomfortable or that are insensitive. They may not be aware that they are doing so, or know what your cultural norms are. While you may feel that it is an unfair burden for you to have to educate them, speaking up can be the fastest way to change the situation and help someone be more empathetic and inclusive in their interactions. Ask for help early if you need it, for any area of your life—interpersonal, research, school, mental health (see chapter 5, "Advisers," on asking your adviser for help and negotiation tips, and chapter 10, "It's Just Grad School," on mental health).

Find community. Seek mentors, including peer mentors, who share your culture and challenges—this is one area where students of color, for example, find a glaring lack.[8] Most institutions have student clubs for international students and various minority groups. There are also many professional groups for minorities—see if one exists for your discipline. For example, you might join the Association of Black Sociologists, the Society of Hispanic Professional Engineers, the Association of Women in Computing, or the Association of American Indian Physicians. As discussed in chapter 11, "Relationships and Family," look for a mom's club, other married couples, religious communities, affinity groups on campus, and so on. If you have difficulty finding people locally, reach out online. Remote friends and support are certainly better than none, and you may be able to forge in-person connections at future conferences or during other travel.

Chapter 13, "Making Changes to Your School," discusses ways you can improve diversity on campus.

EXERCISE 21: WHAT MAKES LIFE MEANINGFUL?

1. Take some time to think and write about what makes your life meaningful. Reflect on the values you brainstormed in chapter 1; your goals and career aspirations from chapter 2; your hobbies, balancing activities, and relationships from chapters 10 and 11. Where is the meaning in your life? How do you maintain that sense of meaning?
2. Meaning is often understood as being entirely objective (e.g., coming from God) or subjective (e.g., we all make our own meaning). An alternative view posits that meaning arises through our interaction with the world—neither objective nor subjective, but still real, like a rainbow. If you are religious, reflect on how your faith interacts with your life and sense of meaning. If you're not, ask yourself where you think meaning comes from and how you encounter meaning in your life.

* David Chapman, "Rumcake and Rainbows," *Meaningness* (blog), accessed September 18, 2023, https://meaningness.com/objective-subjective.

DIFFICULT CONVERSATIONS

Whether you hold minority beliefs, are not yet comfortable being open about your sexuality, have an invisible disability, or have any other personal details that would change how people see you, you may worry about what happens when everyone finds out you're different. How do you deal with your peers, colleagues, and professors potentially interacting with you in different, possibly more negative ways? These concerns can be a major stressor.

First, don't panic. There's no guarantee people *will* treat you differently—or that it will be different bad, not different good. Remember that mental contrasting exercise from chapter 2? Imagine the worst that could happen. Imagine all the obstacles and conflicts. And imagine how you would overcome each one. Plan for the worst and hope for the best. You'll feel more prepared. In the best case, they'll recognize that you are still *you*, they'll be happy to continue supporting you, and they'll be genuinely interested in dialoguing about whatever issues come up. That's the mark of a true mentor or friend. Even if they don't understand, or come from a different point of view, they can still be there for you.

However, concern that you'd lose support and friendships isn't always misplaced in our increasingly polarized country. Especially, for instance, if you're a political conservative in a predominantly liberal department. Remember what your goals are in attending graduate school. Keeping your head down may be the safest way to proceed. Focus on getting your degree and getting out. If difficult conversations come up, use the communication strategies described in chapter 5. Be calm and empathetic.

REMAINING YOURSELF, EVEN AFTER YOUR DEGREE

A couple months before I left Boston, a friend (let's call her Anna) relayed a message to me from another friend: "She's worried you'll waste your degree." I could tell from Anna's tone of voice that she was undeniably worrying about the same potential waste. It was a passive-aggressive way of questioning my life decisions, to be sure—decisions that satisfied me, and that were none of her business. Yes, I had a baby while in grad school; I was six months pregnant when I defended; my post-PhD plan was entirely unconventional, as it involved homeschooling my kids, not landing a full-time job. But instead of seeing all this as a badass feat of time management and excellent life design, Anna took it as proof that childbearing, not science, was my ultimate goal in life, since the two clearly weren't compatible. (That's not mentioning the fact that two of my dissertation committee members were inspiring women with three kids apiece, nor the countless other women who have successfully integrated work and family life.)

The implicit assumption Anna had that "wasting my degree" was even possible was, frankly, an insult. She identified as a feminist. Isn't feminism supposed to be about empowering and supporting women in making life choices that are right for them?

Remember, a big part of the point of grad school is learning. Learning about project management. Developing writing skills. Doing independent research. Asking interesting questions. Pursuing ideas. Managing time, balancing multiple commitments, and being involved in many activities I care about. Whether or not I then use those skills to pursue any of the most common paths out of grad school isn't the point. What I learned will still serve me well in future endeavors—writing papers, essays, blogs, and books; consulting; hiking in the mountains; raising my children; reading philosophy; advocating for changes I care about in my community; and so much more. As discussed in chapter 2, leaving the ivory tower doesn't mean leaving research or a creative, intellectual life.

There are countless paths you can take out of graduate school. All you have to do is find one path that works for you.

chapter 13
Making Changes to Your School

During my final semesters of dissertation writing, I played with my two-year-old more than I wrote. Nearly all my work was relegated to naptimes. I delayed answering friends' questions about what I was doing next—Academic job market? Industry?—and although I met with a few professors about local opportunities, I already had an inkling that I wasn't going to follow up about starting my own lab. I wanted to be present for my children's childhood. At the same time, I wanted to keep working on creative intellectual projects; I had, after all, gone to grad school because it was going to be *fun*.

How was I going to balance everything? Like a snail, I extended my antennae and quested for options. The academic system as it stood didn't jibe with my vision for my life. But what would?

In my seeking, I discovered other scholars who, like me, were disillusioned with academia's status quo. Groups of independent scholars banding together, supporting each other in unique, distributed networks that aimed to reinvent academia altogether. Mothers who chose unconventional paths through their careers and for their children's education. *Maybe*, I thought, *I can make this work*.

No matter what your personal background is, there will inevitably be something about academia that doesn't work for you. Whether it's how academia treats parents, issues of diversity, or simply a niggling feeling that you don't belong, academia has plenty of systemic issues. It wasn't designed with our current expanse of graduate students and student experiences in mind. How can we make graduate school friendlier for all students, rather than assuming everyone can and should mold themselves into the existing structures?

WHO CHANGES WHAT?

Making changes to a system is easier if you have status and power in that system, as Adam Grant explains in his book *Originals*.[1] In the university system, graduate students don't have much power. They're low status compared to professors and administrators. This is why, Leonard Cassuto argues, many of the problems in graduate education will be solved by changes that faculty make. The welfare of students, Cassuto writes, is the responsibility of their professors: "once we admit them to our programs, we've accepted that responsibility."[2] Fixing teaching and mentoring at the graduate level can fix many of the issues that have been inherent in the system for over a hundred years, such as increasing the emphasis on practical skills—for example, communication, public speaking, writing, teaching; returning to scholarship as an engaged practice, in which students are connected with broader audiences for their work outside the ivory tower and with careers outside of higher education; and creative ways of looking after students.

That said, students should not wait around for their professors to wake up to the problems of higher education. You have four options when you're unhappy with the status quo: exit, persist, neglect, or voice (see chapter 5). Only two options change the situation. *Exit* only changes things for you. *Voice* is the only option if you also want to make changes for others. If you find a particular problem you want to tackle, plus the needed energy to tackle it, here are some ways to plunge ahead.

GET INVOLVED ON CAMPUS

Student Government

Student governments are comprised of groups of student volunteers at a college or university, generally elected by the student body, who usually meet on a monthly basis. They serve two functions: (1) to build a strong graduate student community, and (2) to advocate for graduate students. To build community, student governments host campus-wide events, such as orientations and academic seminars. They provide financial and organizational support for student clubs and events; frequently, they collect a graduate student life fee or activities fee and dole it out appropriately. In their advocacy role, student governments provide educational and informational support for graduate students, so students know what their rights are and what resources are available. They work with and advise the university administration and faculty on issues involving graduate students, by ensuring that graduate students are represented appropriately on institute committees, for example. Sometimes, student governments include an individual who is a voting member of the institution's board of trustees, board of regents, or board of governors, which means that student has a very direct influence over what the institution can do. A minority of colleges and universities do not have student governments and are instead run democratically or through a joint student-faculty governance structure.

Student governments often have a direct line to administrators. This gives them an opening to share opinions when decisions about the future of graduate education are being made; institutional committees, discussed below, are similar in this regard. These students can make events happen (or not happen), since they have a direct say in how funds and other resources are allotted on campus. If, for instance, you want your university to better support students seeking nonacademic careers, you could advocate for hosting and funding events and clubs that cater to those sorts of life plans. Student government is likely a good avenue for change if you're interested in building certain kinds of community, or if you want to see certain kinds of events or clubs on campus, though you may also be able to plan such events directly (if you convince those with the purse strings to fund you).

If you want to get involved in student government, consult the website of your school's student government. It will have information about who is in charge and ways to get involved. The simplest first step is to identify current members of the government and contact them for informal informational conversations, so you can ask questions and find out what opportunities are currently available.

Consider your goals and the changes you want to make. After having a few conversations, evaluate whether student government is the most effective way to enact those changes, or whether another avenue could provide faster success.

Graduate Student Unions

At some institutions, graduate student research and teaching assistants have formed unions, reflecting their status as university employees (and the increasing corporatization of universities).[3] The labor graduate students provide drives the university system forward; without graduate students, research projects would stall and ultimately fail. My university did not have a union when I was there, but the students formed one a few years after I graduated.

Unionization is controversial. Students seek collective bargaining toward benefits such as increased stipends, health insurance, and childcare. Administrators frequently oppose unions—for example, on the grounds that they threaten academic freedom and harm the relationships between faculty and students.[4] However, research suggests unionization in fact has a weak positive impact on both.[5]

If your institution does not have a union, you could work toward forming one, if your goal is improving graduate student quality of life. If you are at a public university, check the laws in your state. Some states give collective bargaining rights to graduate student employees at public universities; others deny them. In 2016, the National Labor Relations Board (NLRB) ruled that graduate student assistants at private institutions are considered employees because they provide services for others and have manager-worker relationships with faculty and administrators at the university. Thus, if you are at a private college or university, you should be able to unionize, given sufficient support: either your institution needs to voluntarily recognize your union, or at least 30 percent of students need to petition to unionize, at which point the NLRB will hold an election, and if the majority vote in favor of a union, the NLRB will certify it.[6]

Institutional Committees

Universities have committees for everything: faculty hiring, prospective student recruitment, public relations, climate, liaising between students in a department and faculty, dealing with academic grievances and codes of conduct, ethical review boards, and more. Lots more. *You* get a committee! And *you* get a committee!

Graduate students are frequently represented on such institutional committees. If there is a particular issue you're passionate about, you can try to get on a committee about it. You will be able to voice your opinion, persuade others with institutional power, and influence your institution's policies. There's not much direct reward beyond the experience you get serving on a committee and the satisfaction of having influenced the course of action the committee takes. Your adviser may frown on you spending time on committee work, but if you believe in it and think it will be worthwhile, then pursue it. (See chapter 5, "Advisers," for negotiation tips.)

Serving on committees, by the way, is one of the main components of what faculty call "service"—that is, the stuff they do that's not research or teaching, that contributes to the academic community in some way. Other service activities include peer review, serving as a journal editor, and organizing conferences or conference sessions.

How do you get on a committee? Most institutions keep a list of active committees on their website along with membership lists. Some will also include instructions for applying to join a committee; if not, try contacting current committee members for further information about their particular body's work and how to get involved. Some committees may require an application; for others, you may simply need to volunteer. If there's little or no info online, ask your adviser or admins in your department.

DIVERSITY

Academia has a diversity problem (see chapter 12, "Maintaining Your Sense of Self"). Actually, it has several diversity problems, which I'll tackle in turn: (1) diversity during graduate admissions, (2) diversity during graduate school and when looking at student retention, and (3) diversity in careers and later outcomes. In all three cases, most people would like to see greater diversity. Diverse people pursue different research interests and interrogate research questions in different ways. Diversity leads to innovation.

What's meant by diversity in graduate school? Among faculty on admissions committees, there's wide enthusiasm for it and wide disagreement about what it is: race and ethnicity (including international status), gender, prestige of undergraduate school, class and socioeconomic status.[7] Any and all of these contribute to diversity, as do factors not necessarily mentioned during admissions, such as family and parental status, career goals, sexuality, religion, disability, and age, among others.

Increasing Diversity in Admissions

Increasing diversity and equity on campus starts with admissions. At present, as Julie Posselt writes in her book *Inside Graduate Admissions*, faculty weigh diversity inconsistently during admissions.[8] Most faculty acknowledge that during graduate admissions, being a "diverse" student can help you—diversity represents intellectual opportunity. Students from different backgrounds will interpret and understand course material or texts in different ways. That said, the interaction between diversity and admissions is complex, and many times, admissions committees settle for "safer," less diverse candidates. They are all for diversity and equity in principle but are often ambivalent about specific actions or changes to the system that could actually achieve these aims.

Posselt recommends several changes to the admissions process. First, strengthen the recruitment of diverse applicants. It's hard to get a diverse set of admittees without a diverse pool to draw from. While I was a student at the MIT Media Lab, for instance, the academic program increased outreach efforts to underrepresented populations and created a "students offering support" program that matched applicants with current students, who provided one round of feedback on the prospective student's application materials. Increasingly, many institutions have bridge programs that help promising undergraduates get master's degrees that fast-track them into doctoral programs.

Second, Posselt recommends admissions committees revisit their processes for recruitment, admission, and awarding financial aid, and in particular, that they list the steps that involve subjective judgments—of which there are many—since this can help counteract the implicit biases the admissions committee may have (such as holding diverse or minority students to higher standards). Revisit the role of reviewer ratings of applications and the methods used to obtain these ratings. Open-ended review can lack transparency; try more structured and transparent approaches that define the criteria applicants must meet to be admitted, with rubrics to guide ratings.

Third, examine assumptions about merit and what it means to be a good applicant. Posselt found that diversity was only one aspect of merit; diversity of excellence meant recruiting from a wider range of colleges and universities and understanding that many of the metrics used to evaluate performance (such as standardized test scores and research experience) don't tell the full story. A student's grit and resilience may predict more about their future success than their test scores or research opportunities so far, especially if they come from a less privileged background. In addition, admissions committees need to stop misusing and misunderstanding standardized test scores: they are not measures of intelligence; at best, they measure some skills that are relevant to success in graduate school.

As a student, the easiest places to get involved are on the admissions committee or in helping recruit more diverse applicants.

Diversity and Retention

Around half of graduate students drop out without a degree (see chapter 1). For many students, especially those belonging to racial or ethnic minorities, the high attrition rate is due to finances; research suggests that increasing funding for PhD students will attract and retain more diverse students.[9] For others, the issue is related to a lack of mentoring and support; once again, increasing these leads to better retention.[10] Leonard Cassuto and Robert Weisbuch, in their book *The New PhD: How to Build a Better Graduate Education*, argue that increasing faculty guidance and involving more people, from within academia and without, in advising students will go a long way toward improving outcomes.[11] They discuss how pipeline programs can help underrepresented minority students succeed by providing additional funding, career-development workshops, and a cohort and community with peer-mentoring opportunities. Graduate students can advocate for these changes, but many of them will need to come from faculty and university administrators.

If, as a student, you want to advocate for change, how can you do that? Here's one example: In a 2021 project, Wendy Chu and her coauthors began with community dialogue in the form of town hall meetings among students. These meetings helped them develop a strategic plan, which in their case was a demand letter, a formal document calling for a particular change; other options include student petitions and protests.[12] In this case, they developed a demand letter calling for faculty diversity training, diversifying course syllabi, and skills workshops on cultural competence. Then, they used a range of tactics to continue pushing for change, including (1) setting up a team of student leaders to work toward the proposed changes; (2) obtaining buy-in from department chairs and deans to ensure student activism is recognized, valued, and supported; (3) involving multiple stakeholder groups, such as students as well faculty and existing diversity committees; and (4) monitoring the implementation of change and measuring its impact to determine whether meaningful change has actually been made.

There are smaller actions you can take as a student too. For example, make a point of finding, reading, and citing diverse scholarship in your field from women, underrepresented minorities, students and early career researchers, and colleagues from less prestigious institutions, and including this work in any syllabi you develop or classes you teach. Form peer-mentoring groups with other students, either in the form of a local, in-person group, or a virtual group spanning multiple institutions.

EXERCISE: FREEDOM OF SPEECH

This is a journaling exercise, and here's the prompt to write about.

While universities appreciate attention, they don't like bad press. In recent years, there have been many instances where speakers have been disinvited or faculty members resigned over issues that some hold to be objectionable—sometimes, for issues unrelated to their jobs at the institution. Some students and scholars feel they cannot share their views publicly due to the potential for backlash.

Regardless of your personal politics, it's worth reflecting on what you think the role of academic institutions is, what kind of dialogue and speech ought to take place on campuses, and what kind of intellectual climate you want to support. When a controversial speaker comes to your campus, or when a faculty member expresses a potentially offensive opinion online or in the classroom, how will you respond? What kinds of conversations do you want to take place? When considering your response, reflect on your values and on those of your graduate institution.

* Jeffrey Adam Sachs, "The 'Campus Free Speech Crisis' Ended Last Year," Niskanen Center, January 25, 2019, https://www.niskanencenter.org/the-campus-free-speech-crisis-ended-last-year/; Jacob Hess, "Opinion: The Courage Not to Cancel," *Deseret News*, August 9, 2021, https://www.deseret.com/opinion/2021/8/8/22568732/cancel-culture-at-universities-higher-education-courage-utah-valley-university.

Preparation for Career Diversity

Among people calling for graduate school reform, the consensus is that we need better preparation for career diversity. There are multiple avenues to pursue. For instance, Cassuto and Weisbuch have argued for improved, more collaborative mentoring of graduate students.[13] Besides their primary advisers in academia, graduate students ought to have additional mentors who can expose them to non-academic career paths and opportunities. You can seek out additional mentors on your own—start with informational interviews (see chapter 2, "Career Plans") and try to identify individuals who jibe with you.

In conjunction with improved mentoring, for students who know that they're seeking nonacademic jobs, consider shorter or alternative dissertation formats that can better serve as preparation for alternative careers. This was one area in which the MIT Media Lab excelled. Dissertatons were highly personalized, and many were not your standard academic document. If your institution doesn't already allow alternative dissertation formats, you could advocate for them, though it's worth keeping in mind this is a difficult change that would need the support of faculty and administrators.

Susan Basalla and Maggie Debelius recommend that departments and schools track the careers of all graduate students, whether they follow an academic path or not, for one, five, and ten years after their time in the department, whether they get a degree or not.[14] Maintain a database or social network with this information and a network of alumni who are willing to discuss careers with current students. In addition, departments and schools should create opportunities or policies that allow students to explore careers, subjects, and skills that may be more broad, unrelated to their dissertation, or unrelated to academia—such as encouraging students to use summers for internships rather their own research.

If your school doesn't have a database or network yet, you can ask the alumni office to start one. At some schools, a graduate student is given a stipend to keep the database up to date. You could volunteer for the job. If that's too big a step, you can learn about the careers of alumni from your department, research group, or even past students of your adviser. The department will have a list of alumni; many research groups and individual professors keep lists of past students on their websites. You can try connecting with these alumni using LinkedIn. You may get the information you want about their careers simply by viewing their LinkedIn profiles or current websites. Send an introductory email and ask for an informational interview, as explained in chapter 2.

Finally, when planning careers, most people only think of work outside the home. But choosing to work inside the home is equally valid, even if it is not equally valued in our current culture (part of the unfortunate trend of devaluing care work of all kinds). Many people—women and parents in particular—choose to stay home some or all of the time, often while continuing to do research, consulting, or writing. Some return to full-time work when their children are older. If you think you may choose this path, some useful alternatives to academia have been cropping up in recent years, as discussed below.

FORGING FLEXIBILITY

For many graduate students, flexibility will be the key to success. Many women leave academia for greener pastures, because of their mothering and caregiving responsibilities (see Chapter 11). Academia wasn't designed around women. We can't just hide all evidence of baby making behind six weeks' paid leave; we can't ignore the family we have at home; we can't ignore mental health, or chronic illnesses, or disabilities, or anything else that is incompatible with academia's predominant unbalanced workaholic culture. Instead, we need to reshape academia.

A feminist version of academia—and the workplace at large—has to be compatible with motherhood, parenting, and caregiving. That means increased flexibility. You know that wage gap we keep hearing about, whereby women earn less than men? In 2016, the podcast *Freakonomics* found that one of the primary factors driving the wage gap is women's desire for flexibility.[15] Many mothers would prefer part-time, remote, and other flexible work alternatives to the straightforward full-time-off, full-time-back arrangement.[16]

Flexibility will, honestly, benefit pretty much everyone. What does flexibility look like? I've listed some options below. For all of them, as a student, you can raise awareness about the importance of creating flexible options at your institution. You can organize a petition or protest, or write a demand letter to gain support from other students and influence the administration. If your campus has a graduate student union, speak with them, as they may be able to help. If you get started, you'll find support; many people want change, they just need to know they're not alone.

Remote and Asynchronous Work

One good thing that came out of the COVID-19 pandemic was a greater awareness of remote work and asynchronous work possibilities. Some professors, research groups, and departments have remained flexible about in-person attendance. Some have maintained the accommodations made during lockdowns, such as recording and posting lectures, making all readings available as pdfs, and eschewing timed tests and quizzes (which are more difficult to administer remotely) in favor of alternative ways of evaluating learning.

That said, the reality is that remote work isn't a possibility for many students. If you work in a lab, for instance, there's no replacement at home. But you may be able to negotiate remote working hours with your adviser for the tasks that don't absolutely require you being on campus.

Leaves of Absence

Most universities have leave policies that cover maternity, medical issues, military services, and disabilities; some may also cover personal difficulties such as mental illness or financial stress. Changing or adding leave policies requires buy-in from administrators, but it is doable. Most students would probably support any changes made; it's a matter of getting the momentum to convince the administration that the changes are worth it.

Maternal Labor and Childcare

Many people want to make academia friendlier for parents.[17] Research suggests that pregnant and parenting students are most helped by family-friendly advisers and programs, planning around the timing of having children, and reasonable expectations about their work.[18] Here are a few examples of measures that would help to alleviate some of the challenges currently facing graduate students raising or hoping to start a family:

- Provide paid parental leave for students, and private lactation spaces.
- Provide funding for childcare and family health insurance, since graduate stipends are not large (see chapter 3, "Money and Logistics"). Or, if one parent is staying home with the children instead of purchasing outside childcare, give the funding directly to the family.
- Create coworking spaces that include childcare—for example, on the model adopted by many gyms, which provide childcare while you're working out.[19]
- Allow flexible deadlines when caring for children, especially if there is illness or stress.
- Cultivate a culture welcoming of student parents, such as family-friendly departmental social events (not only evening events, or events at bars). Most student parents are just as productive and motivated as those without children—sometimes even more so, *because* of their children, though the opposite is often assumed.
- Recognize that children have different needs at different ages. Younger children necessarily need more from their parents, and greater flexibility and support should be provided in response.

Changing the Culture

Numerous people have already called for changing the culture of academia to value life balance over workaholism, and quality of work over quantity.[20] Jessica Calarco, for instance, suggests combating the pressure to publish papers by increasing the incentives for good teaching and good mentoring, such as reducing course loads for faculty if they mentor many students. Lisa Barrett argues that we need to consciously change our behavior: "Each of us, the next time we're on a search or tenure-and-promotion committee, can commit to reading applicants' papers instead of counting them. Each of us, when sitting down to write the next manuscript, or even better, to design the next set of experiments, can ask: Will this research contribute something of substance?"[21] As a graduate student, you may be on a search or hiring committee, or on an admissions committee. These are places you can take action.

You can also lead by example. Set your own boundaries between work and nonwork and create a healthy life balance for yourself—as discussed in chapters 10 through 12. Acknowledge others' boundaries and try to ensure your requests for others' time are reasonable. Change the way you talk about your work and life to normalize having boundaries and balance. You can also advocate for policy changes that support balance, such as limits on the number of hours graduate teaching assistants are required to work, or better family leave policies.

Alternative Academic Structures

When reimagining the academic world, we should look to the scholars who are currently at the forefront of such reimagination and who have created communities outside the traditional academic structure, such as those at the Ronin Institute for Independent Scholarship and the Institute for Globally Distributed Open Research and Education.[22] Organizations like these enable independent scholars to join forces by creating new academic networks, helping administer grants (since many funding agencies require an institutional affiliation), assisting independent scholars in finding collaborators and funding in the first place, forming independent IRB systems for human subjects study approval, and more.

While some of these scholars also hold conventional academic positions, many have eschewed traditional institutions in favor of less orthodox and more flexible paths. Personally, I have appreciated finding women like me through the Ronin Institute, who have managed to balance caring for their children and families with part-time work, and later, a return to full-time research.

A small minority of institutions have created part-time opportunities within traditional academia—for instance, providing one full-time faculty position that is shared by a dual-career couple.[23] Part of the problem, however, is funding; most funding agencies assume people are going to be working full-time. Funding agencies should create more grants that pay out less money over longer timelines for part-time research. Institutions could pay each part-time faculty a little less, and then use the money to hire an extra admin or lab manager to help them out, freeing up time for part-time faculty to engage in actual research work. These same faculty could have reduced teaching loads, and they could use shared offices or shared lab spaces. These changes are predominantly beyond the purview of graduate students, but being aware of the options and possibilities can inspire you as you plan your life.

> **EXERCISE 22: THE IDEAL WORKPLACE**
>
> 1. Set a timer for ten minutes: let's think about workplaces! Write about or sketch your ideal graduate school workplace. Where are you? Who is there? What does it look like? What's the ambiance? What about it would suit you better than what you have now?
> 2. Next, review your ideas. What is one small change you can make today that could move you closer to your vision? How might you tackle some of the bigger changes?

chapter 14
What's Next, Revisited

This book has been an invitation for you to consider where you are today, in graduate school and in your personal life, and where you're heading, with the goal of helping you figure out how to live your life in the way that's best for you. With all the tools, exercises, and resources I've shared, I hope you feel thoroughly prepared for whatever's next—whether it's sauntering forth to conquer that degree, or retreating from academia.

Our paths are all different. There's no way of knowing ahead of time where your road is taking you. I certainly didn't. And that's part of the exhilaration of living.

As you look forward, consider what success means for you. What are you doing, today, that you'll look back at and smile, knowing you made the right choices for *you*? That should be your goal. You, making the right choices for you. Making the best decisions you can, balancing what's important to you, living coherently. That's all you can do.

Know full well that other people would make different decisions. And that's fine, because they're not you. They hold different values. Some people will look at the choices you're making, the choices you've made, and furrow their eyebrows. They'll ask, "Aren't you wasting your degree? Shouldn't you be waiting to do that? Isn't X, or Y, or Z a better option? Why is *that* the career you want?" There will be people who question your every move.

Don't listen. You're forging your own path. As Dr. Seuss wrote in his 1990 book *Oh! The Places You'll Go!*,

> You have brains in your head.
> You have feet in your shoes.

> You can steer yourself
> any direction you choose.

Ultimately, the only person who needs to be fully satisfied with how you live your life is you. As you go forward, remember your values. Remember what motivates you.

There are an infinite number of paths to success. Regardless of whether grad school is part of your road, or if what you've gained from this book is the knowledge that grad school isn't where you're headed, I wish you the best of luck.

Glossary

ABD (ALL BUT DISSERTATION): Status in a doctoral program in which a student has completed all necessary coursework, exams, and other requirements—all they need to finish is writing the dissertation.

ADJUNCT/AD HOC FACULTY: Part-time instructors who teach one or more courses; contract workers paid on a semester-by-semester basis; generally do not receive other employment benefits; not on the tenure track.

ADMINISTRATION: Faculty and staff who run the day-to-day operations of the university, including presidents, provosts, chancellors, deans, department chairs, research staff, and department admins.

ADVISER: A professor with a PhD or similar advanced degree who serves as mentor to one or more graduate students. Their role is to guide students through the graduate program, help them find funding, promote their development as scholars, and provide training, resources, or other support.

ASSISTANT PROFESSOR: Academic rank. Usually, beginning professor with zero to seven years of experience; full-time salaried position. First step on the tenure track; after between five and seven years, they can apply for tenure and be promoted to associate professor.

ASSOCIATE PROFESSOR: Academic rank. Typically, professor with five to seven years or more of experience; full-time salaried position. Tenured professor; after more time, can be promoted to full professor.

BROWN BAG (TALK/SEMINAR/SESSION): Event held around lunchtime. Lunch isn't provided, but attendees are welcome to bring food and eat during the event. Frequently involves less formal research talks given by members of the department.

CHALK TALK: Talk given by a job candidate during the academic job search about their future research, often accompanied by a white board or chalkboard but not a digital presentation.

CONFERENCE PAPER: Written report about research presented at a conference, often in a panel format or as an individual presentation. Generally has to pass peer review to be accepted; varies by field whether it describes in-progress or completed work.

CONFERENCE PRESENTATION: Talk about research given at a conference; may be accompanied by slides.

CONFERENCE: A multiday meeting of scholars to share recent research and discuss issues of interest to their field. May include plenary sessions, keynotes, paper presentations, poster sessions, and workshops.

CONTINGENT FACULTY: See *adjunct/ad hoc*.

CV (CURRICULUM VITAE): Detailed document (with no page limit) listing academia-related accomplishments, including education and academic credentials, academic work history, nonacademic work experience, publications, awards and honors, conference presentations, speaking experience, service, and teaching experience.

DEAN: A professor in charge of a department, school, or college within a university or college who sets policies, makes decisions, helps hire faculty, leads committees. Sometimes aided by associate deans.

DOCTORAL CANDIDATES: In some departments, a special title granted to students who have passed qualifying exams and just need to do their dissertations.

DOUBLE-BLIND: In publication and peer review, reviewers don't know who the authors are, and the authors don't know who the reviewers are; can help decrease bias against marginalized groups or specific individuals.

FELLOWSHIP: Money, affiliation, or opportunities to work awarded by an organization or institution to an individual to support them and/or their research. Generally determined on the basis of merit; may have a work requirement, commitment to a particular research project, and quarterly or yearly reporting.

FULL PROFESSOR: Academic rank; associate professors who gain sufficient experience can be promoted to full professor; usually accompanied by a pay increase and higher-level administrative roles.

GRADUATE ASSISTANT: Graduate students who perform research or teaching for a university in exchange for pay (often, a stipend), tuition waivers, and/or other benefits.

GRADUATE STUDENT: Individual with a bachelor's degree who is pursuing a master's or doctoral degree.

GRANT: Money from an organization or institution to support a specific research project or particular parts of a project.

IACUC (INSTITUTIONAL ANIMAL CARE AND USE COMMITTEE): A group of people at a university (e.g., professors, administrators, graduate students) who approve research work involving animals to ensure the research follows international ethical standards and laws.

INCOMPLETE: Grade taken for a class indicating that a student did not finish assignments or missed a substantial number of classes prior to the grading deadline; allowed by an instructor who intends to work with the student to finish the class later.

IRB (INSTITUTIONAL REVIEW BOARD): A group of people at a university (e.g., professors, administrators, graduate students) who approve research work involving human subjects—such as interviews, surveys, experiments, and clinical trials—to ensure the research follows international ethical standards and laws. Sometimes this group is called by a different name: ERB (Ethical Review Board), REB (Research Ethics Board), etc. At MIT, it is called the Committee on the Use of Humans as Experimental Subjects.

JOURNAL PAPER: Written report about research; generally more prestigious than other papers; published in an academic journal run by a scholarly organization, university, or nonprofit foundation after a lengthy peer-review and editorial-review process. Some journals also publish shorter articles, such as commentaries and book reviews.

KEYNOTE: A longer talk (thirty minutes or more) given by a prominent scholar in the field, often a highlight of a conference.

LECTURER: Non-tenure-track professor who focuses on undergraduate teaching; employed on a renewable contract with the option of being promoted later.

LOI (LETTER OF INTEREST): Some funding agencies and organizations require people to submit a LOI to gauge fit for funding prior to requesting a full application.

MENTOR: An individual who helps, advises, or trains another individual, in one or more areas of life.

MONOGRAPH: A scholarly book on a single, specialized topic; frequently the most prestigious form of publication in the humanities.

NAMED PROFESSORSHIP: At some universities, a distinguished professorship funded by private donations and named for someone of note who donated money to support the position.

OPEN ACCESS: In academic publishing, any work available to read or access free of charge; not paywalled.

PEER REVIEW: A process aimed at ensuring rigor in scholarly work, wherein research (whether an article, a manuscript, a book proposal, a grant proposal, or some other work) is sent to other researchers in your field ("peers") for assessment; essentially, to get someone in the field to comment on the significance of the work prior to publication. The reviews cover what the reviewers liked and didn't like, comments, recommendations, suggestions. An editor or funding agency may use reviews to decide to publish or fund a project.

PI (PRINCIPAL INVESTIGATOR): Person in charge of designing, carrying out, overseeing a research project. Generally takes a lead role in writing the grant that funds the research, the IRB applications, and writing the manuscripts. Many universities and funding agencies require PIs to hold a PhD or similar advanced degree, but not all. Sometimes, a student's adviser is called their PI.

PLENARY: Session at a conference that everyone generally attends (e.g., a keynote or a panel).

POSTDOCTORAL FELLOWS (POSTDOCS): Individuals with doctorates working with a professor to gain experience with research and teaching; a temporary position lasting between one and five years.

POSTER PRESENTATION: A presentation at a poster session of information about a scholar's research accompanied by a visual description of the research.

POSTER SESSION: Event in which some researchers display large posters they've made describing their work, while everyone else walks around, looks at the posters, and talks to them about their work.

PRESIDENT: Individual who oversees all research and administrative operations at a university; highest position.

PROFESSOR: Academic in a research and/or teaching position at a university.

PROVOST: Individual who oversees academics at a university; senior position; works with the president to develop policies and institute plans.

RA (RESEARCH ASSISTANT): Individual receiving a stipend, tuition waiver, and/or other benefits in exchange for work on research for a professor. Commonly, a position filled by graduate students as a way to fund their studies.

R&R (REVISE AND RESUBMIT): One of four outcomes of the peer-review process in academic publishing, indicating that the authors should incorporate the feedback from the reviewers and resubmit the paper or book manuscript to the same venue again; also known as accept with major revisions. The other outcomes are accept, accept with minor revisions, or reject.

RESUME: A brief (between one and two pages), persuasive document explaining your skills and qualifications to potential employers.

RFP (REQUEST FOR PROPOSALS): A list of research areas that funding agencies and organizations would like to fund, with priorities and guidelines.

R1: Loose classification of universities or departments as having a heavy emphasis on research and preparation of graduate students for academic careers, as opposed to teaching or preparation for trades or industry.

ROUNDTABLE: A form of academic discussion focused on a specific topic, in which all participants have equal say. May be moderated much like a panel discussion.

SABBATICAL: For a professor, paid or unpaid leave away from their usual job at their institution, often used for writing projects or for research/travel.

SCHOLARSHIP: Money awarded by an organization or institution to an individual, based on merit, need, or some other qualifying factor, that can be used to pay for schooling or living expenses. Does not have to be repaid, unlike a loan.

SERVICE: A catch-all term for work done for the university, the department, the discipline, or the community that's not research or teaching, such as serving on committees.

SINGLE-BLIND: In publication and peer review, reviewers know who the authors are, but authors don't know who the reviewers are.

STIPEND: Money paid out to an individual to help cover living expenses, often as payment for a graduate assistantship or from a fellowship. May be taxed differently than hourly wages.

SUPERVISOR: See *adviser*.

SYMPOSIUM: Much like a conference, but often smaller, though it varies by discipline.

TA (TEACHING ASSISTANT): Individual receiving a stipend, tuition waiver, and/or other benefits in exchange for helping a processor teach classes (also called a graduate assistant or proctor). They may give lectures, grade exams and papers, and lead review sessions. Commonly, a position filled by graduate students as a way to fund their studies.

TEACHING LOAD (e.g., 4-4, 2-2-2, 3:3 with two preps): The number of classes a faculty member is expected to teach each semester or each quarter during the academic year. The terminology "with preps" indicates that some of the classes taught will be multiple sections of the same class, meaning there's less preparation time.

TEMPORARY FACULTY: See *adjunct/ad hoc*.

TENURE: Job security for professors; the right to hold jobs for life without risk of being fired so long as they don't violate any university policies. More recently, some universities have post-tenure review processes to ensure tenured faculty are not unsatisfactory workers. It usually takes five to seven years for a tenure-track professor to go up for tenure.

TENURE-TRACK FACULTY: Assistant professors who, after working on research, teaching, and service for five to seven years, can be promoted to tenured faculty, or denied tenure (so they have to find a job elsewhere). Universities vary in their requirements for hiring and promotion.

UNDERGRADUATE STUDENTS (UNDERGRADS): People pursuing an associate's or bachelor's degree.

VISITING PROFESSOR: A temporary teaching position at a university, often for one or two years; like an adjunct with a fancier title. May be like a postdoc but for teaching, or may be held by a professor with a job elsewhere who is visiting while on sabbatical at their normal institution. More common in the social sciences and humanities.

WORKSHOP PAPER: Written description of work in progress submitted to a conference workshop session, which is generally a smaller gathering of researchers on a focused topic that is more hands-on with more discussion.

Notes

INTRODUCTION

1. Julie R. Posselt, *Inside Graduate Admissions: Merit, Diversity, and Faculty Gatekeeping* (Cambridge, MA: Harvard University Press, 2016).
2. National Center for Education Statistics, *The Condition of Education: Postbaccalaureate Enrollment*, U.S. Department of Education, Institute of Education Sciences, May 2023, https://nces.ed.gov/programs/coe/indicator_chb.asp.
3. Chris Woolston, "PhDs: The Tortuous Truth," *Nature* 575 (2019): 403–406, https://doi.org/10.1038/d41586-019-03459-7.
4. Woolston, "PhDs."
5. Woolston.
6. Ronald G. Ehrenberg, Harriet Zuckerman, Jeffrey A. Groen, and Sharon M. Brucker, *Educating Scholars: Doctoral Education in the Humanities* (Princeton, NJ: Princeton University Press, 2009).
7. Michael T. Nettles and Catherine M. Millett, *Three Magic Letters: Getting to Ph.D.* (Baltimore, MD: Johns Hopkins University Press, 2006).
8. Christopher L Caterine, *Leaving Academia: A Practical Guide* (Princeton, NJ: Princeton University Press, 2020).
9. Scott Jaschik, "The Shrinking Ph.D. Job Market," *Inside Higher Ed*, April 3, 2016, https://www.insidehighered.com/news/2016/04/04/new-data-show-tightening-phd-job-market-across-disciplines.

1. WHAT'S NEXT

1. "Data & Insights," Council of Graduate Schools, accessed July 24, 2023, https://www.cgsnet.org/ckfinder/userfiles/files/DataSources_2010_03.pdf.
2. Amanda I. Seligman, *Is Graduate School Really for You? The Whos, Whats, Hows, and Whys of Pursuing a Master's or Ph.D.* (Baltimore, MD: Johns Hopkins University Press, 2012).

3. Maggie Kuo, "What Comes After a Ph.D.? Check Out the Data," *Science*, July 24, 2017, https://www.science.org/content/article/what-comes-after-phd-check-out-data. Kuo's article is based on the National Science Foundation's annual Survey of Earned Doctorates, conducted in 2017. See "About This Report," National Science Foundation, accessed July 24, 2023, https://www.nsf.gov/statistics/2017/nsf17306/report/about-this-report.cfm.
4. Bill Burnett and Dave Evans, *Designing Your Life: How to Build a Well-Lived, Joyful Life* (New York: Knopf, 2016), 82.
5. Burnett and Evans, *Designing Your Life*, 83.
6. Christopher P. Niemiec, Richard M. Ryan, and Edward L. Deci, "The Path Taken: Consequences of Attaining Intrinsic and Extrinsic Aspirations in Post-College Life," *Journal of Research in Personality* 73, no. 3 (June 2009): 291–306, https://doi.org/10.1016/j.jrp.2008.09.001.
7. "Number of Jobs, Labor Market Experience, Marital Status, and Health: Results From a National Longitudinal Survey," Bureau of Labor Statistics, U.S. Department of Labor, news release USDL-21-1567, August 31, 2021, https://www.bls.gov/news.release/archives/nlsoy_08312021.pdf.
8. Leonard Cassuto, "Ph.D. Attrition: How Much Is Too Much?," *Chronicle of Higher Education*, July 1, 2013, https://www.chronicle.com/article/PhD-Attrition-How-Much-Is/140045/.
9. Robert Sowell, Ting Zhang, Nathan Bell, Kenneth Redd, and Margaret F. King, *Ph.D. Completion and Attrition: Analysis of Baseline Demographic Data from the Ph.D. Completion Project* (Washington, DC: Council of Graduate Schools, 2008), https://cgsnet.org/wp-content/uploads/2022/01/phd_completion_and_attrition_analysis_of_baseline_demographic_data-2.pdf.
10. "Master's Completion Project," Council of Graduate Schools, accessed July 24, 2023, https://cgsnet.org/masters-completion-project.
11. Holly Else, "Nearly Half of U.S. Female Scientists Leave Full-Time Science After First Child," *Nature*, February 19, 2019, https://www.nature.com/articles/d41586-019-00611-1.
12. Susan Basalla and Maggie Debelius, *"So What Are You Going to Do with That?": Finding Careers Outside Academia*, 3rd ed. (Chicago: University of Chicago Press, 2014), 2.
13. Seligman, *Is Graduate School Really for You?*
14. Seligman, xvii.
15. Sophie Moullin, Jane Waldfogel, and Elizabeth Washbrook, *Baby Bonds: Parenting, Attachment and a Secure Base for Children* (London: Sutton Trust, 2014).
16. Jacqueline Kory-Westlund, "Wasting My Degree: Why Is Having Kids, Moving Out of the City, and Following an Unusual Path a Waste?," *MIT Grad Blog*, March 18, 2019, https://oge.mit.edu/wasting-my-degree/; Jacqueline Kory-Westlund, "PhD and a Baby: Debugging Code and Changing Diapers," *MIT Grad Blog*, March 28, 2018, https://oge.mit.edu/phd-and-a-baby/; Jacqueline Kory-Westlund, "Parenting While Researching? It Takes Support, Kid-Friendly Systems, and a Lot of Luck," in *Graduate Students at Work: Exploited Scholars of Neoliberal Higher Ed*, ed. Tessa Brown (Lawrence: Kansas University Press), 170–172.

2. CAREER PLANS

1. Lori Turk-Bicakci, Andrea Berger, and Clarisse Haxton, "The Nonacademic Careers of STEM PhD Holders," STEM at American Institutes for Research, issue brief (April 2014), https://www.air.org/sites/default/files/downloads/report/STEM%20nonacademic%20careers%20April14.pdf.
2. Colleen Flaherty, "A Non-Tenure-Track Profession?," *Inside Higher Ed*, October 11, 2018, https://www.insidehighered.com/news/2018/10/12/about-three-quarters-all-faculty-positions-are-tenure-track-according-new-aaup; Nathan M. Greenfield, "American Professors Report Declining Salaries, Rising University Debt," *University World News*, August 14, 2021, https://www.universityworldnews.com/post.php?story=20210813112321174; Colleen Flaherty, "Faculty Salaries Dip This Year," *Inside Higher Ed*, April 12, 2021, https://www.insidehighered.com/news/2021/04/13/faculty-salaries-decreased-year.
3. Scott Jaschik, "The Shrinking Ph.D. Job Market," *Inside Higher Ed*, April 3, 2016, https://www.insidehighered.com/news/2016/04/04/new-data-show-tightening-phd-job-market-across-disciplines.
4. Katie Langin, "In a First, U.S. Private Sector Employs Nearly as Many Ph.D.s as Schools Do," *Science*, March 12, 2019. https://www.science.org/content/article/first-us-private-sector-employs-nearly-many-phds-schools-do.
5. Trevor Griffey, "The Decline of Faculty Tenure: Less From an Oversupply of PhDs, & More from the Systematic De-valuation of PhD as a Prereq for College Teaching—LAWCHA," *LaborOnline*, January 9, 2017, https://www.lawcha.org/2017/01/09/decline-faculty-tenure-less-oversupply-phds-systematic-de-valuation-phd-credential-college-teaching/.
6. "Data Snapshot: Full-Time Women Faculty and Faculty of Color," American Association of University Professors, December 9, 2020, https://www.aaup.org/news/data-snapshot-full-time-women-faculty-and-faculty-color; "Data Snapshot: Contingent Faculty in US Higher Ed," American Association of University Professors, October 11, 2018, https://www.aaup.org/news/data-snapshot-contingent-faculty-us-higher-ed; "Data Snapshot: Contingent Faculty in US Higher Ed," American Association of University Professors, 2016, https://www.aaup.org/sites/default/files/10112018%20Data%20Snapshot%20Tenure.pdf.
7. This is discussed in Susan Basalla and Maggie Debelius, *"So What Are You Going to Do with That?" Finding Careers Outside Academia*, 3rd ed. (University of Chicago Press, 2014), and in Christopher L. Caterine, *Leaving Academia: A Practical Guide* (Princeton, NJ: Princeton University Press, 2020).
8. Caterine, *Leaving Academia*.
9. Aaron Clauset, Samuel Arbesman, and Daniel B. Larremore, "Systematic Inequality and Hierarchy in Faculty Hiring Networks," *Science Advances* 1, no. 1 (2015): e1400005, https://doi.org/10.1126/sciadv.1400005.
10. Melinda Clark, Anthony Miller, Jamie Berry, and Ken Cheng, "Mental Contrasting with Implementation Intentions Increases Study Time for University Students," *British Journal of Educational Psychology* 91, no. 3 (2021): e12396, https://doi.org/10.1111/bjep.12396;

Angela Lee Duckworth, Heidi Grant, Benjamin Loew, Gabriele Oettingen, and Peter M. Gollwitzer, "Self-Regulation Strategies Improve Self-Discipline in Adolescents: Benefits of Mental Contrasting and Implementation Intentions," *Educational Psychology* 31, no. 1 (2011): 17-26, https://doi.org/10.1080/01443410.2010.506003; Angela Lee Duckworth, Teri Kirby, Anton Gollwitzer, and Gabriele Oettingen, "From Fantasy to Action: Mental Contrasting with Implementation Intentions (MCII) Improves Academic Performance in Children," *Social Psychological and Personality Science* 4, no. 6 (2013): 745-753, https://doi.org/10.1177/1948550613476307; Gabriele Oettingen, Heather Barry Kappes, Katie B. Guttenberg, and Peter M. Gollwitzer, "Self-Regulation of Time Management: Mental Contrasting with Implementation Intentions," *European Journal of Social Psychology* 45, no. 2 (2015): 218-229, https://doi.org/10.1002/ejsp.2090.

11. Clauset, Arbesman, and Larremore, "Systematic Inequality and Hierarchy in Faculty Hiring Networks"; James H. Fowler, Bernard Grofman, and Natalie Masuoka, "Social Networks in Political Science: Hiring and Placement of Ph.D.s, 1960-2002," *PS: Political Science & Politics* 40, no. 4 (2007): 729-739; Bo Mai, Jiaying Liu, and Sandra González-Bailón, "Network Effects in the Academic Market: Mechanisms for Hiring and Placing PhDs in Communication (2007-2014)," *Journal of Communication* 65, no. 3 (2015): 558-583; Robert J. Speakman, Carla S. Hadden, Matthew H. Colvin, Justin Cramb, K. C. Jones, Travis W. Jones, Isabelle Lulewicz, et al., "Market Share and Recent Hiring Trends in Anthropology Faculty Positions," *PLOS ONE* 13, no. 9 (September 12, 2018): e0202528, https://doi.org/10.1371/journal.pone.0202528.

12. Sean C. McConnell, Erica L. Westerman, Joseph F. Pierre, Erin J. Heckler, and Nancy B. Schwartz, "United States National Postdoc Survey Results and the Interaction of Gender, Career Choice and Mentor Impact," *ELife*, December 18, 2018, https://doi.org/10.7554/eLife.40189; Maya Denton, Maura Borrego, and David B. Knight, "U.S. Postdoctoral Careers in Life Sciences, Physical Sciences and Engineering: Government, Industry, and Academia," *PLOS ONE* 17, no. 2 (February 2, 2022): e0263185, https://doi.org/10.1371/journal.pone.0263185.

13. Chris Woolston, "Postdoc Survey Reveals Disenchantment with Working Life," *Nature*, November 18, 2020, https://doi.org/10.1038/d41586-020-03191-7.

14. Peter J. Feibelman, *A PhD Is Not Enough! A Guide to Survival in Science* (New York: Basic Books, 2011).

15. Woolston, "Postdoc Survey Reveals Disenchantment with Working Life."

16. Basalla and Debelius, *"So What Are You Going to Do with That?"*

17. Caterine, *Leaving Academia*.

18. Here's one anonymously shared story from someone who enjoys the flexibility of adjuncting: The PhD Story (@thephdstory), "I Wish There Were More Op-Eds on Adjuncting...," Twitter, May 15, 2020, 12:00 p.m., https://twitter.com/thephdstory/status/1261325636217434112.

19. Rebbecca Kaplan, "The Confessions of a Ph.D. on Life as an Admissions Counselor," *Inside Higher Ed*, October 31, 2019, https://www.insidehighered.com/advice/2019/10/31/advantages-those-phd-working-admissions-opinion.

20. Jennifer Polk, "Where to Look for #Altac PhDs at Universities," Google Docs, July 15, 2020, https://docs.google.com/document/d/1Ovc1sJ6b825LdQT1lEU29Em1cICfH0MHtUfrvmBvnvg/edit?usp=sharing.
21. Joyce B. Main, Sarah Prenovitz, and Ronald G. Ehrenberg, "In Pursuit of a Tenure-Track Faculty Position: Career Progression and Satisfaction of Humanities and Social Sciences Doctorates," *Review of Higher Education* 42, no. 4 (2019): 1309–1336.
22. Basalla and Debelius, *"So What Are You Going to Do with That?"*
23. Basalla and Debelius.
24. Junming Huang, Alexander J. Gates, Roberta Sinatra, and Albert-László Barabási, "Historical Comparison of Gender Inequality in Scientific Careers across Countries and Disciplines," *Proceedings of the National Academy of Sciences* 117, no. 9 (2020): 4609–4616, https://doi.org/10.1073/pnas.1914221117.
25. Holly Else, "Nearly Half of US Female Scientists Leave Full-Time Science After First Child," *Nature*, February 19, 2019, https://doi.org/10.1038/d41586-019-00611-1.
26. Anabel Cossette Civitella, "Women Academics Are Still Outnumbered at the Higher Ranks," *University Affairs*, June 13, 2018, https://www.universityaffairs.ca/news/news-article/women-academics-are-still-outnumbered-at-the-higher-ranks/.
27. Henrik Kleven, Camille Landais, Johanna Posch, Andreas Steinhauer, and Josef Zweimüller, "Child Penalties Across Countries: Evidence and Explanations," Working Paper 25524, National Bureau of Economic Research (February 2019), https://doi.org/10.3386/w25524.
28. Caterine, *Leaving Academia*.
29. Bill Burnett and Dave Evans, *Designing Your Life: How to Build a Well-Lived, Joyful Life* (New York: Knopf, 2016).
30. Darcie Fitzpatrick, "AEIOU Observation Framework: A Heuristic Framework Used for Ethnographic Observations," Open Practice Library, November 30, 2018, https://openpracticelibrary.com/practice/aeiou-observation-framework/.
31. Leonard Cassuto, *The Graduate School Mess* (Cambridge, MA: Harvard University Press, 2015).
32. Lou Adler, "New Survey Reveals 85% of All Jobs Are Filled Via Networking," LinkedIn, February 29, 2016, https://www.linkedin.com/pulse/new-survey-reveals-85-all-jobs-filled-via-networking-lou-adler.
33. Caterine, *Leaving Academia*; Burnett and Evans, *Designing Your Life*.

3. MONEY AND LOGISTICS

1. Melanie Hanson, "Average Cost of a Master's Degree [2022]," Education Data Initiative, November 13, 2022, https://educationdata.org/average-cost-of-a-masters-degree; Melanie Hanson, "Average Cost of a Doctorate Degree: Ph.D., Psy.D. & More [2023]," Education Data Initiative, December 10, 2022, https://educationdata.org/average-cost-of-a-doctorate-degree.
2. Wynne Parry, "The Real Cost of Grad School in the US," *Chemical & Engineering News*, November 2, 2021, https://cen.acs.org/education/graduate-education/real-cost-grad-school-US/99/i41.

3. Melanie Hanson, "Average Graduate Student Loan Debt [2023]," Education Data Initiative, May 23, 2023, https://educationdata.org/average-graduate-student-loan-debt.
4. Amanda I. Seligman, *Is Graduate School Really for You? The Whos, Whats, Hows, and Whys of Pursuing a Master's or Ph.D.* (Baltimore, MD: Johns Hopkins University Press, 2012).
5. Ben Luthi, "How Much Do Graduate Students Get Paid?," *Juno*, September 22, 2021, https://joinjuno.com/financial-literacy/student-loans/how-much-do-graduate-students-get-paid.
6. People share their experiences with different funding models in this twitter thread: Dr. Casey Fiesler (@cfiesler), "I'd Like to Do a Video About PhD Funding . . . ," Twitter, December 30, 2020, 9:20 a.m., https://twitter.com/cfiesler/status/1344287334154563585.
7. Cal Newport, *Deep Work: Rules for Focused Success in a Distracted World* (New York: Grand Central Publishing, 2016).
8. Emily Roberts, "This Grad Student and Her Family Lived on Her Stipend While Banking Her Spouse's," *Personal Finance for PhDs*, February 21, 2021, http://pfforphds.com/this-grad-student-and-her-family-lived-on-her-stipend-while-banking-her-spouses/.
9. Jessica McCrory Calarco, *A Field Guide to Grad School: Uncovering the Hidden Curriculum* (Princeton, NJ: Princeton University Press, 2020).
10. Teresa Crew, *Higher Education and Working-Class Academics: Precarity and Diversity in Academia* (Cham, CH: Palgrave Pivot, 2020), https://link.springer.com/book/10.1007/978-3-030-58352-1.
11. Seligman, *Is Graduate School Really for You?*
12. Calarco, *A Field Guide to Grad School.*
13. "How the Debt Snowball Method Works," Ramsey Solutions, May 3, 2023, https://www.ramseysolutions.com/debt/how-the-debt-snowball-method-works.

4. MAKING GRAD SCHOOL WORK FOR YOU

1. Ayelet Fishbach, *Get It Done: Surprising Lessons from the Science of Motivation* (New York: Little, Brown Spark, 2022).
2. Daniel H. Pink, *Drive: The Surprising Truth About What Motivates Us* (New York: Riverhead Books, 2011); Adam Grant, *Originals: How Non-Conformists Move the World*, ill. ed. (New York: Viking, 2016).
3. Daniel M. Wegner, David J. Schneider, Samuel R. Carter, and Teri L. White, "Paradoxical Effects of Thought Suppression," *Journal of Personality and Social Psychology* 53, no. 1 (1987): 5–13.
4. Leonard Cassuto, *The Graduate School Mess* (Cambridge, MA: Harvard University Press, 2015).
5. William Stixrud and Ned Johnson, *The Self-Driven Child: The Science and Sense of Giving Your Kids More Control Over Their Lives* (New York: Viking, 2018); Pink, *Drive*; Edward L. Deci, Richard Koestner, and Richard M. Ryan, "A Meta-Analytic Review of Experiments Examining the Effects of Extrinsic Rewards on Intrinsic Motivation," *Psychological Bulletin* 125, no. 6 (1999): 627.

6. Carol S. Dweck, *Mindset: The New Psychology of Success* (New York: Random House, 2006).
7. L. S. Vygotsky, *Mind in Society: The Development of Higher Psychological Processes* (Cambridge, MA: Harvard University Press, 1978).
8. Mihaly Csikszentmihalyi, *Flow: The Psychology of Optimal Experience* (New York: Harper and Row, 1990); Mihaly Csikszentmihalyi, *Finding Flow: The Psychology of Engagement with Everyday Life* (New York: Basic Books, 1997).
9. Peter Gray, *Free to Learn: Why Unleashing the Instinct to Play Will Make Our Children Happier, More Self-Reliant, and Better Students for Life* (New York: Basic Books, 2013).
10. James Carse, *Finite and Infinite Games* (New York: Free Press, 2011).
11. Daniel Greenberg, *Free at Last: The Sudbury Valley School* (Framingham, MA: Sudbury Valley School, 1995).
12. Kerry McDonald, *Unschooled: Raising Curious, Well-Educated Children Outside the Conventional Classroom* (Chicago: Chicago Review Press, 2019).
13. Sara, "Reading Doesn't Need to Be Taught: How Unschoolers Learn to Read," *Happiness Is Here* (blog), accessed November 10, 2019, https://happinessishereblog.com/reading-doesnt-need-taught-unschoolers-learn-read/.
14. Emily Oster, *Cribsheet: A Data-Driven Guide to Better, More Relaxed Parenting, from Birth to Preschool* (London: Penguin, 2019).
15. Christine Lui, "Imposter Syndrome Isn't the Problem—Toxic Workplaces Are," *Quartz*, May 23, 2018, https://qz.com/work/1286549/imposter-syndrome-lets-toxic-work-culture-off-the-hook/.
16. Dr. Zoë Ayres (@ZJAyres), "An Impostor Syndrome Printable...," Twitter, September 17, 2020, 8:11 a.m., https://twitter.com/ZJAyres/status/1306566378376359937.
17. Amanda I. Seligman, *Is Graduate School Really for You? The Whos, Whats, Hows, and Whys of Pursuing a Master's or Ph.D.* (Baltimore, MD: Johns Hopkins University Press, 2012).
18. Jessica McCrory Calarco, *A Field Guide to Grad School: Uncovering the Hidden Curriculum* (Princeton, NJ: Princeton University Press, 2020).

5. ADVISERS

1. David L. Brunsma, David G. Embrick, and Jean H. Shin, "Graduate Students of Color: Race, Racism, and Mentoring in the White Waters of Academia," *Sociology of Race and Ethnicity* 3, no. 1 (2017): 1–13; Sonia N. Young, William R. Vanwye, Mark A. Schafer, Troy A. Robertson, and Ashley Vincent Poore, "Factors Affecting PhD Student Success," *International Journal of Exercise Science* 12, no. 1 (2019): 34–45; Sarvenaz Sarabipour, Sarah J. Hainer, Feyza Nur Arslan, Charlotte M. de Winde, Emily Furlong, Natalia Bielczyk, Nafisa M. Jadavji, Aparna P. Shah, and Sejal Davla, "Building and Sustaining Mentor Interactions as a Mentee," *FEBS Journal* 289, no. 6 (2022): 1374–1384, https://doi.org/10.1111/febs.15823.
2. Jessica McCrory Calarco, *A Field Guide to Grad School: Uncovering the Hidden Curriculum* (Princeton, NJ: Princeton University Press, 2020).
3. Some of these questions are adapted from Andrew Kuznetsov, "Questions to Ask a Prospective Ph.D. Advisor on Visit Day, with Thorough and Forthright Explanations," *Machine*

Learning Blog, Carnegie Mellon University, March 2, 2020, https://blog.ml.cmu.edu/2020/03/02/questions-to-ask-a-prospective-ph-d-advisor-on-visit-day-with-thorough-and-forthright-explanations/.
4. John Long, email message to author, March 5, 2012.
5. Albert O. Hirschman, *Exit, Voice, and Loyalty: Responses to Decline in Firms, Organizations, and States* (Cambridge, MA: Harvard University Press, 1970); Adam Grant and Sheryl Sandberg, *Originals: How Non-Conformists Move the World*, ill. ed. (New York: Viking, 2016).
6. Chris Cramer, "My Advisor Is a Monster (What Do I Do?)," Supercomputing Institute, University of Minnesota, April 22, 2015, http://pollux.chem.umn.edu/ProblemAdvisors.html.
7. Chris Voss and Tahl Raz, *Never Split the Difference: Negotiating As If Your Life Depended On It* (New York: Harper Business, 2016). Lots of good advice can be found in the *Edge Newsletter*, put out by Voss's company and available at https://blog.blackswanltd.com/the-edge.
8. Grant and Sandberg, *Originals*.
9. Edward L. Deci and Richard M. Ryan, "Self-Determination Theory," *Handbook of Theories of Social Psychology* 1, no. 20 (2012): 416–436; Edward L. Deci and Richard M. Ryan, "Self-Determination Theory: When Mind Mediates Behavior," *Journal of Mind and Behavior* 1, no. 1 (1980): 33–43.
10. Amanda I. Seligman, *Is Graduate School Really for You? The Whos, Whats, Hows, and Whys of Pursuing a Master's or Ph.D.* (Baltimore, MD: Johns Hopkins University Press, 2012).

6. LABS, CLASSES, AND TEACHING

1. Jessica McCrory Calarco, *A Field Guide to Grad School: Uncovering the Hidden Curriculum* (Princeton, NJ: Princeton University Press, 2020).
2. Mario Luis Small, *Someone to Talk To* (New York: Oxford University Press, 2017), chap. 8.
3. Elisa J. Grant-Vallone and Ellen A. Ensher, "Effects of Peer Mentoring on Types of Mentor Support, Program Satisfaction and Graduate Student Stress." *Journal of College Student Development* 41, no. 6 (2000): 637-642; Diane L. Lorenzetti, Leah Shipton, Lorelli Nowell, Michele Jacobsen, Liza Lorenzetti, Tracey Clancy, and Elizabeth Oddone Paolucci, "A Systematic Review of Graduate Student Peer Mentorship in Academia," *Mentoring & Tutoring: Partnership in Learning* 27, no. 5 (2019): 549-576, https://doi.org/10.1080/13611267.2019.1686694.
4. Thanks to Deb Roy, who taught our cohort's PhD seminar that year, for the inspiring suggestion.
5. Amanda I. Seligman, *Is Graduate School Really for You? The Whos, Whats, Hows, and Whys of Pursuing a Master's or Ph.D.* (Baltimore, MD: Johns Hopkins University Press, 2012).
6. Keith J. Topping, "Trends in Peer Learning," *Educational Psychology* 25, no. 6 (2005): 631-645.
7. Seligman, *Is Graduate School Really for You?*

8. Ayelet Fishback, *Get It Done: Surprising Lessons from the Science of Motivation* (New York: Little, Brown Spark, 2022).
9. Rob Johnson, Anthony Watkinson, and Michael Mabe, *The STM Report, 5th Edition: An Overview of Scientific and Scholarly Publishing 1968–2018* (The Hague: International Association of Scientific, Technical and Medical Publishers, 2018).
10. Arif Jinha, "Article 50 Million: An Estimate of the Number of Scholarly Articles in Existence," *Learned Publishing* 23, no. 3 (2010): 258-263, https://doi.org/10.1087/20100308.
11. Calarco, *A Field Guide to Grad School: Uncovering the Hidden Curriculum*.
12. John Biggs, "Aligning Teaching for Constructing Learning," *Higher Education Academy* 1, no. 4 (2003): 1-4; Grant P. Wiggins and Jay McTighe, *Understanding by Design*, 2nd ed. (Alexandria, VA: Association for Supervision and Curriculum Development, 2005).
13. Lorin W. Anderson and David R. Krathwohl, *A Taxonomy for Learning, Teaching, and Assessing: A Revision of Bloom's Taxonomy of Educational Objectives* (Boston: Longman, 2001); Benjamin Bloom, *Taxonomy of Educational Objectives: The Classification of Educational Goals* (New York: David McKay Co., 1956).
14. Scott Freeman, Sarah L. Eddy, Miles McDonough, Michelle K. Smith, Nnadozie Okoroafor, Hannah Jordt, and Mary Pat Wenderoth, "Active Learning Increases Student Performance in Science, Engineering, and Mathematics," *Proceedings of the National Academy of Sciences* 111, no. 23 (2014): 8410-8415; Carl E. Wieman, "Large-Scale Comparison of Science Teaching Methods Sends Clear Message," *Proceedings of the National Academy of Sciences* 111, no. 23 (2014): 8319-8320; Jana Hackathorn, Erin D. Solomon, Kate L. Blankmeyer, Rachel E. Tennial, and Amy M. Garczynski, "Learning by Doing: An Empirical Study of Active Teaching Techniques," *Journal of Effective Teaching* 11, no. 2 (2011): 40-54; Jeffrey S. Lantis, Kent J. Kille, and Matthew Krain, "Active Teaching and Learning: The State of the Literature," *Oxford Research Encyclopedia of International Studies*, March 1, 2010, https://doi.org/10.1093/acrefore/9780190846626.013.427.
15. Henri Lipmanowicz and Keith McCandless, *The Surprising Power of Liberating Structures: Simple Rules to Unleash a Culture of Innovation* (Seattle: Liberating Structures Press, 2013).
16. Therese Huston, *Teaching What You Don't Know* (Cambridge, MA: Harvard University Press, 2009); James M. Lang, *Small Teaching: Everyday Lessons from the Science of Learning* (Hoboken, NJ: John Wiley and Sons, 2021).
17. Judith M. Harackiewicz, Elizabeth A. Canning, Yoi Tibbetts, Cynthia J. Giffen, Seth S. Blair, Douglas I. Rouse, and Janet S. Hyde, "Closing the Social Class Achievement Gap for First-Generation Students in Undergraduate Biology," *Journal of Educational Psychology* 106, no. 2 (2014): 375.

7. RESEARCH, THESES, AND DISSERTATIONS

1. Jessica McCrory Calarco, *A Field Guide to Grad School: Uncovering the Hidden Curriculum* (Princeton, NJ: Princeton University Press, 2020).

2. Amanda I. Seligman, *Is Graduate School Really for You? The Whos, Whats, Hows, and Whys of Pursuing a Master's or Ph.D.* (Baltimore, MD: Johns Hopkins University Press, 2012).
3. Taylor Evans, "U-PhD-ate: Call Me Candidate," *Stylishly Taylored* (blog), November 10, 2019, https://www.stylishlytaylored.com/post/phdcandidate.
4. beckmw, "How Long Is the Average Dissertation?," *R Is My Friend* (blog), April 15, 2013, https://beckmw.wordpress.com/2013/04/15/how-long-is-the-average-dissertation/; beckmw, "Average Dissertation and Thesis Length, Take Two," *R Is My Friend* (blog), July 15, 2014, https://beckmw.wordpress.com/2014/07/15/average-dissertation-and-thesis-length-take-two/.
5. Leonard Cassuto, *The Graduate School Mess* (Cambridge, MA: Harvard University Press, 2015).
6. Vera John-Steiner, *Notebooks of the Mind: Explorations of Thinking* (Albuquerque: University of New Mexico Press, 1985).
7. Adam Grant, *Originals: How Non-Conformists Move the World*, ill. ed. (New York: Viking, 2016).
8. This is known as the Zeigarnik effect. While some replications of the original work failed, others have succeeded; the context of remembering, what counted as complete for any given task, as well as a person's motivation to remember or keep something active in mind all were relevant.
9. Here's a useful analysis of different databases: Alberto Martin-Martin, Enrique Orduna-Malea, Mike Thelwall, and Emilio Delgado-Lopez-Cozar, "Google Scholar, Web of Science, and Scopus: Which Is Best for Me?," *LSE Impact Blog*, December 3, 2019, https://blogs.lse.ac.uk/impactofsocialsciences/2019/12/03/google-scholar-web-of-science-and-scopus-which-is-best-for-me/.
10. Grant, *Originals*.
11. Bill Burnett and Dave Evans, *Designing Your Life: How to Build a Well-Lived, Joyful Life* (New York: Knopf, 2016), 38.
12. Mark De Rond and Alan N. Miller, "Publish or Perish: Bane or Boon of Academic Life?," *Journal of Management Inquiry* 14, no. 4 (2005): 321–329; Seema Rawat and Sanjay Meena, "Publish or Perish: Where Are We Heading?," *Journal of Research in Medical Sciences: The Official Journal of Isfahan University of Medical Sciences* 19, no. 2 (February 2014): 87–89.
13. Rob Johnson, Anthony Watkinson, and Michael Mabe, *The STM Report, 5th Edition: An Overview of Scientific and Scholarly Publishing 1968–2018* (The Hague: International Association of Scientific, Technical and Medical Publishers, 2018).
14. Arif Jinha, "Article 50 Million: An Estimate of the Number of Scholarly Articles in Existence," *Learned Publishing* 23, no. 3 (July 2010): 258–263, https://doi.org/10.1087/20100308.
15. "New Report Examines Reproducibility and Replicability in Science, Recommends Ways to Improve Transparency and Rigor in Research," National Academies of Sciences, Engineering, and Medicine, April 7, 2019, https://www.nationalacademies.org/news/2019/05/new-report-examines-reproducibility-and-replicability-in-science-recommends-ways-to-improve-transparency-and-rigor-in-research; Monya Baker, "Reproducibility Crisis,"

Nature 533, no. 26 (2016): 353-366; Daniele Fanelli, "Opinion: Is Science Really Facing a Reproducibility Crisis, and Do We Need It To?," *Proceedings of the National Academy of Sciences* 115, no. 11 (2018): 2628-2631; Bradford J. Wiggins and Cody D. Christopherson, "The Replication Crisis in Psychology: An Overview for Theoretical and Philosophical Psychology," *Journal of Theoretical and Philosophical Psychology* 39, no. 4 (2019): 202; Przemysław G. Hensel, "Reproducibility and Replicability Crisis: How Management Compares to Psychology and Economics—A Systematic Review of Literature," *European Management Journal* 39, no. 5 (2021): 577-594.

16. "What Is Preregistration?," Center for Open Science, accessed May 11, 2022, https://www.cos.io/initiatives/prereg; Brian A. Nosek, Charles E. Ebersole, Alexander C. DeHaven, and David T. Mellor, "The Preregistration Revolution," *Proceedings of the National Academy of Sciences* 115, no. 11 (2018): 2600-2606, https://www.pnas.org/doi/10.1073/pnas.1708274114.

17. Seligman, *Is Graduate School Really for You?*

8. MANAGING PROJECTS AND MANAGING TIME

1. As recommended by Jessica McCrory Calarco, *A Field Guide to Grad School: Uncovering the Hidden Curriculum* (Princeton, NJ: Princeton University Press, 2020).
2. Frederick Brooks Jr., *The Mythical Man-Month: Essays on Software Engineering*, anniv. ed. (Reading, MA: Addison-Wesley Professional, 1995).
3. Melinda Clark, Anthony Miller, Jamie Berry, and Ken Cheng, "Mental Contrasting with Implementation Intentions Increases Study Time for University Students," *British Journal of Educational Psychology* 91, no. 3 (2021): e12396, https://doi.org/10.1111/bjep.12396; Gabriele Oettingen, Heather Barry Kappes, Katie B. Guttenberg, and Peter M. Gollwitzer, "Self-Regulation of Time Management: Mental Contrasting with Implementation Intentions," *European Journal of Social Psychology* 45, no. 2 (2015): 218-229, https://doi.org/10.1002/ejsp.2090; Angela Lee Duckworth, Teri Kirby, Anton Gollwitzer, and Gabriele Oettingen, "From Fantasy to Action: Mental Contrasting with Implementation Intentions (MCII) Improves Academic Performance in Children," *Social Psychological and Personality Science* 4, no. 6 (2013): 745-753, https://doi.org/10.1177/1948550613476307; Angela Lee Duckworth, Heidi Grant, Benjamin Loew, Gabriele Oettingen, and Peter M. Gollwitzer, "Self-regulation Strategies Improve Self-discipline in Adolescents: Benefits of Mental Contrasting and Implementation Intentions," *Educational Psychology* 31, no. 1 (2011): 17-26, https://doi.org/10.1080/01443410.2010.506003.
4. Ayelet Fishbach, *Get It Done: Surprising Lessons from the Science of Motivation* (New York: Little, Brown Spark, 2022).
5. Nira Liberman and Yaacov Trope, "The Psychology of Transcending the Here and Now," *Science* 322, no. 5905 (2008): 1201-1205, https://doi.org/10.1126/science.1161958; Yaacov Trope and Nira Liberman, "Construal-Level Theory of Psychological Distance," *Psychological Review* 117, no. 2 (2010): 440-463, https://doi.org/10.1037/a0018963.

6. Bec Crew, "Here's How to Deal with Failure, Say Senior Scientists," *Nature Index*, July 5, 2019, https://www.natureindex.com/news-blog/how-to-deal-with-failure-rejection-academic-research-say-senior-scientists.
7. Cal Newport, *Deep Work: Rules for Focused Success in a Distracted World* (New York: Grand Central Publishing, 2016), 7.
8. Cal Newport, *The Time-Block Planner: A Daily Method for Deep Work in a Distracted World* (Edmonton, AB: Portfolio, 2020).
9. "The Pomodoro® Technique," Cirillo Consulting GmbH, accessed May 19, 2022, https://francescocirillo.com/products/the-pomodoro-technique.
10. Chris McChesney, Sean Covey, and Jim Huling, *The 4 Disciplines of Execution: Achieving Your Wildly Important Goals* (New York: Free Press, 2012); Newport, *Deep Work*.
11. Stever Robbins, "Tips for Mastering E-Mail Overload," HBS Working Knowledge, October 25, 2004, https://hbswk.hbs.edu/archive/tips-for-mastering-e-mail-overload.
12. Newport, *Deep Work*.
13. Newport.
14. Fuschia Sirois and Timothy Pychyl, "Procrastination and the Priority of Short-Term Mood Regulation: Consequences for Future Self," *Social and Personality Psychology Compass* 7, no. 2 (2013): 115-127; Piers Steel, "The Nature of Procrastination: A Meta-Analytic and Theoretical Review of Quintessential Self-Regulatory Failure," *Psychological Bulletin* 133, no. 1 (2007): 65.
15. Piers Steel, *The Procrastination Equation: How to Stop Putting Things Off and Start Getting Stuff Done* (New York: Harper Perennial, 2012).
16. Angela L. Duckworth, Katherine L. Milkman, and David Laibson, "Beyond Willpower: Strategies for Reducing Failures of Self-Control," *Psychological Science in the Public Interest* 19, no. 3 (2018): 102-129.
17. Erika L. Kirgios, Graelin H. Mandel, Yeji Park, Katherine L. Milkman, Dena M. Gromet, Joseph S. Kay, and Angela L. Duckworth, "Teaching Temptation Bundling to Boost Exercise: A Field Experiment," *Organizational Behavior and Human Decision Processes* 161, no. 1 (2020): 20-35; Katherine L. Milkman, Julia A. Minson, and Kevin G. M. Volpp, "Holding the Hunger Games Hostage at the Gym: An Evaluation of Temptation Bundling," *Management Science* 60, no. 2 (2014): 283-299.
18. Piers Steel, *The Procrastination Equation: How to Stop Putting Things Off and Start Getting Stuff Done*, 2nd ed. (New York: Pearson Life, 2012), 147.
19. Michael J. A. Wohl, Timothy A. Pychyl, and Shannon H. Bennett, "I Forgive Myself, Now I Can Study: How Self-Forgiveness for Procrastinating Can Reduce Future Procrastination," *Personality and Individual Differences* 48, no. 7 (2010): 803-808; Fuschia M. Sirois, "Procrastination and Stress: Exploring the Role of Self-Compassion," *Self and Identity* 13, no. 2 (2014): 128-145.
20. Fuschia Sirois and Timothy Pychyl, "Procrastination and the Priority of Short-Term Mood Regulation: Consequences for Future Self," *Social and Personality Psychology Compass* 7, no. 2 (2013): 115-127.

8. Managing Projects and Managing Time 267

21. Fishbach, *Get It Done*.
22. Yaacov Trope and Nira Liberman, "Construal-Level Theory of Psychological Distance," *Psychological Review* 117, no. 2 (2010): 440–463, https://doi.org/10.1037/a0018963.
23. Kirk Warren Brown, Richard M. Ryan, and J. David Creswell, "Addressing Fundamental Questions About Mindfulness," *Psychological Inquiry* 18, no. 4 (2007): 272–281; Nathaniel Elkins-Brown, Rimma Teper, and Michael Inzlicht, "How Mindfulness Enhances Self-Control," in *Mindfulness in Social Psychology*, ed. Johan C. Karremans and Esther K. Papies (New York: Routledge, 2017), 65–78.
24. Malte Friese, Julius Frankenbach, Veronika Job, and David D. Loschelder, "Does Self-Control Training Improve Self-Control? A Meta-Analysis," *Perspectives on Psychological Science* 12, no. 6 (2017): 1077–1099, https://doi.org/10.1177/1745691617697076; Mark Muraven, "Building Self-Control Strength: Practicing Self-Control Leads to Improved Self-Control Performance," *Journal of Experimental Social Psychology* 46, no. 2 (2010): 465–468, https://doi.org/10.1016/j.jesp.2009.12.011.
25. Peter Gray, "The Value of Play I: The Definition of Play Gives Insights," *Psychology Today*, November 19, 2008, https://www.psychologytoday.com/us/blog/freedom-learn/200811/the-value-play-i-the-definition-play-gives-insights.
26. "Theory," Center for Self-Determination Theory, accessed July 8, 2022, https://selfdeterminationtheory.org/theory/.
27. Thanks to this series of blog posts for articulating many of my feelings on the matter of "shoulds": Nate Soares, " 'Should' Considered Harmful," *Minding Our Way*, May 25, 2015, https://mindingourway.com/should-considered-harmful/.
28. Daniel H. Pink, *Drive: The Surprising Truth About What Motivates Us* (New York: Riverhead Books, 2011).
29. Mark R. Lepper, David Greene, and Richard E. Nisbett, "Undermining Children's Intrinsic Interest with Extrinsic Reward: A Test of the 'Overjustification' Hypothesis," *Journal of Personality and Social Psychology* 28, no. 1 (1973): 129–137, https://doi.org/10.1037/h0035519; Mark R. Lepper and David Greene, "Turning Play into Work: Effects of Adult Surveillance and Extrinsic Rewards on Children's Intrinsic Motivation," *Journal of Personality and Social Psychology* 31, no. 3 (1975): 479–486, https://doi.org/10.1037/h0076484; Mark R. Lepper, Mark Keavney, and Michael Drake, "Intrinsic Motivation and Extrinsic Rewards: A Commentary on Cameron and Pierce's Meta-Analysis," *Review of Educational Research* 66, no. 1 (1996): 5–32, https://doi.org/10.3102/00346543066001005.
30. Nathalie Tasler, "ADHD and Time Management," *Adventures in Academic Development* (blog), April 25, 2021, https://acdevadventures.blog/2021/04/25/time-management-myths/; Ari Tuckman, "ADHD Minds Are Trapped in Now (& Other Time Management Truths)," *ADDitude*, July 30, 2019, https://www.additudemag.com/time-management-skills-adhd-brain/; "Time Management and Productivity Advice for Adults with ADHD," *ADDitude*, accessed May 24, 2022, https://www.additudemag.com/category/manage-adhd-life/getting-things-done/time-productivity/.

9. YOUR WORK AND THE WORLD

1. Leonard Cassuto, *The Graduate School Mess* (Cambridge, MA: Harvard University Press, 2015). See especially the introduction, "In Search of a Usable Future."
2. Douglas P. Peters and Stephen J. Ceci, "Peer-Review Practices of Psychological Journals: The Fate of Published Articles, Submitted Again," *Behavioral and Brain Sciences* 5, no. 2 (June 1982): 187–195, https://doi.org/10.1017/S0140525X00011183; Richard Smith, "Classical Peer Review: An Empty Gun," *Breast Cancer Research* 12, no. S4 (2010): S13, https://doi.org/10.1186/bcr2742; Julia Belluz and Steven Hoffman, "Let's Stop Pretending Peer Review Works," *Vox*, December 7, 2015, https://www.vox.com/2015/12/7/9865086/peer-review-science-problems.
3. Mike Taylor, "The Ironies of Academic Publishing: The System Is Stupid and It's Time for a New Manifesto," *LSE Impact Blog*, July 26, 2012, https://blogs.lse.ac.uk/impactofsocialsciences/2012/07/26/ironies-academic-publishing-new-manifesto/; Devon Price, "Academic Publishing Is an Exploitative Farce," Medium, February 10, 2022, https://devonprice.medium.com/academic-publishing-is-an-exploitative-farce-b367ceadd3c5; Tim Crane, "The Peer Review Industry: Implausible and Outrageous," *TLS*, October 23, 2018, https://www.the-tls.co.uk/articles/peer-review-industry-implausible-outrageous-essay-tim-crane/; Samuel Gershman, "The Exploitative Economics of Academic Publishing," *Footnote*, March 18, 2014, https://footnote.co/the-exploitative-economics-of-academic-publishing.
4. To explore some of these publications, see the website of the Directory of Open Access Journals at https://doaj.org/.
5. http://whopayswriters.com/.
6. Peter J. Feibelman, *A PhD Is Not Enough! A Guide to Survival in Science* (New York: Basic Books, 2011).
7. Rainer Bäuerle, Christoph Schwarze, and Arnim von Stechow, *Meaning, Use, and Interpretation of Language* (Berlin: Walter de Gruyter, 2012).
8. Stephen King, *On Writing: A Memoir of the Craft* (London: Hodder and Stoughton, 2010). I first learned about the 10 percent cut from Brandon Sanderson on the *Writing Excuses* podcast. See "How Do I Make This Pretty?," November 15, 2015, in *Writing Excuses*, MP3 audio, 23:28, https://writingexcuses.com/writing-excuses-10-46-how-do-i-make-this-pretty/.
9. Christopher L. Caterine, *Leaving Academia: A Practical Guide* (Princeton, NJ: Princeton University Press, 2020).
10. Jacqueline Kory-Westlund, "The Words Aren't Right Yet: How Revision and Resubmission Led to Resilience," Jakory.com, June 28, 2020, https://jakory.com/blog/2020/words-arent-right-yet-paper-revision-resubmission-led-resilience/.
11. Tracy Kidder and Richard Todd, *Good Prose: The Art of Nonfiction* (New York: Random House Trade Paperbacks, 2013).
12. Kameron Hurley, "How Pro Writers Deal with Pro Criticism," Kameronhurley.com, July 13, 2017, https://www.kameronhurley.com/pro-writers-deal-pro-criticism/.

13. Steven R. Shaw, "How Not to Suck at Reviewing Articles for Scholarly Journals," *Research to Practice* (blog), July 4, 2015, https://researchtopracticeconnections.wordpress.com/2015/07/04/how-not-to-suck-at-reviewing-articles-for-scholarly-journals/.
14. Feibelman, *A PhD Is Not Enough!*
15. Alexandre Heeren, Grazia Ceschi, David P. Valentiner, Vincent Dethier, and Pierre Philippot, "Assessing Public Speaking Fear with the Short Form of the Personal Report of Confidence as a Speaker Scale: Confirmatory Factor Analyses Among a French-Speaking Community Sample," *Neuropsychiatric Disease and Treatment*, no. 9 (May 2013): 609-618, https://doi.org/10.2147/NDT.S43097.
16. Adam Grant, *Originals: How Non-Conformists Move the World*, ill. ed. (New York: Viking, 2016).

10. IT'S JUST GRAD SCHOOL

1. Chris Woolston, "PhDs: The Tortuous Truth," *Nature*, no. 575 (2019): 403-406, https://doi.org/10.1038/d41586-019-03459-7.
2. Amanda I. Seligman, *Is Graduate School Really for You? The Whos, Whats, Hows, and Whys of Pursuing a Master's or Ph.D.* (Baltimore, MD: Johns Hopkins University Press, 2012), see especially chap. 3.
3. Seligman, *Is Graduate School Really for You?*
4. Robert M. Sapolsky, *Why Zebras Don't Get Ulcers: The Acclaimed Guide to Stress, Stress-Related Diseases, and Coping*, 3rd ed. (New York: Macmillan, 2004).
5. "Data & Insights," Council of Graduate Schools, accessed August 11, 2023, https://cgsnet.org/data-insights/.
6. Cal Newport, *Deep Work: Rules for Focused Success in a Distracted World* (New York: Grand Central Publishing, 2016).
7. Keeren Sundara Rajoo, Daljit Singh Karam, and Mohd Zaki Abdullah, "The Physiological and Psychosocial Effects of Forest Therapy: A Systematic Review," *Urban Forestry & Urban Greening* 54 (October 2020): 126744, https://doi.org/10.1016/j.ufug.2020.126744.
8. Credit to Sonia Roberts for this helpful bit of advice.
9. Seligman, *Is Graduate School Really for You?*, 29.

11. RELATIONSHIPS AND FAMILY

1. Amanda I. Seligman, *Is Graduate School Really for You? The Whos, Whats, Hows, and Whys of Pursuing a Master's or Ph.D.* (Baltimore, MD: Johns Hopkins University Press, 2012).
2. Shari Wilson, "Love In (and Out of) Academe," *Inside Higher Ed*, November 28, 2005, https://www.insidehighered.com/views/2005/11/28/love-and-out-academe.
3. Tina Lasisi, "Harm Masquerading as Help: Isolation, Abuse, and Crisis in Grad School by Tina Lasisi," *Voices of Academia* (blog), October 8, 2021, https://voicesofacademia.com

/2021/10/08/harm-masquerading-as-help-isolation-abuse-and-crisis-in-grad-school-by-tina-lasisi/.
4. "Money Ruining Marriages in America: A Ramsey Solutions Study," Ramsey Solutions, February 6, 2018, https://www.ramseysolutions.com/company/newsroom/releases/money-ruining-marriages-in-america.
5. Chris Woolston, "PhDs: The Tortuous Truth," *Nature*, no. 575 (2019): 403–406, https://doi.org/10.1038/d41586-019-03459-7.
6. "Parenting Students' Experience and Challenges at UC," University of California Institutional Research and Academic Planning, January 2019, https://www.ucop.edu/institutional-research-academic-planning/_files/uc-parenting-students.pdf.
7. "What Is the Average Age of a Graduate Student?," Grad School Hub, last modified June 3, 2021, https://www.gradschoolhub.com/faqs/what-is-the-average-age-of-a-graduate-student/.
8. Kendall Powell, "Why Scientist-Mums in the United States Need Better Parental-Support Policies," *Nature*, no. 569 (2019): 149–151, https://doi.org/10.1038/d41586-019-01315-2.
9. Justin Wolfers, "A Family-Friendly Policy That's Friendliest to Male Professors," *New York Times*, June 24, 2016, https://www.nytimes.com/2016/06/26/business/tenure-extension-policies-that-put-women-at-a-disadvantage.html.
10. Allison C. Morgan, Samuel F. Way, Michael J. D. Hoefer, Daniel B. Larremore, Mirta Galesic, and Aaron Clauset, "The Unequal Impact of Parenthood in Academia," *Science Advances* 7, no. 9 (2021): eabd1996, https://www.science.org/doi/10.1126/sciadv.abd1996.
11. Stephanie Spies-Upton and Morgan Hill, "Perspectives on Parenting as a Graduate Student Amid the Pandemic," *The Gavel* (blog), APA Div. 18: Psychologists in Public Service, July 2021, https://www.apadivisions.org/division-18/publications/newsletters/gavel/2021/07/parenting-as-grad-student.
12. Ronke M. Olabisi, "The Pregnancy Drop: How Teaching Evaluations Penalize Pregnant Faculty," *Humanities and Social Sciences Communications* 8, no. 1 (2021): 1–10, https://doi.org/10.1057/s41599-021-00926-3.
13. Mary Ann Mason, "In the Ivory Tower, Men Only," *Slate*, June 17, 2013, https://slate.com/human-interest/2013/06/female-academics-pay-a-heavy-baby-penalty.html.
14. Shelley J. Correll, Stephen Benard, and In Paik, "Getting a Job: Is There a Motherhood Penalty?," *American Journal of Sociology* 112, no. 5 (2007): 1297–1338, https://doi.org/10.1086/511799.
15. The Pregnant Scholar (homepage), accessed June 16, 2022, https://thepregnantscholar.org/.
16. Nandini Pandey, "Not Bringing Home a Baby," Medium, August 22, 2019, https://eidolon.pub/not-bringing-home-a-baby-b6dc15a3701.
17. "Infertility," National Center for Health Statistics, Centers for Disease Control and Prevention, last modified December 7, 2022, https://www.cdc.gov/nchs/fastats/infertility.htm.
18. "Miscarriage," March of Dimes, accessed June 16, 2022, https://www.marchofdimes.org/complications/miscarriage.aspx.

12. MAINTAINING YOUR SENSE OF SELF

1. Amanda I. Seligman, *Is Graduate School Really for You? The Whos, Whats, Hows, and Whys of Pursuing a Master's or Ph.D.* (Baltimore, MD: Johns Hopkins University Press, 2012), xvii.
2. Bill Burnett and Dave Evans, *Designing Your Life: How to Build a Well-Lived, Joyful Life* (New York: Knopf, 2016).
3. Pew Research Center, *America's Changing Religious Landscape* (Washington, DC: Pew Research Center, 2015), https://www.pewresearch.org/religion/wp-content/uploads/sites/7/2015/05/RLS-08-26-full-report.pdf.
4. David DeSteno, *How God Works: The Science Behind the Benefits of Religion* (New York: Simon & Schuster, 2021).
5. National Science Foundation, *2016 Doctorate Recipients from U.S. Universities* (Alexandria, VA: National Science Foundation, 2018), https://www.nsf.gov/statistics/2018/nsf18304/static/report/nsf18304-report.pdf.
6. "Graduate Degree Fields," National Center for Education Statistics, May 2023, https://nces.ed.gov/programs/coe/indicator/ctb.
7. Nancy Padilla-Coreano, "Five Ways I Navigated Grad School as a Minority," Neuronline, January 23, 2019, https://neuronline.sfn.org/professional-development/five-ways-i-navigated-grad-school-as-a-minority.
8. David L. Brunsma, David G. Embrick, and Jean H. Shin, "Graduate Students of Color: Race, Racism, and Mentoring in the White Waters of Academia," *Sociology of Race and Ethnicity* 3, no. 1 (2017): 1–13; Kimberly A. Truong, Samuel D. Museus, and Keon M. McGuire, "Vicarious Racism: A Qualitative Analysis of Experiences with Secondhand Racism in Graduate Education," *International Journal of Qualitative Studies in Education* 29, no. 2 (2016): 224–247.

13. MAKING CHANGES TO YOUR SCHOOL

1. Adam Grant, *Originals: How Non-Conformists Move the World*, ill. ed. (New York: Viking, 2016).
2. Leonard Cassuto, *The Graduate School Mess* (Cambridge, MA: Harvard University Press, 2015), 16.
3. Robert A. Rhoads and Gary Rhoades, "Graduate Employee Unionization as Symbol of and Challenge to the Corporatization of U.S. Research Universities," *Journal of Higher Education* 76, no. 3 (2005): 243–275, https://doi.org/10.1080/00221546.2005.11772282.
4. Abby Jackson, "America's Most Elite Colleges Have Joined Forces to Bust a Union," *Business Insider*, March 2, 2016, https://www.businessinsider.com/nine-elite-universities-filed-an-amicus-brief-against-allowing-graduate-students-the-ability-to-unionize-2016-3; Alana Semuels, "Will Grad Students Lose the Right to Unionize Under Trump?," *The Atlantic*, June 28, 2017, https://www.theatlantic.com/business/archive/2017/06/graduate-students-unions/531975/.

5. Sean Rogers, Adrienne E. Eaton, and Paula B. Voos, "Effects of Unionization on Graduate Student Employees: Faculty-Student Relations, Academic Freedom, and Pay," ILRReview 66, no. 2 (2013): 487–510, https://ecommons.cornell.edu/handle/1813/71794.
6. Cara Chang and Meimei Xu, "'Our Success or Failure Is Tied Together': Grad Student Union Activism Picks Up in Biden Era," Harvard Crimson, April 12, 2021, https://www.thecrimson.com/article/2021/4/12/grad-union-solidarity/.
7. Julie R. Posselt, *Inside Graduate Admissions: Merit, Diversity, and Faculty Gatekeeping* (Cambridge, MA: Harvard University Press, 2016).
8. Julie R. Posselt, *Inside Graduate Admissions: Merit, Diversity, and Faculty Gatekeeping* (Cambridge, MA: Harvard University Press, 2016).
9. Walter G. Ecton and Shaun M. Dougherty, "Focus on Finances to Promote Doctoral Student Diversity," Brookings Institution, October 18, 2021, https://www.brookings.edu/blog/brown-center-chalkboard/2021/10/18/focus-on-finances-to-promote-doctoral-student-diversity/; Walter G. Ecton, Christopher T. Bennett, H. Kenny Nienhusser, Milagros Castillo-Montoya, and Shaun M. Dougherty, "If You Fund Them, Will They Come? Implications From a PhD Fellowship Program on Racial/Ethnic Student Diversity," *AERA Open* 7 (January 2021): 23328584211040484, https://doi.org/10.1177/23328584211040485.
10. Sonia N. Young, William R. Vanwye, Mark A. Schafer, Troy A. Robertson, and Ashley Vincent Poore, "Factors Affecting PhD Student Success," *International Journal of Exercise Science* 12, no. 1 (2019): 34–45; David L. Brunsma, David G. Embrick, and Jean H. Shin, "Graduate Students of Color: Race, Racism, and Mentoring in the White Waters of Academia," *Sociology of Race and Ethnicity* 3, no. 1 (2017): 1–13.
11. Leonard Cassuto and Robert Weisbuch, *The New PhD: How to Build a Better Graduate Education* (Baltimore, MD: Johns Hopkins University Press, 2021).
12. Wendy Chu, Mackenzie J. Hart, Kristin N. Kirchner, Mariajosé J. Paton, and Conner J. Black, "Addressing Race and Diversity in Graduate Education: Practices from Student Activism," *Journal of Diversity in Higher Education* 15, no. 1 (2021): 7–11.
13. Cassuto and Weisbuch, *The New PhD*; Robert Weisbuch and Leonard Cassuto, *Reforming Doctoral Education, 1990 to 2015: Recent Initiatives and Future Prospects* (New York: Andrew W. Mellon Foundation, 2016); Leonard Cassuto, "Foreword," in *The Reimagined PhD: Navigating 21st Century Humanities Education*, ed. Leanne M. Horinko, Jordan M. Reed, and James M. Van Wyck (New Brunswick, NJ: Rutgers University Press, 2021), i–ii; Cassuto, "The Graduate School Mess."
14. Susan Basalla and Maggie Debelius, *"So What Are You Going to Do with That?" Finding Careers Outside Academia*, 3rd ed. (Chicago: University of Chicago Press, 2014).
15. Stephen J. Dubner, "The True Story of the Gender Pay Gap," January 7, 2016, in *Freakonomics*, produced by Greg Rosalsky, podcast, MP3 audio, 43:27, https://freakonomics.com/podcast/the-true-story-of-the-gender-pay-gap/.
16. Jane Miller and Amy Adkins, "Kids Are a Company's Greatest Competition," *Business Journal* (blog), Gallup, October 5, 2016, https://news.gallup.com/businessjournal/196058/kids-company-greatest-competition.aspx.

17. See, for example, Ellie Harrison, Siobhan O'Brien, and Tiffany Taylor, "Breaking Barriers for Women: How to Build Effective Parental Leave," *Times Higher Education*, May 26, 2022, https://www.timeshighereducation.com/campus/breaking-barriers-women-how-build-effective-parental-leave; Kendall Powell, "Why Scientist-Mums in the United States Need Better Parental-Support Policies," *Nature* 569, no. 7754 (2019): 149–151, https://doi.org/10.1038/d41586-019-01315-2.
18. Rebecca G. Mirick and Stephanie P. Wladkowski, "Making It Work: Pregnant and Parenting Doctoral Students' Attributions of Persistence," *Advances in Social Work* 19, no. 2 (2019): 349–368, https://doi.org/10.18060/23220.
19. Mimi Kirk, "The Latest Trend in Co-working: Child Care," *Bloomberg*, March 27, 2019, https://www.bloomberg.com/news/articles/2019-03-27/co-working-spaces-for-parents-offer-child-care-too.
20. Lisa Feldman Barrett, "The Publication Arms Race," *APS Observer* 32, no. 7 (2019), https://www.psychologicalscience.org/observer/the-publications-arms-race; Laura McKenna, "How Hard Do Professors Actually Work?," *The Atlantic*, February 7, 2018, https://www.theatlantic.com/education/archive/2018/02/how-hard-do-professors-actually-work/552698/; Jessica McCrory Calarco, *A Field Guide to Grad School: Uncovering the Hidden Curriculum* (Princeton, NJ: Princeton University Press, 2020); Michael John Bartlett, Feyza Nur Arslan, Adriana Bankston, and Sarvenaz Sarabipour, "Ten Simple Rules to Improve Academic Work-Life Balance," *PLOS Computational Biology* 17, no. 7 (2021): e1009124, https://doi.org/10.1371/journal.pcbi.1009124.
21. Feldman Barrett, "The Publication Arms Race."
22. The websites of the Ronin Institute and the Institute for Globally Distributed Open Research and Education are, respectively, at https://ronininstitute.org/ and https://igdore.org/.
23. Laura Malisheski, "Part-Time Science in Perspective," *Science*, December 7, 2007, https://www.science.org/content/article/part-time-science-perspective.

Resources

LIFE PLANNING

Books on Careers and Life Design

Berdahl, Loleen, and Jonathan Malloy. *Work Your Career: Get What You Want from Your Social Sciences or Humanities PhD*. Toronto: University of Toronto Press, 2018.

Blake, Jenny. *Pivot: The Only Move That Matters Is Your Next One*. New York: Penguin, 2017. How to decide what to do next.

Bridges, William. *Transitions: Making Sense of Life's Changes*. Boston: Da Capo Lifelong Books, 2004. Psychological process of transition, not simply a change. Only way out is through.

Brown, Brené. *Braving the Wilderness: The Quest for True Belonging and the Courage to Stand Alone*. New York: Random House, 2017.

Burnett, Bill, and Dave Evans. *Designing Your Life: How to Build a Well-Lived, Joyful Life*. New York: Knopf, 2016.

Seligman, Martin E. P. *Flourish: A Visionary New Understanding of Happiness and Well-Being*. New York: Atria Books, 2011.

Podcasts and Videos About Academic Life and Life Planning

Dear Grad Student: http://deargradstudent.buzzsprout.com/.
The Effort Report: https://effortreport.libsyn.com/.
The Professor Is In: https://theprofessorisin.com/podcast/.
Secret Life of a Grad Student: https://secretlifeofagradu.wixsite.com/home.
You've Got This: https://www.drkatielinder.com/ygt/.
Martin Seligman, "Flourishing—a New Understanding of Wellbeing": https://www.youtube.com/watch?v=eoLbwEVnfJA.

Strengths, Values, and Personality

Authentic Happiness Questionnaire Center: https://www.authentichappiness.sas.upenn.edu/testcenter. Includes questionnaires about happiness, character strengths, grit, flourishing, and more.

CliftonStrengths assessment: https://www.gallup.com/cliftonstrengths/en/252137/home.aspx. Get the book from a library to read about strengths; pay for the test if you like.

Personality tests such as the Myers-Briggs Type Indicator, the Jersey Temperament Sorter, and the Big 5 Personality Index can give you insight into how you work best.

Podcasts, Videos, and Websites About Career Options for Academics

AltAcChats YouTube channel: https://www.youtube.com/channel/UC5ZxeDDSE4WPzFNqxJYGJQg/about.

Careers in Your Ears: https://anchor.fm/careersinyourears.

Cheeky Scientist: https://cheekyscientist.com/podcasts/cheeky-scientist-radio/.

Hub&Spoken, episode 135: "Lessons on Moving from Academia into Industry," https://www.youtube.com/watch?v=CCsjPMDGrrA.

PhD Career Stories: https://phdcareerstories.com/.

Recovering Academic: https://recoveringacademic.net/.

Roots to STEM Podcast: https://podcasts.apple.com/us/podcast/roots-to-stem-podcast/id1542318998.

Self-Compassionate Professor: https://danielledelamare.com/?page_id=375.

STEMulating Conversations with Dr. Q: http://stemulatingconvo.libsyn.com/.

What Are You Going to Do with That?: https://podcasts.apple.com/us/podcast/what-are-you-going-to-do-with-that/id1613578382.

Leaving Academia

General Books on Leaving Academia

Basalla, Susan, and Maggie Debelius. *"So What Are You Going to Do with That?" Finding Careers Outside Academia*. 3rd ed. Chicago: University of Chicago Press, 2014.

Bolles, Richard N., and Katharine Brooks. *What Color Is Your Parachute? 2021: Your Guide to a Lifetime of Meaningful Work and Career Success*. Berkeley, CA: Ten Speed Press, 2020.

Brooks, Katharine. *You Majored in What? Designing Your Path from College to Career*. New York: Plume, 2009.

Caterine, Christopher L. *Leaving Academia: A Practical Guide*. Princeton, NJ: Princeton University Press, 2020.

Fruscione, Joseph, and Kelly J. Baker, eds. *Succeeding Outside the Academy: Career Paths Beyond the Humanities, Social Sciences, and STEM*. Lawrence: University Press of Kansas, 2018.

Kelly, Kevin, Kathryn E. Linder, Thomas J. Tobin, and Joshua Kim. *Going Alt-Ac: A Guide to Alternative Academic Careers*. Sterling, VA: Stylus Publishing, 2020.

Kelsky, Karen. *The Professor Is In: The Essential Guide to Turning Your Ph.D. into a Job*. Ill. ed. New York: Crown, 2015.

Miller, Kathleen, Julie Chmiel, Lauren Whitehead, and Jet, eds. *Moving On: Essays on the Aftermath of Leaving Academia*. Self-published, Amazon Digital Services, 2014. Kindle.

Peabody, Rebecca. *The Unruly PhD: Doubts, Detours, Departures, and Other Success Stories*. London: Palgrave Macmillan, 2016.

Pryal, Katie Rose Guest. *The Freelance Academic: Transform Your Creative Life and Career*. Chapel Hill, NC: Blue Crow Books, 2019.

Books for STEM Fields

Abou-Chahine, Fawzi. *A Jobseeker's Diary: Unlocking Employment Secrets*. Self-published, Chahine Communications, 2021.

Bielczyk, Natalia. *What Is Out There for Me? The Landscape of Post-PhD Career Tracks*. Self-published, Welcome Solutions, 2019.

Gallagher, Ashleigh H., and M. Patrick Gallagher. *The Portable PhD: Taking Your Psychology Career Beyond Academia*. Washington, DC: American Psychological Association, 2020.

Giltner, David M. *Turning Science into Things People Need: Voices of Scientists Working in Industry*. Denver, CO: Wise Media Group, 2017.

Janssen, Kaaren, and Richard Sever, eds. *Career Options for Biomedical Scientists*. Ill. ed. Cold Spring Harbor, New York: Cold Spring Harbor Laboratory Press, 2014.

Nelson, M. R. *Navigating the Path to Industry: A Hiring Manager's Advice for Academics Looking for a Job in Industry*. Middletown, DE: Annorlunda Books, 2014.

Sinche, Melanie V. *Next Gen PhD: A Guide to Career Paths in Science*. Repr. ed. Cambridge, MA: Harvard University Press, 2018.

Books for Social Sciences and Humanities

Rogers, Katina L. *Putting the Humanities PhD to Work: Thriving in and Beyond the Classroom*. Durham, NC: Duke University Press Books, 2020.

Trester, Anna Marie. *Bringing Linguistics to Work: A Story Listening, Story Finding, and Story Telling Approach to Your Career*. Morrisville, NC: Lulu Publishing, 2017.

Urban, Jennifer Brown, and Miriam R. Linver, eds. *Building a Career Outside Academia: A Guide for Doctoral Students in the Behavioral and Social Sciences*. Washington, DC: American Psychological Association, 2018.

Resumes and the Job Search

Jellison, Jerald M. *Life After Grad School: Getting from A to B.* New York: Oxford University Press, 2010.

Klaus, Peggy. *Brag! The Art of Tooting Your Own Horn Without Blowing It.* Brentwood, TN: Warner Business Books, 2008. Useful on talking about yourself.

Polk, Jennifer, and L. Maren Wood. "Powering Up Your Résumé for a Nonfaculty Job Search." *Inside Higher Ed*, October 18, 2018. https://www.insidehighered.com/advice/2018/10/18/tips-improving-your-r%C3%A9sum%C3%A9-alt-ac-position-opinion.

Wendleton, Kate. *Through the Brick Wall: How to Job-Hunt in a Tight Market.* New York: Random House, 1992.

Whitcomb, Susan Britton. *Resume Magic: Trade Secrets of a Professional Resume Writer.* 2nd ed. Indianapolis, IN: Jist Works, 2003.

Communities of Former Academics and Resources for Exploring Careers

Beyond the Professoriate: https://beyondprof.com.
Free the PhD: https://www.freethephd.com/.
From PhD to Life: https://fromphdtolife.com/.
Jobs on Toast: http://jobsontoast.com/.
The Professor Is In: https://theprofessorisin.com/.
Roostervane: https://roostervane.com/.
The Versatile PhD: https://versatilephd.com/.

Finding Jobs

80,000 Hours career planning: https://80000hours.org/.
Imagine PhD career exploration tool: https://www.imaginephd.com/.
MyIDP science career planning tool: https://myidp.sciencecareers.org/.
Impact Opportunity lists jobs with nonprofits and foundations: https://impactopportunity.org/jobs/.
USA Jobs lists internships and jobs with the federal government: https://www.usajobs.gov/.
On Think Tanks lists various think tanks, and includes job postings: https://onthinktanks.org/jobs/.
The New York Foundation for the Arts lists jobs and internships in the arts: https://www.nyfa.org/jobs/.
The Association of Independent Research Institutes has information on individual organizations and institutes—including some internship or job opportunities—such as the Smithsonian,

National Institute of Standards and Technology, the National Institutes of Health, the National Science Foundation, the National Endowment for the Humanities, research centers such as Pew and Gallup, and independent research centers: https://www.airi.org/.

A Guide to Careers in Science Policy: https://ccst.us/wp-content/uploads/CCST-Alumni-Science-Policy-Career-Guide-Feb-2020.pdf.

Many university career centers list free resources on their websites; check yours, and check others. too: search "university career resources" online.

Use job sites and social media, such as LinkedIn, Career Builder, and ZipRecruiter.

Academic Careers

Books on the Academic Job Search

Cahn, Steven, and Catharine R. Stimpson. *From Student to Scholar: A Candid Guide to Becoming a Professor.* New York: Columbia University Press, 2008.

Heiberger, Mary Morris, Julia Miller Vick, Jennifer S. Furlong, and Rosanne Lurie. *The Academic Job Search Handbook.* 5th ed. Philadelphia: University of Pennsylvania Press, 2016.

Hutchinson, Hillary, and Mary Beth Averill. *Scaling the Ivory Tower: Your Academic Job Search Workbook.* Self-published, 2020.

Semenza, Gregory Colon, and Greg M. Colon Semenza. *Graduate Study for the Twenty-First Century: How to Build an Academic Career in the Humanities.* New York: Palgrave Macmillan, 2005.

Articles About Doing a Postdoc

Bodewits, Karin. "Three Bad Reasons to Do a Postdoc." *Science*, February 10, 2020. https://www.science.org/content/article/three-bad-reasons-do-postdoc.

Langin, Katie. "Want to Avoid a 'Default Postdoc?' Try an Internship." *Science*, May 7, 2018. https://www.science.org/content/article/want-avoid-default-postdoc-try-internship.

Powell, Devin. "The Price of Doing a Postdoc." *Science*, January 10, 2017. https://www.science.org/content/article/price-doing-postdoc.

Articles About Academic Job Searches and Academic Careers

Nagpal, Radhika. "The Awesomest 7-Year Postdoc or: How I Learned to Stop Worrying and Love the Tenure-Track Faculty Life." *Guest Blog, Scientific American*, July 21, 2013. https://blogs.scientificamerican.com/guest-blog/the-awesomest-7-year-postdoc-or-how-i-learned-to-stop-worrying-and-love-the-tenure-track-faculty-life/.

Sura, Shayna A., Lauren L. Smith, Monique R. Ambrose, C. Eduardo Guerra Amorim, Annabel C. Beichman, Ana C. R. Gomez, Mark Juhn, Gaurav S. Kandlikar, Julie S. Miller, Jazlyn Mooney, Riley O. Mummah, Kirk E. Lohmueller, and James O. Lloyd-Smith. "Ten Simple Rules for Giving an Effective Academic Job Talk." *PLOS Computational Biology* 15, no. 7 (2019): e1007163. https://doi.org/10.1371/journal.pcbi.1007163.

Books on the Tenure Track

Brennan, Jason. *Good Work If You Can Get It: How to Succeed in Academia*. 4th ed. Baltimore, MD: Johns Hopkins University Press, 2020.

Gasman, Marybeth. *Candid Advice for New Faculty Members: A Guide to Getting Tenure and Advancing Your Academic Career*. Gorham, ME: Myers Education Press, 2021.

James, Russell. *Tenure Hacks: The 12 Secrets of Making Tenure*. Self-published, CreateSpace Independent Publishing Platform, 2014.

Lang, James M. *Life on the Tenure Track: Lessons from the First Year*. Annot. ed. Baltimore, MD: Johns Hopkins University Press, 2005.

Perlmutter, David D. *Promotion and Tenure Confidential:* Cambridge, MA: Harvard University Press, 2010.

Rockquemore, Kerry Ann, and Tracey Laszloffy. *The Black Academic's Guide to Winning Tenure—Without Losing Your Soul*. Boulder, CO: Lynne Rienner Publishers, 2008.

Finding an Academic Job

AAAS Science Careers: https://jobs.sciencecareers.org/jobs/.
Academic Keys: https://www.academickeys.com/.
AGU Career Center: https://findajob.agu.org/.
Chronicle of Higher Ed: https://jobs.chronicle.com/jobs/.
FindAPhD: https://www.findaphd.com/.
HigherEdJobs: https://www.higheredjobs.com/.
Jobrxiv: https://jobrxiv.org/.
Nature Careers: https://www.nature.com/naturecareers.
ResearchGate: https://www.researchgate.net/.
Scholarshipdb.net: https://scholarshipdb.net/.

For online job postings in higher education, websites for finding postdocs, and so on, browse https://jobs.sciencecareers.org/ careers.

There may be field-specific sites and listservs too, such as https://www.epimonitor.net/ in epidemiology and https://bioloxy.com/ in biology.

There are other sites if you're job seeking outside the United States, such as Euraxess in Europe (https://euraxess.ec.europa.eu/) and Jobs.ac.uk in the United Kingdom (https://www.jobs.ac.uk/).

On Twitter, try the hashtags #phdopps and #postdocopps; check accounts like @postdocpal, @thepostdoctoral, and @PostdocO.

ACADEMIC SOCIAL MEDIA

If you'd like to ask for advice, people are your best resources. Besides asking folks local to you (e.g., in your lab, cohort, department, or school), ask online. There are academic communities on Twitter, LinkedIn, Facebook, Bluesky, Mastodon, and probably every other social media platform.

- Try these hashtags: #AcademicTwitter, #AcademicChatter, #PhDlife, #gradschool, #GradLife, #phdlife, #PhDchat, #PhDVoice, #AcademicVoices, #OpenAcademics, and #Momademia
- Find sub-communities, such as #scicomm for science communication, or #BlackinX and @BlackinXNetwork, or #VanguardSTEM for women of color in STEM
- A few good academic accounts: @AcademicChatter, @thoughtsofaphd, @OpenAcademics, @PhDVoice, @HappyResearchers, @academicvoices, @PhDBalance
- Some have associated websites, such as Open Academics (https://www.oacommunity.org/), Voices of Academia (https://voicesofacademia.com/), Vanguard STEM (https://www.vanguardstem.com/), and PhDBalance (https://www.phdbalance.com/)
- Daniel Quintana's Twitter for Scientists website offers a lot of great advice for how to navigate that online forum: https://t4scientists.com/.

Memoirs and Novels About Grad School

Cornthwaite, Christopher. *Doctoring: Building a Life with a PhD*. Self-published, 2020.

Fedunkiw, M. P. *A Degree of Futility*. Altona, MB: FriesenPress, 2014.

Harad, Alyssa. *Coming to My Senses: A Story of Perfume, Pleasure, and an Unlikely Bride*. Repr. ed. New York: Penguin Books, 2012.

Neff, Rachel. *Chasing Chickens: When Life After Higher Education Doesn't Go the Way You Planned*. Lawrence: University Press of Kansas, 2019.

Snyder, Don J. *The Cliff Walk: A Memoir of a Job Lost and a Life Found*. Boston: Little, Brown and Company, 2014.

MONEY

Budgeting, Side Hustles, Dealing with Debt

Altmix, Matt. "Different Approaches to Budgeting—Episode 176." *How to Money* (blog), March 18, 2020. https://www.howtomoney.com/different-approaches-to-budgeting/.

Barret, Lauren. "Grad School ROI Calculator: Is Graduate School Worth It?" *Money Under 30*, last modified September 5, 2023. https://www.moneyunder30.com/is-graduate-school-worth-the-cost.

Ramsey, Dave. *The Total Money Makeover: Classic Edition: A Proven Plan for Financial Fitness.* Nashville, TN: Thomas Nelson, 2013.

Personal Finance for PhDs (includes a podcast!): http://pfforphds.com/.

You Need a Budget: https://www.youneedabudget.com/.

Twitter thread of academics explaining their side hustles: https://twitter.com/sophiaupshaw/status/1274042697322545152.

Understanding Money

DeMarco, M. J. *The Millionaire Fastlane: Crack the Code to Wealth and Live Rich for a Lifetime.* Phoenix, AZ: Viperion Publishing, 2011.

Kiyosaki, Robert T. *Rich Dad Poor Dad: What the Rich Teach Their Kids About Money That the Poor and Middle Class Do Not!* 2nd ed. Scottsdale, AZ: Plata Publishing, 2017.

Mr. Money Mustache: https://www.mrmoneymustache.com/.

The Motley Fool: https://www.fool.com/.

Primers on Investing

Feroldi, Brian. *Why Does the Stock Market Go Up? Everything You Should Have Been Taught About Investing in School, But Weren't.* Glen Allen, VA: Choose Fi Media, 2022.

Maggiulli, Nick. *Just Keep Buying: Proven Ways to Save Money and Build Your Wealth.* New York: HarperBusiness, 2022.

Budgeting Tools

Clarity Money: https://claritymoney.com/.

EveryDollar: https://www.ramseysolutions.com/ramseyplus/everydollar.

Gnucash accounting software: https://www.gnucash.org/.

Goodbudget: https://goodbudget.com/.
Mint: https://mint.intuit.com/.
YNAB: https://www.ynab.com/our-app-lineup/.

Finding Fellowships and Scholarships

- UCLA GRAPES database: https://grad.ucla.edu/funding/#/.
- Unigo: https://www.unigo.com/.
- Fastweb: https://www.fastweb.com/.
- Go Grad: https://www.gograd.org/financial-aid/scholarships/.
- Sallie Mae Grad school scholarship search: https://www.salliemae.com/student-loans/graduate-school-information/graduate-school-scholarships/.
- A list of over three hundred postdoctoral fellowships in STEM, medicine, humanities, social sciences from the Office of the Vice Provost for Research at Johns Hopkins University: https://research.jhu.edu/rdt/funding-opportunities/postdoctoral/.

Ask admins or professors in your department about internal lists of grants or fellowships; some universities keep a webpage with current opportunities.

Look at the CVs of more advanced grad students, postdocs, and professors in your field to see what fellowships and awards they've received.

Professional organizations in your field may have funding opportunities. For example, the Association for Women in Science has awards for graduate students and early career scholars.

Writing Research Proposals and Grants

Coley, Soraya M., Cynthia A. Scheinberg, and Yulia A. Levites Strekalova. *Proposal Writing: Effective Grantsmanship for Funding*. 6th ed. Los Angeles: SAGE, 2021.

Crawley, Gerard M., and Eoin O'Sullivan. *The Grant Writer's Handbook: How to Write a Research Proposal and Succeed*. London: Imperial College Press, 2015.

Gerin, William, Christine Kapelewski Kinkade, and Niki L. Page. *Writing the NIH Grant Proposal: A Step-by-Step Guide*. 3rd ed. Thousand Oaks, CA: SAGE, 2017.

Hall, Mary S., and Susan Howlett. *Getting Funded: The Complete Guide to Writing Grant Proposals*. 4th ed. Portland: Portland State University, Extended Studies, Continuing Education Press, 2003.

Karsh, Ellen, and Arlen Sue Fox. *The Only Grant-Writing Book You'll Ever Need*. 5th ed. New York: Basic Books, 2019.

Li, Ping, and Karen Marrongelle. *Having Success with NSF: A Practical Guide*. Hoboken, NJ: Wiley-Blackwell, 2012.

Schimel, Joshua. *Writing Science: How to Write Papers That Get Cited and Proposals That Get Funded*. Ill. ed. Oxford: Oxford University Press, 2011.

Teitel, Martin. *"Thank You for Submitting Your Proposal": A Foundation Director Reveals What Happens Next*. Medfield, MA: Emerson and Church Publishers, 2006.

Many people share their fellowships application materials online—for example, you can find my own NSF GFRP materials at https://jakory.com/resources/nsf-grfp-application-materials/.

NEGOTIATION, DECIDING ON YES, AND SAYING NO

Breitman, Patti, and Richard Carlson. *How to Say No Without Feeling Guilty: And Say Yes to More Time, and What Matters Most to You*. New York: Harmony, 2001.

Camp, Jim. *Start with NO . . . The Negotiating Tools That the Pros Don't Want You to Know*. New York: Currency, 2002.

Cloud, Henry, and John Townsend. *Boundaries Updated and Expanded Edition: When to Say Yes, How to Say No to Take Control of Your Life*. Grand Rapids, MI: Zondervan, 2017.

McKeown, G. *Essentialism: The Disciplined Pursuit of Less*. New York: Currency, 2014.

Stone, Douglas, Bruce Patton, Sheila Heen, and Roger Fisher. *Difficult Conversations: How to Discuss What Matters Most*. Anniv. ed. New York: Penguin Books, 2010.

Voss, Chris, and Tahl Raz. *Never Split the Difference: Negotiating as If Your Life Depended on It*. New York: HarperBusiness, 2016.

Voss's company, the Black Swan Group, also maintains a weekly blog full of negotiation tips and tactics: https://blog.blackswanltd.com/the-edge.

StarterStory.com provides templates for how to politely say no to all kinds of requests: https://www.starterstory.com/how-to-say-no.

Advisers

Bramson, Robert M. *Coping with Difficult People: The Proven-Effective Battle Plan that Has Helped Millions Deal with the Troublemakers in Their Lives at Home and at Work*. New York: Dell, 2012.

Cramer, Chris. "My Advisor Is a Monster (What Do I Do?)." Chemistry, University of Minnesota, April 22, 2015. http://pollux.chem.umn.edu/ProblemAdvisors.html.

Feamster, Nick. "Managing Your Advisor." *How to Do Great Research* (blog), August 14, 2013. https://greatresearch.org/2013/08/14/managing-your-advisor/.

LEARNING MIND-SET: CURIOSITY, NATURAL LEARNING, MOTIVATION, PERSEVERANCE, FLOW

Coyle, Daniel. *The Talent Code: Greatness Isn't Born. It's Grown. Here's How.* New York: Bantam, 2009.

Csikszentmihalyi, Mihaly. *Flow: The Psychology of Optimal Experience.* New York: Harper and Row, 1990.

Duckworth, Angela. *Grit: The Power of Passion and Perseverance.* New York: Scribner, 2018.

Dweck, Carol S. *Mindset: The New Psychology of Success.* New York: Ballantine Books, 2007.

Dweck—The Growth Mindset: https://www.mindsetworks.com/science/.

Gatto, John T. *Dumbing Us Down: The Hidden Curriculum of Compulsory Schooling.* Gabriola Island, BC: New Society Publishers, 2017.

Gray, Peter. *Free to Learn: Why Unleashing the Instinct to Play Will Make Our Children Happier, More Self-Reliant, and Better Students for Life.* New York: Basic Books, 2015.

Greenberg, Daniel. *Free at Last: The Sudbury Valley School.* Framingham, MA: Sudbury Valley School Press, 1995.

Kohn, Alfie. *Punished By Rewards: The Trouble with Gold Stars, Incentive Plans, A's, Praise, and Other Bribes.* 25th anniv. ed. Boston: HarperOne, 2018.

Kotler, Steven. *The Rise of Superman: Decoding the Science of Ultimate Human Performance.* Boston: New Harvest, 2014.

McDonald, Kerry. *Unschooled: Raising Curious, Well-Educated Children Outside the Conventional Classroom.* Chicago: Chicago Review Press, 2019.

Pink, Daniel H. *Drive: The Surprising Truth About What Motivates Us.* New York: Riverhead Books, 2011.

Stixrud, William, and Ned Johnson, *The Self-Driven Child: The Science and Sense of Giving Your Kids More Control Over Their Lives.* Repr. ed. New York: Penguin Books, 2018.

RESEARCH SKILLS

Guides to Grad School

Batchelder, Edward, and John Palattella. *Real Guide to Grad School, 2001–2002: The Humanities.* New York: Contentville Press, 2001.

Bellemare, Marc F. *Doing Economics: What You Should Have Learned in Grad School—but Didn't.* Cambridge, MA: MIT Press, 2022.

Bloom, Dale F., Jonathan D. Karp, and Nicholas Cohen. *The Ph.D. Process: A Student's Guide to Graduate School in the Sciences.* New York: Oxford University Press, 1999.

Boynton, Petra M. *The Research Companion: A Practical Guide for Those in the Social Sciences, Health and Development.* 2nd ed. London: Routledge, 2016. https://doi.org/10.4324/9781315688909.

Brown, Gavin, ed. *How to Get Your PhD: A Handbook for the Journey*. New York: Oxford University Press, 2021.
Feibelman, Peter J. *A PhD Is Not Enough! A Guide to Survival in Science*. New York: Basic Books, 2011.
Grayson, Malika. *Hooded: A Black Girl's Guide to the Ph.D.* Atlanta: Malika Grayson, 2020.
Karp, Jason. *How to Survive Your PhD: The Insider's Guide to Avoiding Mistakes, Choosing the Right Program, Working with Professors, and Just How a Person Actually Writes a 200-Page Paper*. Naperville, IL: Sourcebooks, 2009.
Lantsoght, Eva O. L. *The A–Z of the PhD Trajectory*. Cham, CH: Springer, 2018. https://link.springer.com/book/10.1007/978-3-319-77425-1.
Petre, Marian, and Gordon Rugg. *The Unwritten Rules of PhD Research*. 2nd ed. Maidenhead, UK: Open University Press, 2010.
Shore, Zachary. *Grad School Essentials: A Crash Course in Scholarly Skills*. Oakland: University of California Press, 2016.

Websites Explaining Grad School Skills

Pat Thompson: https://patthomson.net/category/thesis/.
Raul Pacheco-Vega: http://www.raulpacheco.org/resources/ and https://twitter.com/raulpacheco/status/1266868032065896451.
Thesis Whisperer, Dr. Inger Mewburn: https://thesiswhisperer.com/useful-resources-for-students-and-supervisors/.

Reading and Literature Reviews

Adler, Mortimer J., Charles Van Doren, and Edward Holland. *How to Read a Book: The Classic Guide to Intelligent Reading*. Unabridged MP3CD—rev. ed. Ashland, OR: Blackstone Audio, 2010.
Machi, Lawrence A., and Brenda T. McEvoy. *The Literature Review: Six Steps to Success*. 3rd ed. Thousand Oaks, CA: Corwin, 2016.

Tools for Finding Relevant Research

Connected Papers—find and explore academic papers: https://www.connectedpapers.com/.
ResearchRabbit—discover and visualize papers: https://www.researchrabbit.ai/.
Scholarcy—online summarizing tool: https://www.scholarcy.com/.
Scite—see how research has been cited, see context in which papers were cited: https://scite.ai/.
Speechify—text to speech, reads aloud: https://speechify.com/.

Doing Quality Work

Jussim, Lee, Jon A. Krosnick, and Sean T. Stevens, eds. *Research Integrity: Best Practices for the Social and Behavioral Sciences*. New York: Oxford University Press, 2022.

National Academies of Sciences, Engineering, Policy and Global Affairs, Engineering Committee on Science, Board on Research Data and Information, Division on Engineering and Physical Sciences, Committee on Applied and Theoretical Statistics, Board on Mathematical Sciences and Analytics, et al. *Improving Reproducibility and Replicability. Reproducibility and Replicability in Science*. Washington, DC: National Academies Press, 2019. https://www.ncbi.nlm.nih.gov/books/NBK547525/.

It's also worth consulting the websites of the Open Science Framework (https://osf.io/) and the Center for Open Science (https://www.cos.io).

COMMUNICATING RESEARCH

Books on Writing, Generally

Kidder, Tracey, and Richard Todd. *Good Prose: The Art of Nonfiction*. New York: Random House, 2013.

King, Stephen. *On Writing: A Memoir of the Craft*. London: Hodder & Stoughton, 2010.

Klinkenborg, Verlyn. *Several Short Sentences About Writing*. New York: Vintage, 2013.

Lamott, Anne. *Bird by Bird: Some Instructions on Writing and Life*. New York: Anchor, 1995. (Especially the essay "Shitty First Drafts.")

Pinker, Steven. *The Sense of Style: The Thinking Person's Guide to Writing in the 21st Century*. New York: Penguin, 2014.

Stone, Sheila Heen Douglas. *Thanks for the Feedback*. New York: Penguin, 2015.

Podcasts on Writing

Writing Excuses: https://writingexcuses.com/.

Books on Academic Writing and Publishing

Alley, Michael. *The Craft of Scientific Writing*. 4th ed. New York: Springer, 2018.

Belcher, Wendy Laura. *Writing Your Journal Article in Twelve Weeks: A Guide to Academic Publishing Success*. 2nd ed. Chicago: University of Chicago Press, 2019.

Boice, Robert. *Professors as Writers: A Self-Help Guide to Productive Writing*. Stillwater, OK: New Forums Press, 1990.

Dunleavy, Patrick, and Jane Tinkler. *Maximizing the Impacts of Academic Research*. London: Red Globe Press, 2020.

Heard, Stephen B. *The Scientist's Guide to Writing: How to Write More Easily and Effectively Throughout Your Scientific Career*. Princeton, NJ: Princeton University Press, 2016.

Joireman, Jeff, and Paul A. M. Van Lange. *How to Publish High-Quality Research*. Washington, DC: American Psychological Association, 2014.

McCloskey, Deirdre. *Economical Writing*. 2nd ed. Prospect Heights, IL: Waveland Press, 1999.

Sarnecka, Barbara W. *The Writing Workshop: Write More, Write Better, Be Happier in Academia*. Self-published, 2019. https://osf.io/n8pc3/.

Silvia, Paul J. *How to Write a Lot: A Practical Guide to Productive Academic Writing*. Washington, DC: APA LifeTools, 2018.

Sword, Helen. *Air & Light & Time & Space: How Successful Academics Write*. Cambridge, MA: Harvard University Press, 2017.

Writing Theses and Dissertations

Bolker, Joan. *Writing Your Dissertation in Fifteen Minutes a Day: A Guide to Starting, Revising, and Finishing Your Doctoral Thesis*. New York: Holt Paperbacks, 1998.

Dunleavy, Patrick. *Authoring a PhD Thesis: How to Plan, Draft, Write and Finish a Doctoral Dissertation*. Houndsmills, UK: Red Globe Press, 2003.

Evans, David, Paul Gruba, and Justin Zobel. *How to Write a Better Thesis*. 3rd ed. Carlton, AU: Melbourne University Publishing, 2012.

Rank, Scott. *How to Finish Your Dissertation in Six Months, Even if You Don't Know What to Write*. Self-published, Scholarpreneur Press, 2015.

White, Guy E. *The Dissertation Warrior: The Ultimate Guide to Being the Kind of Person Who Finishes a Doctoral Dissertation or Thesis*. Happy Valley, OR: Triumphant Heart International, 2017.

Length of Average Dissertations and Theses by Field

"Average Dissertation and Thesis Length, Take Two." *R Is My Friend* (blog), July 15, 2014. https://beckmw.wordpress.com/2014/07/15/average-dissertation-and-thesis-length-take-two/.

"How Long Is the Average Dissertation?" *R Is My Friend* (blog), April 15, 2013. https://beckmw.wordpress.com/2013/04/15/how-long-is-the-average-dissertation/.

Other Media About Academic Writing

Calarco, Jessica McCrory. *A Field Guide to Grad School: Uncovering the Hidden Curriculum*. Princeton, NJ: Princeton University Press, 2020. Chapters on academic writing, including sample outlines for social science papers, a guide to submitting an academic article, and sample cover letters, peer review, and resubmission letters.

Cayley, Rachael. *Explorations of Style: A Blog About Academic Writing*: https://explorationsofstyle.com/.

"How Do I Write a Scientific Paper?" SciDev.Net, February 7, 2013. https://www.scidev.net/global/practical-guides/how-do-i-write-a-scientific-paper/.

Pomona College Writing Center resources: https://www.pomona.edu/administration/writing-center/student-resources/general-writing-resources

Twitter thread by Lucy Foulkes on academic writing: https://twitter.com/lfoulkesy/status/1522260225599975424?s=20.

Writing Reviews

Shaw, Steven R. "How Not to Suck at Reviewing Articles for Scholarly Journals." *Researchtopractice* (blog), July 4, 2015. https://researchtopracticeconnections.wordpress.com/2015/07/04/how-not-to-suck-at-reviewing-articles-for-scholarly-journals/.

Science Writing and Writing for the Media

Blum, Deborah, Mary Knudson, and Robin Marantz Henig, eds. *A Field Guide for Science Writers: The Official Guide of the National Association of Science Writers*. 2nd ed. Oxford: Oxford University Press, 2005.

Carpenter, Siri. *The Craft of Science Writing: Selections from The Open Notebook*. Madison, WI: Open Notebook, 2020.

Cormick, Craig. *The Science of Communicating Science: The Ultimate Guide*. Ill. ed. Clayton, AU: CSIRO Publishing, 2019.

Golash-Boza, Tanya. "How Can an Academic Publish an Op/Ed?" *Get a Life, PhD* (blog), November 27, 2012. http://getalifephd.blogspot.com/2012/11/how-can-academic-publish-oped.html.

Lewenstein, Bruce V. "Am I Making Myself Clear?" *Journal of Clinical Investigation* 120, no. 2 (2010): 400. https://doi.org/10.1172/JCI42033.

Liz Neeley on storytelling and science communication: "Your Brain on Storytelling." *Short Wave*, National Public Radio, January 14, 2020. https://www.npr.org/2020/01/13/795977814/your-brain-on-storytelling.

Zimmer, Carl. "Science Writing: Guidelines and Guidance" *Carl Zimmer* (blog), accessed July 24, 2022. https://carlzimmer.com/science-writing-guidelines-and-guidance/.

The Scholars Strategy Network connects researchers with journalists and policymakers: https://scholars.org/.

The OpEd Project helps researchers turn their work into narratives for short articles and reports: https://www.theopedproject.org/.

Website listing how much different venues pay writers: http://whopayswriters.com/.

Graphics, Data Visualization, Design, Slides

Tufte, Edward R. *Envisioning Information*. 9th ed. Cheshire, CT: Graphics Press, 2003.

Tufte, Edward R. *The Visual Display of Quantitative Information*. 2nd ed. Cheshire, CT: Graphics Press, 2001.

Williams, Robin. *The Non-designer's Design Book*. 4th ed. San Francisco: Peachpit Press, 2014.

Mike Morrison on how to create a better research poster in less time (#betterposter): https://www.youtube.com/watch?v=1RwJbhkCA58.

Colorblind Palettes

Goedhart, Joachim. "Data Visualization with Flying Colors." *The Node*, August 29, 2019. https://thenode.biologists.com/data-visualization-with-flying-colors/research/.

Nichols, David. "Coloring for Colorblindness." Davidmathlogic.com, accessed July 24, 2022. http://www.davidmathlogic.com/colorblind/.

Poster Software

Adobe Illustrator
Adobe Photoshop
Affinity Designer
Canva
Google Slides
Inkscape
LibreOffice
Microsoft Publisher
Overleaf
Pages
PowerPoint
Scribus

Talking

Alley, Michael. *The Craft of Scientific Presentations: Critical Steps to Succeed and Critical Errors to Avoid*. 2nd ed. New York: Springer, 2011.

Booth, Vernon. *Communicating in Science: Writing a Scientific Paper and Speaking at Scientific Meetings*. 2nd ed. Cambridge: Cambridge University Press, 1993.

Gallo, Carmine. *Talk Like TED: The 9 Public Speaking Secrets of the World's Top Minds*. New York: Macmillan, 2014.

Patrick Winston on how to speak: https://youtu.be/Unzc731iCUY.
Three Minute Thesis: https://threeminutethesis.uq.edu.au/.

TEACHING

Course and Syllabus Design

Biggs, John. "Aligning Teaching for Constructing Learning." *Higher Education Academy* 1, no. 4 (2003): 1–4.

Eng, Norman. *Teaching College: The Ultimate Guide to Lecturing, Presenting, and Engaging Students.* Self-published, 2017.

Henri Lipmanowicz, Henri, and Keith McCandless. *The Surprising Power of Liberating Structures: Simple Rules to Unleash a Culture of Innovation.* Seattle, WA: Liberating Structures Press, 2013.

Slattery, Jeanne M., and Janet F. Carlson. "Preparing an Effective Syllabus: Current Best Practices." *College Teaching* 53, no. 4 (2005): 159–164.

Suskie, Linda. *Assessing Student Learning: A Common Sense Guide.* 2nd ed. San Francisco: Jossey-Bass, 2009.

Wiggins, Grant P., and Jay McTighe. *Understanding by Design.* 2nd ed. Alexandria, VA: Association for Supervision and Curriculum Development, 2005.

Many disciplines have teaching journals, websites, and Facebook groups where people share ideas about how to teach the subject.

Inclusive Syllabi

Many universities have examples of inclusive policies online; search for such terms as "inclusive syllabus examples," and see the following examples:

- "Syllabus Preparation and Language." University of Kansas, last modified January 2022. https://flexteaching.ku.edu/syllabus-language.
- "Syllabus Statements." Lewis-Clark State College, accessed September 23, 2023. https://www.lcsc.edu/teaching-learning/inspiration-for-teaching-and-learning/syllabus-statements.

Science of Learning

Halpern, Diane F., and Milton D. Hakel. "Applying the Science of Learning to the University and beyond: Teaching for Long-Term Retention and Transfer." *Change: The Magazine of Higher Learning* 35, no. 4 (2003): 36–41.

Lang, James M. *Small Teaching: Everyday Lessons from the Science of Learning.* Hoboken, NJ: John Wiley & Sons, 2021.

Teaching Strategies

Armstrong, Kacie L. *Teaching Gradually: Practical Pedagogy for Graduate Students, by Graduate Students.* Sterling, VA: Stylus Publishing, 2021.

Beuning, Penny J., Dave Z. Besson, and Scott A. Snyder. *Teach Better, Save Time, and Have More Fun: A Guide to Teaching and Mentoring in Science.* Tucson, AZ: Research Corporation for Science Advancement, 2014.

Davis, Barbara Gross. *Tools for Teaching.* Hoboken, NJ: John Wiley & Sons, 2009.

Huston, Therese. *Teaching What You Don't Know.* Cambridge, MA: Harvard University Press, 2009.

Lang, James M. *On Course: A Week-by-Week Guide to Your First Semester of College Teaching.* Cambridge, MA: Harvard University Press, 2008.

PRODUCTIVITY

Books

Carroll, Ryder. *The Bullet Journal Method: Track the Past, Order the Present, Design the Future.* Ill. ed. New York: Portfolio, 2018.

Elrod, Hal, and Robert Kiyosaki. *The Miracle Morning: The Not-So-Obvious Secret Guaranteed to Transform Your Life.* Self-published, 2012.

Fiore, Neil A. *The Now Habit: A Strategic Program for Overcoming Procrastination and Enjoying Guilt-Free Play.* Rev. ed. New York: TarcherPerigee, 2007.

Newport, Cal. *Deep Work: Rules for Focused Success in a Distracted World.* New York: Grand Central Publishing, 2016.

Steel, Piers. *The Procrastination Equation: How to Stop Putting Things Off and Start Getting Stuff Done.* 2nd ed. New York: Pearson Life, 2012.

Apps and Websites

Forest—focus timer: https://www.forestapp.cc/.
Freedom—app and website blocker: https://freedom.to/.
Piers Steel's list of anti-procrastination apps: https://procrastinus.com/anti-procrastination-apps/.

Podcasts About Productivity and Life Skills

Accidental Creative: https://podcasts.apple.com/us/podcast/accidental-creative-creativity/id93424211.
Beyond the To-Do List: https://beyondthetodolist.com/.
Brilliant Balance: https://cherylanneskolnicki.com/podcast/.
Defining Success: https://podcasts.apple.com/us/podcast/defining-success-podcast/id619459909.

ADHD

"Time Management and Productivity Advice for Adults with ADHD." *ADDitude*, accessed May 24, 2022. https://www.additudemag.com/category/manage-adhd-life/getting-things-done/time-productivity/.
Tuckman, Ari. "ADHD Minds Are Trapped in Now (& Other Time Management Truths)." *ADDitude*, July 30, 2019. https://www.additudemag.com/time-management-skills-adhd-brain/.

Time-Management Apps

Coach.me
Finish
Listastic
TeuxDeux
2Do
30/30

Time Estimation

Brooks, Frederick Jr. *The Mythical Man-Month: Essays on Software Engineering*. Anniv. ed. Reading, MA: Addison-Wesley Professional, 1995.
Pink, Daniel H. *When: The Scientific Secrets of Perfect Timing*. New York: Riverhead Books, 2018.
Sharot, Tali. *The Optimism Bias: A Tour of the Irrationally Positive Brain*. Repr. ed. New York: Vintage, 2012.

Motivation and Meeting Goals

Barker, Eric. *Barking Up the Wrong Tree: The Surprising Science Behind Why Everything You Know About Success Is (Mostly) Wrong*. New York: HarperOne, 2017.
Fishbach, Ayelet. *Get It Done: Surprising Lessons from the Science of Motivation*. New York: Little, Brown Spark, 2022.

Scheduling and Task Tracking

Asana
Bullet journals
Evernote
Gantt charts
Google Calendar, iCal, or Outlook Calendar
Google Keep
Microsoft ToDo
Notion
Paper to-do planners
Passion planner
Todoist
Trello
Whiteboards
Everything notebook, Dr Raul Pacheco Vega: http://www.raulpacheco.org/resources/the-everything-notebook/.
Kevin Burgio's organization spreadsheet: https://twitter.com/KRBurgio/status/1225528578063904769.
(Many of the digital tools listed above sync with Google Calendar, iCal, or Outlook Calendar.)

Scheduling Meetings

Doodle: https://doodle.com/en/.
WhenIsGood: https://whenisgood.net/.
When2Meet: https://www.when2meet.com/.

Digital Notetaking and Record Keeping

Evernote
Google docs
Notion
OneNote
Personal wiki such as tiddlywiki
Rocketbook
Trello
Typora
List of free and low-cost digital tools, software, images, teaching resources, and more: https://docs.google.com/document/d/1IFbHIN5OOAO0qz-VfCU9nEx4-x6CfArj1-d8ylA2vsU/.

Home Management

Flylady home cleaning system: http://www.flylady.net/.
Brenneman, Kim. *Home Management: Plain and Simple*. Self-published, Home Plain and Simple, 2017.
White, Dana K. *How to Manage Your Home Without Losing Your Mind: Dealing with Your House's Dirty Little Secrets*. Nashville, TN: Thomas Nelson, 2016.

Meal Prep

Denise Bustard, grad student turned food blogger: https://sweetpeasandsaffron.com/.
Karrie Truman's *Happy Money Saver*: https://happymoneysaver.com.
Low-cost recipes on food blogs like Beth Moncel's *Budget Bytes*: https://www.budgetbytes.com/.
Shelly King offers tips for how to make a variety of slow-cooker meals that can be frozen for later: https://stockpilingmoms.com/20-slow-cooker-freezer-meals-in-4-hours/.

BALANCING LIFE

Brooks, Arthur C. "'Success Addicts' Choose Being Special Over Being Happy." *The Atlantic*, July 30, 2020. https://www.theatlantic.com/family/archive/2020/07/why-success-wont-make-you-happy/614731/.
Hutchinson, D. *Lead with Balance: How to Master Work-Life Balance in an Imbalanced Culture*. Advantage, 2016.
Kelly, Matthew. *Off Balance: Getting Beyond the Work-Life Balance Myth to Personal and Professional Satisfaction*. New York: Penguin Random House, 2011.
Merrill, A. Roger, and Rebecca Merrill. *Life Matters: Creating a Dynamic Balance of Work, Family, Time, & Money*. New York: McGraw Hill, 2004.
Shlain, Tiffany. *24/6: The Power of Unplugging One Day a Week*. New York: Gallery Books, 2019.
Warhurst, Chris, Doris Ruth Eikhof, and Axel Haunschild. *Work Less, Live More? Critical Analyses of the Work-Life Boundary*. London: Palgrave Macmillan, 2008.

Mental Health

These are a few phone numbers in the United States you can call if you want or need to talk to someone right now:

> National Suicide Prevention Hotline: 1-800-273-8255 (TALK)
> National Domestic Violence Hotline: 1-800-799-7233
> Lifeline Crisis Chat: https://www.contact-usa.org/chat.html
> Crisis Text Line: Text REASON to 741741

Self-Harm Hotline: 1-800-DONT CUT (1-800-366-8288)
National Council on Alcoholism & Drug Dependency: 1-800-622-2255

Books on Resilience in Academia and Mental Well-Being

Ayres, Zoe. *Managing Your Mental Health During Your PhD: A Survival Guide*. London: Springer Nature, 2022.

Boynton, Petra. *Being Well in Academia: Ways to Feel Stronger, Safer and More Connected*. New York: Routledge, 2020.

Brown, Brené. *The Gifts of Imperfection: Let Go of Who You Think You're Supposed to Be and Embrace Who You Are*. Danvers, MA: Hazelden Publishing, 2010.

Ivens, Sarah. *Forest Therapy: Seasonal Ways to Embrace Nature for a Happier You*. London: Piatkus, 2018.

Pryal, Katie Rose Guest. *Life of the Mind Interrupted: Essays on Mental Health and Disability in Higher Education*. Chapel Hill, NC: Blue Crow Books, 2018.

Shanok, Arielle, and Nicole Benedicto Elden, eds. *Thriving in Graduate School: The Expert's Guide to Success and Wellness*. Lanham, MD: Rowman and Littlefield, 2021.

Tugend, Alina. *Better By Mistake: The Unexpected Benefits of Being Wrong*. New York: Riverhead Books, 2011.

Young, Valerie. *The Secret Thoughts of Successful Women: Why Capable People Suffer from the Impostor Syndrome and How to Thrive in Spite of It*. Sydney: Currency, 2011.

Websites, Blogs, and Podcasts

Academic Mental Health Collective: https://amhcollective.com/.

How God Works: https://davedesteno.com/podcast.

Hyperbole and a Half: Adventures in Depression: http://hyperboleandahalf.blogspot.com/2011/10/adventures-in-depression.html.

Papa PhD podcast: https://papaphd.com.

PhDisabled: What It's Like Doing Academia with Disability and Chronic Illness: https://phdisabled.wordpress.com/.

Resilience in Academic Writing Blog: https://www.nicolesheawrites.com/resilient-academic-writing-blog.

Voices of Academia blog and podcast: https://voicesofacademia.com/.

You can also search the app stores for apps that promote skills, activities, and mind-sets associated with good mental health, such as gratitude practice, meditation, focus, and exercise.

Marriage and Personal Responsibility

Chapman, Gary. *The 5 Love Languages: The Secret to Love That Lasts*. Repr. ed. Northfield, MI: Northfield Publishing, 2014.

Finkel, Eli J. *The All-or-Nothing Marriage: How the Best Marriages Work*. Repr. ed. New York: Dutton, 2017.

Peterson, Jordan B. *12 Rules for Life: An Antidote to Chaos*. London: Penguin, 2019.

Schlessinger, Laura. *The Proper Care and Feeding of Husbands*. New York: HarperCollins, 2009.

Pregnancy and Birth

Books

England, Pam, and Rob Horowitz. *Birthing from Within: An Extra-Ordinary Guide to Childbirth Preparation*. Albuquerque, NM: Partera Press, 1998.

Oster, Emily. *Expecting Better: Why the Conventional Pregnancy Wisdom Is Wrong and What You Really Need to Know*. London: Orion, 2013.

Weschler, Toni. *Taking Charge of Your Fertility: The Definitive Guide to Natural Birth Control, Pregnancy Achievement, and Reproductive Health*. 20th anniv. ed. New York: William Morrow Paperbacks, 2015.

Websites

KellyMom: https://kellymom.com/.
March of Dimes: https://www.marchofdimes.org.
The Pregnant Scholar: https://thepregnantscholar.org/.

Parenting in Academia

Books

Connelly, Rachel, and Kristen Ghodsee. *Professor Mommy: Finding Work-Family Balance in Academia*. Lanham, MD: Rowman and Littlefield, 2011.

Evans, Elrena, and Miriam Peskowitz. *Mama, PhD: Women Write About Motherhood and Academic Life*. Edited by Caroline Grant. New Brunswick, NJ: Rutgers University Press, 2008.

Mason, Mary Ann, Nicholas H. Wolfinger, and Marc Goulden. *Do Babies Matter? Gender and Family in the Ivory Tower*. New Brunswick, NJ: Rutgers University Press, 2013.

Ward, Kelly, Lisa Wolf-Wendel, and Lisa Banning. *Academic Motherhood: How Faculty Manage Work and Family.* New Brunswick, NJ: Rutgers University Press, 2012.

Essays

Kory-Westlund, Jacqueline. "Balancing My PhD with a Baby: Debugging Code and Changing Diapers." *Jakory.Com* (blog), March 31, 2018. https://jakory.com/blog//2018/balance-phd-with-baby-debugging-code-changing-diapers/.

Kory-Westlund, Jacqueline. "Wasting My Degree: Kids and the Alt-Ac/Post-Ac Life." *Jakory.Com* (blog), March 18, 2019. https://jakory.com/blog/2019/wasting-my-mit-phd-degree/.

Social Media

SciMom Chats: https://www.mothersinscience.com/scimomchats

On Twitter: @mothersinsci, @parent_phd, @Momademia.

Thread on women managing children and academia: https://twitter.com/M_Chapleau/status/1292596770418102273.

Finding Community

Books, Essays, and Organizations

DeSteno, David. *How God Works: The Science Behind the Benefits of Religion.* New York: Simon and Schuster, 2021.

Donovan, Roxanne. "Six Ways to Create Sister Circles in Academe—WOC Guest Post." *The Professor Is In*, January 22, 2020. https://theprofessorisin.com/2020/01/22/six-ways-to-create-sister-circles-in-academe-woc-guest-post/.

Institute for Globally Distributed Open Research and Education: https://igdore.org/.

Jussim, Lee. "Introducing The Society for Open Inquiry in the Behavioral Sciences." *Unsafe Science*, July 8, 2022. https://unsafescience.substack.com/p/introducing-the-society-for-open.

Ronin Institute: https://ronininstitute.org/.

Warnick, Melody. *This Is Where You Belong: Finding Home Wherever You Are.* Repr. ed. New York: Penguin Books, 2017.

Podcasts

LGBTQ+ Stem Cast: https://anchor.fm/lgbtqstemcast.

PhDivas: https://phdivaspodcast.wordpress.com/.

CHANGING ACADEMIA

Books

Berg, Maggie, and Barbara K. Seeber. *The Slow Professor: Challenging the Culture of Speed in the Academy*. Reprint edition. Toronto: University of Toronto Press, 2017.

Brown, Tessa, ed. *Essential Work, Exploited Workers: Graduate Student Labor in the Corporate University*. Lawrence: Kansas University Press, in press.

Cassuto, Leonard. *The Graduate School Mess*. Cambridge, MA: Harvard University Press, 2015.

Cassuto, Leonard, Robert Townsend, Robert Weisbuch, Michael J. McGandy, Augusta Rohrbach, Joseph M. Vukov, Melissa Dalgleish, Karen Wilson, Stephen Aron, and Vernita Burrell. *The Reimagined PhD: Navigating 21st Century Humanities Education*. New Brunswick, NJ: Rutgers University Press, 2021.

Cassuto, Leonard, and Robert Weisbuch. *The New PhD: How to Build a Better Graduate Education*. Baltimore, MD: Johns Hopkins University Press, 2021.

Crew, Teresa. *Higher Education and Working-Class Academics: Precarity and Diversity in Academia*. Cham, CH: Palgrave Pivot, 2020. https://link.springer.com/book/10.1007/978-3-030-58352-1.

Hinchey, Patricia, and Isabel Kimmel. *The Graduate Grind: A Critical Look at Graduate Education*. New York: Routledge, 2001.

Tyehimba, Agyei. *The Blueprint: A Black Student Union Handbook*. Scotts Valley, CA: CreateSpace Independent Publishing Platform, 2013.

Weisbuch, Robert, and Leonard Cassuto. *Reforming Doctoral Education, 1990 to 2015: Recent Initiatives and Future Prospects*. New York: Andrew W. Mellon Foundation, 2016. https://www.humanitiescareers.pitt.edu/sites/default/files/A.W.Mellon%2C%20Reforming%20Doctoral%20Education%2C%201990%E2%80%932015.pdf.

Can Academics Be Activists?

Bartel, Anna Sims, and Debra A. Castillo. *The Scholar as Human: Research and Teaching for Public Impact*. Ithaca, NY: Cornell University Press, 2021.

Beaulieu, Marianne, Mylaine Breton, and Astrid Brousselle. "Conceptualizing 20 Years of Engaged Scholarship: A Scoping Review." *PLOS ONE* 13, no. 2 (2018): e0193201. https://doi.org/10.1371/journal.pone.0193201.

Boyer, Ernest L. *Scholarship Reconsidered: Priorities of the Professoriate*. Princeton, NJ: Princeton University Press, 1990.

Boyte, Harry C., and Eric Fretz. "Civic Professionalism." *Journal of Higher Education Outreach and Engagement* 14, no. 2 (2010): 67–90.

Index

academia, 1, 5, 12, 19, 37, 49-50, 100, 106, 187, 211, 247; alternative paths in, 233, 245; careers in (*see* careers: academic); and creativity, 124; culture of, 6, 19, 21, 39, 58, 74, 94, 150, 165, 203, 243-245, 299; leaving, 24, 31-33, 36, 38-41, 44-45, 88, 95, 100, 165, 204, 229, 241-242, 276-277; and overwork, 74, 132; and parenting (*see* parenting); and research, 109, 165, 167, 239, 241; success in, 150, 193, 209, 227, 239, 242, 280, 288, 296; systemic issues in, 193, 233, 237, 239, 296. *See also* graduate school

academic publishing. *See* publishing

accessibility, 184-185

accountability, 138, 154, 196

accounting, 58, 60, 282

achievement, 75, 187

ADHD (attention deficit hyperactivity disorder), 113, 162, 293

administrators, 66, 104-105, 234-237, 239, 241, 243, 283; careers as, 37-38; opposition to student unions, 236; questions for, 91-92

admissions, 53, 56, 85, 245; diversity in, 237-239; financial package, 53, 65

admissions committees, 238

adjunct teaching. *See* teaching, adjunct

advisers, 1-2, 5, 9, 19, 21, 30, 35, 42, 55-56, 66, 85-97, 99-101, 103-104, 105, 111, 114, 117, 125, 127, 133-134, 137-138, 143, 146, 150, 155, 175, 200, 208, 217, 229, 236-237, 241, 284; abusive, 96-97, 100; asking questions of, 95; breaking up with, 101; and dissertation or thesis committees, 121-123, during dissertation work, 129-130, 138, 140-142; expectations for, 93-94; feedback from, 79-81, 93; interviewing prospective, 85, 88-90; meetings with, 94, 135, 201; negotiating with, 97-98, 243; picking, 86-88, 101; and power, 80, 99; problems with, 22, 94, 95-97, 100, 130, 141, 150, 201; relationships with, 86, 88, 92-93; and research dissemination, 165-170, 172, 178-180; and research ideas, 129-130; and managing undergraduates, 161-162

alumni, 35, 38, 46, 68, 88, 90, 208, 241

anxiety, 3, 14, 162, 185, 193-195

applications, academic job, 34-35

applications, committee, 237

applications, funding, 53, 55-56, 172, 175, 284

applications, graduate school, 19, 63, 85, 238

applications, internship, 26

applications, job, 43, 45, 192

archives, 122, 124, 126, 135, 149, 200; digital, 126-127

arts, 10, 34-36, 38, 53, 87, 111, 119-120, 165-166, 198
assessments, 110, 112-113, 135, 143, 149, 166; designing inclusive, 113
assignments. *See* courses: assignments in
assistantships. *See* research assistantships; teaching assistantships
attention, 43, 73, 152, 162, 200, 221
authorship, 114, 170, 179-180. *See also* coauthor; writing
autonomy, 91, 98, 120, 160

babies. *See* children: as babies
balance, 5-6, 19, 22, 33, 42, 63, 72, 93, 163, 192-195, 205-208, 213, 224, 232, 244-245, 293, 295, 297; activities for, 197-198; and advisors, 90, 92-93; and family, 207-208, 298; finding, 1, 195-197, 233; and health, 3, 193, 203-204; and living situations, 64; and managing undergraduates, 161; work versus nonwork, 3, 30, 47, 193-195, 199-201, 207-208
bibliography, 110, 114, 120. *See also* citations
blogging, 5, 24, 33, 68, 76-77, 117, 127, 164-165, 170-171, 175, 177, 232
book reviews, 166, 168, 251
books, publishing, 165, 166-168. *See also* writing
book chapters, 168
boundaries, 81, 92, 197, 201, 245, 284; with advisors, 92-93
budgeting, 4-5, 43, 57–63, 65, 75, 105, 133, 202, 212, 282-283; creating a, 58-60; evaluating your, 60; and food, 51, 62, 65-66, 295; and housing, 62-64. *See also* finances
burnout, 194, 205

Calarco, Jessica McCrory, 56, 63, 81, 86, 80, 104, 109, 111-112, 114, 116, 122, 144, 244
campus visits, 34

careers, 1, 3-6, 11-14, 17, 19-23, 25-29, 30, 61, 63, 71, 75-77, 81, 86, 92, 99, 129, 186, 199-200, 202-203, 215, 224, 229, 233-234, 235, 239, 247; academic, 3, 11, 19, 22-24, 31-38, 67-68, 75, 79, 101, 103-104, 110-111, 132, 213, 215; administration, 37-38; advancement, 132, 207; advisor support for, 86, 88-89; and balance, 207-208, 210-211, 213, 230, 233; centers or counselors on campus, 26, 55, 68, 99; consulting, 170; diversity of, 237, 241-242; and freedom of speech, 240; government, 12, 25, 35-36, 38-39; full-time (*see* work: full-time); goals for, 18, 25, 68-70; and international students, 49; and job searches, 42-49, 61, 92, 181, 192, 210, 213-214; nonacademic, 25, 38-49, 241; part-time (*see* work: part-time); planning, 25-27, 33, 40-41, 67-68, 88, 94-95, 242; preparation for, 25, 42-43, 54, 67-68, 70, 75-76, 79, 93, 106-108, 111; research, 11, 25, 31-32, 67, 167, 202; resources for, 275-279, 283; skills for, 42-44, 78-79; switching, 20-23, 68, 94, 134, 165, 167; and the two-body problem, 213-214, 245
Cassuto, Leonard, 42, 70, 164-165, 234, 239, 241
Caterine, Christopher, 31-32, 36, 39-40, 42, 44, 47, 174
challenge, 2, 18, 44, 48, 77, 122, 125, 150, 162, 171, 185, 230, 244; financial, 51; graduate school as a, 195, 224-225, 228; theories about, 71
changing direction, 20-23, 39, 48, 68, 94, 129, 134, 129, 165, 167, 248
children, 3, 13, 67, 73, 81, 93, 121, 223, 232-233; as babies, 24, 105, 113, 215, 218-221, 297; course policies about, 113; and finances, 61-62 (*see also* childcare; finances); and leaving academia, 21, 39, 231-233; and managing time and work, 24, 42, 81, 143, 163, 200, 208, 220-222, 242; research

with, 128–130, 149, 161, 164, 168, 171, 217; resources about, 285, 295, 297–298; support for academics with, 243–245; and travel, 222
childcare, 52–53, 60, 209, 217, 220, 222, 236, 243–244
church. *See* religion
Cirillo, Francesco, 153
citations. *See* references
classes. *See* courses
classmates. *See* students
coauthors, 66, 114, 179–180, 203, 239. *See also* writing
code of conduct, 97, 236
cohort. *See* students
collaboration, 89–90, 103, 140, 179–180, 184, 201, 241, 245
colleagues, 1, 28, 32, 34–35, 61, 76, 179, 186–187, 208, 231, 240
colleges, 1–2, 9, 14, 23, 26, 48, 108, 157, 161, 224, 238, 276; community, 19, 26; professors at, 24, 32; and student government, 234–235; and student unions, 236; teaching and working at, 34, 45, 111, 213, 291–292; and towns, 62–63
colleges, liberal arts, 34, 53, 111
colleges, community, 19, 26, 34, 111
commentaries, 132, 166, 168
commitment, 32, 54, 81, 96, 150, 158, 191, 195–196, 232
committee, dissertation. *See* dissertation committee
committee, exam. *See* exam committee
committee, hiring. *See* hiring committee
committee, institutional. *See* institutional committee
committee, thesis. *See* dissertation committee
commutes, 61, 63–64, 197; and balance, 192, 196–197; working during, 110, 152
communication, 43, 49, 162, 171, 234; and advisors, 92; difficulties with, 201, 231; of research, 5, 24, 68, 165, 171, 174, 177; resources for, 281, 287–290; and teaching, 110
community, 5, 34, 198, 232, 237; academic, 35, 37, 186; building student, 234–235; finding, 63, 200, 203, 213, 227–230, 281, 298
companies, 2, 26–27, 38–39, 45–48, 80; funding from, 53; professional, 166; publishing, 168
competence, 71, 81, 160, 215, 221, 239. *See also* expertise
competition, 71, 75
compromise, 208, 213, 223
computer engineering, 24
computer science, 24, 208
computers, 44, 65, 69, 78, 134, 161
comprehensive exams. *See* exams
conference calls, 219, 221
conference program committee, 169
conferences, 44, 78, 89, 126–127, 165–166, 169–170, 176, 187, 207, 230, 237; costs of, 66; funding for, 53, 55, 66, 91; panels at, 82; papers at, 165, 167, 169; posters at, 165, 169, 186; presenting at, 127, 169–170, 181–186; reviewing for, 79, 81, 179; submitting to, 140, 172; travel for, 216, 222; what to wear to, 170
confidence, 74, 124, 181
conflict, 87, 94; and advisers, 96–97, 100; and author order, 180; and committees, 122; and hard conversations, 99–100, 231; resolution strategies, 95–97
cost of living, 34, 55, 57, 63
courses, 5, 11, 19, 26, 43, 45, 66, 74–77, 89, 92, 101–104, 106–110, 119, 122, 125, 128, 131–132, 143, 145, 147, 154, 168, 175, 193, 199, 210, 227, 229; assignments and work in, 107–108, 115–117, 140; choosing, 86, 99, 106–107; discussions, 112; exams in, 107; extracurricular, 50, 68, 77, 198, 205, 210; and group projects, 108; inclusive, 113, 240;

courses (*continued*)
required, 106; and scheduling, 150-151, 161, 192, 203, 220; teaching (*see* teaching). *See also* reading

coursework. *See* courses

co-working spaces, 244

Creative Commons, 183

creativity, 50, 160, 234, 277; and life, 38, 232-233; and research, 119, 124-125, 127

criticism. *See* feedback

critiques. *See* reviews

Csikszentmihalyi, Mihaly, 71

cumulative exams. *See* exams

curiosity, 22, 72-73, 82, 96, 130, 171, 229, 285

curriculum vitae (CV), 26, 34, 36, 95, 122, 166-168, 283; preparing a, 44-45, 187

data, 78, 109, 116, 132-134, 136-137, 143, 149, 151, 153, 179, 215; access to, 66; presentation of, 172, 176, 184, 290; quantity of, 133, 149

data analysis, 1, 10, 78, 109, 114, 133-136, 154, 216-217

data collection, 2, 115, 124, 135-136, 143, 149-150, 161, 174, 217

data papers, 166

datasets, 120; funding for, 53

de Palma, Nick, 124

deadlines, 3, 105-106, 139, 145, 154-155, 194, 203, 211, 244; and boundaries, 81, 176, 192, 199; degree, 121, 141; funding, 56; setting, 79, 149, 156; tracking, 56, 107, 144-145, 162; and undergraduates, 161

debt, 22, 36, 52-53, 91, 94; and budgets, 60; living free from, 58; paying down, 61, 64-65; resources for dealing with, 282. *See also* finances

Deci, Edward, 160

defense. *See* dissertations: defense

degrees, 3, 72, 86-87, 89, 106-107, 152, 161, 181, 193, 226-227; completion of, 3, 21, 214, 227, 231, 239, 247; and finances, 20, 52, 63, 67; and life plans, 4, 9-12, 19, 25, 41, 203, 207-209, 231-232, 241, 298; requirements for, 75, 77, 99; timelines for, 93, 121, 145-148, 150; time to, 11-12, 70, 140, 150. *See also* graduate programs

degrees, associates, 2

degrees, doctoral, 2-3, 11-12, 28-30, 35, 52, 61, 72, 75, 86, 89, 102, 106, 115, 118-119, 129, 145, 150, 158, 160, 195, 199, 205; and funding (*see* funding: degree or program); humanities, 11; and life plans, 1, 19-21, 23, 31-32, 37-38, 40, 203, 231; resources for earning, 275-299; steps to earn, 67, 106, 115, 118-120, 145-146; support during (*see* support)

degrees, graduate. *See* graduate programs

degrees, master's, 11, 21, 52-53, 89, 115, 119-120, 125, 129, 238

degrees, professional, 3, 11

degrees, undergraduate, 106

department head, 96

Department of Defense, 53

depression, 3, 14, 162, 193-195, 201, 296

design, 38, 43, 45, 68, 110, 186, 290-291; life, 12, 40, 46, 130, 151, 193, 232, 275

discipline. *See* self-discipline

director of graduate studies, 96

disabilities, 162, 229, 231, 237, 242-243, 296; accommodations for, 107; learning with, 113, 162

dissertations, 5, 31, 42, 57, 81, 103, 118-121, 130-131, 143, 149, 158, 164, 172-173, 208-209, 233; approval of, 133, 138, 140-142; and class assignments, 108; defense of, 119, 140-142; format of, 120-121, 137, 241; and life goals, 33; and passion, 129; and perfectionism, 202; proposals for, 3, 123-124, 217, 229;

prospectus, 123; publishing, 167; purpose of, 28; and reading, 109; revisions of, 138, 141; scale and scope of, 119-120, 128; skills from, 43, 75; timelines for, 94, 106, 121, 145-147; topics for, 87, 97, 114-115, 123, 125-129; tracking tasks for, 144, 151; writing your, 135-137, 152-155, 180, 288. *See also* research

dissertation committees, 5, 31, 87, 93, 119, 133, 135, 146-147, 217, 232; choosing, 99, 115, 121-123; connections of, 122; expertise of, 121-122; feedback from, 120, 124, 136, 138, 140-142, 149; fit of, 122; responsiveness from, 122; working with your, 121, 124, 128, 139, 149-150

diversity, 90, 187, 228-230, 233, 237-241; admissions (*see* admissions: diversity in); career (*see* careers: diversity in); committee (*see* institutional committees: diversity)

diversity statements, 113

D'Mello, Sidney, 153

doctor of education (EdD), 11

doctor of law (JD), 11

doctor of medicine (MD), 11

doctor of philosophy (PhD). *See* degrees, doctoral

doctoral students, 3, 31, 52, 115; and careers, 5; questions to ask as, 29-30

doctoral degrees. *See* degrees, doctoral

doctoral programs. *See* degrees, doctoral

documentation, 97, 133-134

Dropbox, 134

dyslexia, 162

early childhood education, 135

EdD. *See* doctor of education

editing. *See* writing: revision of

editors, 76, 139, 168, 175-176

Eisenhower Matrix, 154

email, 75, 80, 95, 97, 110, 177, 186, 201, 205, 214, 222; and admins, 105; and advisors, 86, 92, 100, 217; and committees, 122-123, 135; managing, 144, 152-155, 199, 219, 221; and networking, 46, 187, 242; writing effective, 94, 155

emotional intelligence, 43

emotions, 74, 130, 150, 156, 193-194, 204, 212, 218; negative, 156, 158, 228

employers, 45, 56, 62, 187; funding from, 53

EndNote, 110

engagement, 41, 71, 77, 151; and communication, 171; and teaching, 112

exam committee, 67, 116-118

exams, 115-118; examples of, 117-118; format of, 116-117; oral, 117; passing, 117; picking a committee for, 116; preparing for, 116, 118; topics on, 116, 118

excellence, 71, 74, 202; versus success, 71-72

expertise, 81, 116, 120, 139, 141, 166, 173; and careers, 20, 23, 45, 47; and choosing committees, 121-122; and getting advice, 67, 87, 101, 104, 135; and judging ideas, 128-129

expectations, 80, 151, 157, 201, 203; and academic careers, 34; and academic culture, 18, 79, 108, 111, 175, 182, 208; and advisors, 89, 92-96, 155; and balance, 195; and committees, 123; and dating, 211; and dissertations, 28, 124; and family, 218-219, 243; and independent research, 120, 125; and learning, 75; and teaching, 113; and undergraduates, 161; and working hard, 191

expectancy, 156, 158

Excel, 172

exercise, 196-198, 205

experiments, 43, 72, 75, 120, 133, 136, 150, 170, 179, 193; planning and scheduling, 100, 135, 149, 152, 179, 244

exploitation, in teaching, 111. *See also* labor

extroversion, 210

faculty, 3, 28, 31-32, 39, 67, 96-97, 101-102, 104-105, 120, 127, 146, 170, 210, 215, 229, 233-241, 243-246; and advisers (*see* advisers); careers as (*see* careers: academic); and committees (*see* committees); contingent, 32, 36; courses with, 26, 77, 107, 128; full-time, 3-4, 32; and funding, 34, 54, 66; and life balance, 199, 208, 221, 224; networking with, 169; part-time, 37; and teaching, 110-111; working with (*see* advisers); and writing, 175, 179

failure, 5, 10, 32, 39, 74, 149-151, 208

faith. *See* religion

family, 1-2, 5, 30, 46, 57, 121, 195, 207, 215, 220, 223, 237, 245; and academia, 34, 49, 106, 140, 211, 229, 232, 243-244; and finances, 19, 61-64, 218; and life goals, 33, 211; managing, 163; 192-193, 198, 200-201, 208-209, 212-214, 224; support from, 9, 75, 213, 227, 230; and values, 13-14, 17, 24, 40, 205-209, 242. *See also* children; parenting; pregnancy

feedback, 86, 88, 169-170; and admissions applications, 238; and advisors (*see* advisors: feedback from); and committees (*see* dissertation committees: feedback from); dealing with negative, 150, 166, 178; giving, 79, 81, 179, 229; and exams, 117; and funding applications, 55- 56; lack of, 201; and job applications, 45; positive, 75, 88; public, 186; and talks or presentations, 182; and thesis or dissertation proposals, 124; writing, 76, 79, 105, 166, 175-179, 201; work, 66, 88

feelings. *See* emotions

fellowships, 36, 51, 53–54, 58, 164; applying for, 55–56, 172, 175, 284; finding, 283

feminism, 232, 242

fertility, 215, 218, 297

Fiebelman, Peter J., 35, 172, 181

field. *See* discipline

field exams. *See* exams

fieldwork, 26, 148-149, 216-217, 222

figures, 23, 79, 120, 136, 153, 184; creating, 134, 172

finances, 11, 22, 33, 53, 57-58, 203, 239; administrators of, 105; and emergencies, 60-61; and family goals, 212; and frugality, 61-62, 65; and health insurance, 62; and investing, 55, 61; and realtors, 51, 57. *See also* budgeting; fellowships; funding; grants; rent; stipend; tuition

Fishbach, Ayelet, 13, 68-69, 108, 145, 149-150, 157-159, 160

fixed mindset, 71

flexibility, 24, 40-41, 64, 68, 94, 152-153, 203, 220, 242-244; and meetings, 221

flipped classroom, 113

flow, 41, 71, 73, 151, 159, 285

focus, 13, 151-153, 192, 200; and writing, 138

freedom of speech, 236, 240

friends, 140, 159-160, 199, 209-210, 231; and childcare, 222; and food, 62; and relationships, 214; and reviews, 178; support from (*see* social support); and writing, 172-173

fun, 1, 6, 24, 26, 33, 156-157, 174, 222; and infinite games, 73; reading for, 72, 196-197; and writing, 23, 174

funding, 3, 35, 51, 53, 80, 103, 150, 166, 239, 245; and autonomy, 120; applying for, 55-56, 58, 107; childcare, 244; conference, 66; and costs of research, 65-66; degree or program, 11; finding, 53-54, 86, 91, 283; postdoc, 35-36; student event, 235; and timelines, 121. *See also* budgeting; fellowships; finances; grants

future work. *See* research: future

gap years, 196

general exams. *See* exams

Google Calendar, 144, 294
Google Docs, 180
Google Drive, 134
Google Scholar, 126, 127
Google Slides, 290
goals, 151, 154, 182, 211, 223, 235, 237;
    achieving, 137-138, 144-145, 152-153,
    157-160, 201-202, 293-294; acting in line
    with our, 74; changing, 22; financial, 58,
    61; life and career, 6, 13-14, 19, 25, 32-33,
    40, 68, 71, 77, 80, 165, 197, 224-225;
    remembering, 68–70, 225-226; revisiting,
    69-70, 77, 82, 197, 230-231; setting, 78,
    158; shared, 211-212; support for
    achieving, 69, 86, 94, 201, 209; teaching
    and learning, 112
GPA, 107
governance, student. *See* student governance
grades, 70-71, 107, 110, 113
graphs. *See* figures
graduate assistantships, 52-53. *See also*
    research assistantship; teaching
    assistantship
graduate oral exams. *See* exams
graduate programs, 1-2, 40, 62, 86-87, 119,
    243; admissions to, 4, 228, 234; and career
    preparation, 25; and funding (*see*
    funding); leaving, 22; and outside
    employment, 61; practice-focused, 10-11,
    19; research-focused, 11-12, 19; time limits
    for, 150. *See also* doctoral programs;
    master's programs
graduate school, 1, 3-5; affording (*see*
    finances); and balance (*see* balance);
    applications for (*see* applications,
    graduate school); diversity in (*see*
    diversity); happiness in (*see* happiness); as
    a job, 199-200; leaving, 21-23, 38, 95, 97,
    204-205, 229; problems with, 4, 233-234,
    237; progress in, 79, 105, 126, 145, 148,
    150, 156, 158, 205-206; reasons to attend,
    1, 6, 11-12, 14, 19, 28, 55, 67, 69, 231; stress
    in (*see* stress); success in, 5-6, 30, 33, 56,
    71-72, 86, 91, 209, 232, 239, 247-248;
    types of, 10-11
graduate students. *See* students
graduate student unions, 94, 111, 235-236
graduates. *See* alumni
graduation, 14, 31, 94, 140, 145, 201, 210
grants, 34, 37, 53-54, 66, 89, 92, 175, 208, 245;
    administration of, 245; applying for,
    55–56, 172, 283-284
growth mindset, 71
group projects, 108

happiness, 32, 90, 228, 275-276
health, 193, 199, 204-205; mental, 3, 13, 21-22,
    33, 63, 97, 113, 150, 162, 193-195, 200-201,
    203-204, 227, 229, 242; physical, 159,
    193-194, 200, 217, 227; resources for,
    295-297; social, 193, 200
health insurance, 32, 37, 52-53, 55, 60-62, 91,
    110, 200, 216, 218, 236, 244
help, asking for, 76-77, 95, 99, 175
hiring committees, 34-35, 70, 236, 245
hobbies, 48, 92, 191-193, 198-199, 201, 207,
    224, 230
housing, 51, 59, 61-64; buying, 57–58; on
    campus, 63-64; costs of, 62-64; off
    campus, 64
humanities, 3-4, 10-12, 31-32, 36, 53, 79, 87,
    90, 104, 107, 119-120, 132, 134-135,
    167-168, 180, 193, 195, 203; resources for
    the, 275, 277, 279, 283, 285, 299
Hurley, Kameron, 177
husband. *See* partner
hypotheses, 106, 115, 128, 131-133, 136, 179,
    182, 186

iCal, 144
iCloud, 134
ideas. *See* research, ideas

illness. *See* health
impact, 168, 171; advisor, 5, 101
imposter syndrome, 49, 150, 194, 196, 202; dealing with, 74-75
impulsiveness, 156
independent scholars, 24, 233, 245-246
indexes, digital, 126-127
Institute for Globally Distributed Open Research and Education (IGDORE), 245, 298
institutional committees, 37, 43, 81, 88, 92, 149, 198, 235-237; and admissions (*see* admissions committee); and diversity, 239; and tenure or promotion, 244
Institutional Review Board (IRB), 122, 149, 236, 245
instructor of record, 110
international students, 49, 230, 237
internships, 26-27, 36, 44, 48, 54, 241, 278-279
interviews, 86, 90, 101; academic job, 34, 66; administrator, 91-92; advisor, 87-90; alumni, 90; ethnographic, 132; graduate admissions, 85, 228; informational, 27, 46-47, 241, 242; nonacademic job, 26, 43, 48; podcast, 61, 165, 181; press, 116, 186; radio, 165, 181; research, 54, 88, 114, 122, 132, 135, 143; student, 91
investing. *See* finances: investing
inclusivity, 229, 291; in teaching, 113
interdisciplinary, 103, 117, 165, 208
introversion, 112-113, 209
isolation, 104-105, 200, 227

JD. *See* doctor of law
job interviews. *See* interviews: job
job market, 3, 5, 42, 45, 94, 121, 195, 203; academic, 3, 22, 31, 33-36, 70, 202, 213. *See also* careers
job search. *See* careers: and job searches
jobs. *See* careers

journals, 4, 124, 240; academic, 66, 109, 126-127, 131-133, 167-169, 187, 202, 237; bullet, 292, 294; career, 40; Good Time, 41, 151; publishing in academic, 165-166, 168-172, 175, 203, 287; research, 127; reviews for academic, 79, 176, 179, 289; teaching 112, 291
JSTOR, 126

Keynote, 182
Kidder, Tracy, 176-177

lab, 64, 72, 81, 85, 104, 132, 149, 193, 246; scientists, 4; time working in, 92-93, 151, 192, 199, 205, 208
lab group. *See* research group
lab rotations, 75, 90, 102
lab sciences, 4, 102, 105, 125, 131
lab skills, 43, 107, 114, 122, 217
lab techs and managers, 22, 105, 245
laboratory. *See* lab
labor, 35, 52, 80, 86, 235-236, 243, 299
LaTeX, 121, 139-140, 180
learning, 1, 4, 14, 37, 43, 72-74, 82, 85, 97, 113, 138, 174, 177, 179, 222, 232; active, 112; evaluating, 243; and failure, 150; finding opportunities for, 76-79; and new research, 126-127, 169; new skill, 19, 23, 29, 40, 68, 70, 76-77, 133-134, 232; resources about, 285, 292; and skill plans, 19, 77-79
learning mind-sets, 5, 49, 70-74, 76, 132, 150; cultivating, 72-73; resources about, 285
learning objectives, 112
learning support on campus, 37, 67, 113, 162
lecturers, 32
lectures, 76, 80, 82, 107, 112, 131, 210; guest, 82, 112; teaching via, 110, 112, 291; video, 19, 243
lease, 64
leaves of absence, 2, 22, 105, 157, 204, 215, 243; maternity, 6, 100, 204, 215, 217-218, 244-245; paternity, 215

letter of recommendation. *See* recommendation letter
LGBTQIA, 228-229, 298
librarians, 76, 121
libraries, 2, 19, 25, 38, 62, 72, 121, 126, 135, 138, 149, 158; programming, 133
life, 1-2, 4-6, 19, 50, 61, 70, 72, 94, 99, 163, 191-193, 203-204, 207-208, 210-211, 224, 231-232, 245, 247-248; coherency in, 5, 12-13, 40, 225-226, 247; designing your, 6, 12, 40, 46, 130, 151, 193, 232; figuring out what to do in, 12, 14, 17-18, 21, 25, 39, 204, 247; goals for (*see* goals: life and career); meaning in, 4, 12, 198, 227-228, 230
life balance. *See* balance
loans, 54, 58, 66; payment of, 57; student, 52, 56-57, 60, 204; and taxes, 56–57

magazines, 165, 167, 170
marriage, 2, 5, 209, 212-213. *See also* partner; relationships
master's degrees. *See* degrees, master's
master's students, 19, 21, 87, 89, 102, 104, 106, 119, 145, 203, 238; funding for, 52-53
master's thesis. *See* thesis
maternity. *See* pregnancy
maternity leave. *See* leaves of absence: maternity
Matlab, 133, 172
MBA (master's of business administration), 10, 21, 25
mediation, 96, 100
Medicaid, 61, 216, 218
meetings, 43, 47, 96, 100, 119, 128, 143, 155, 169, 187, 210, 217, 219, 235; academic hiring, 34; advisor, 92, 94, 96, 100-101, 135, 201; committee, 123, 135; group, 82, 89, 108; managing children during, 221-222; professional, 43; scheduling, 81, 144, 201-202, 208, 294; streamlining, 94, 155, 162; virtual, 123, 187, 221-222

men, 39, 215, 229
Mendeley, 110
mental contrasting, 149, 231
mental health. *See* health: mental
mental health professional, 139, 162
mentoring, 92, 239-240; conference programs for, 170; graduate student, 37, 86-88, 234; lack of, 201; learning, 75, 86, 292; peer, 104, 230, 239-240; and teaching, 43; undergraduate, 31, 64, 161-162
mentors, 41, 86, 122, 161, 230-231, 240-241; academic, 31, 39, 42, 86, 200, 234, 244; advise from, 42, 56, 99; postdocs as, 35;
merit, 172, 238; and funding, 53-54
methodology, 25, 44, 88, 121-122, 132-133, 141, 166, 184; classes on, 107; help with, 87; preregistration of, 133; teaching, 111; writing about, 136, 164, 173, 179
milestones, 5, 81, 135, 148, 151, 156, 205; degree, 67, 118-119, 135, 145-146, 149; setting, 148, 156, 160, 201; writing, 137-138. *See also* timelines
mindfulness, 113, 158-159
minorities, 3, 39, 49, 94, 113, 127, 200, 227-230, 238-240; and difficult conversations, 231
MIT, 28, 51, 85, 103, 228; student blog, 24, 68, 76
MIT Media Lab, 2, 28-29, 31, 55, 67, 103, 114, 120, 238, 241
money. *See* finances
motherhood. *See* parenting. *See also* children; leaves of absence; maternity
motivation, 1, 4, 6, 9-11, 18, 30, 33, 67, 69-70, 73-74, 107-108, 149-151, 154, 156-161, 203, 205; extrinsic, 70; intrinsic, 70, 160-161; resources about, 285, 293
multidisciplinary, 165

National Labor Relations Board, 236
National Science Foundation (NSF), 53, 56, 66

National Institutes of Health (NIH), 53
negotiation, 5, 24, 79-82, 96-100, 114, 130, 141, 229, 235, 243; and hard conversations, 100, 231; job offer, 49; tactics for, 97-98, 284
networking, 27, 36, 46, 68, 233, 245, 281; and conferences, 66; and fellowships, 54; and hiring decisions, 35; with alumni, 90, 241
neurodivergence, 162, 229
Newport, Cal, 152-156, 197
nonprofits, 36, 38-39, 168; funding from, 53; jobs and internships with, 36, 278; volunteering for, 198

off campus, 64, 77, 157, 194, 197. *See also* housing
on campus, 76, 143, 150, 161, 197, 227, 230; getting involved, 198, 205, 234-235; living, 63-64. *See also* housing
OneDrive, 134
opportunities, 21, 29, 54, 64, 66, 81, 86, 98, 113, 125, 128, 135, 141, 166, 177-178, 214, 222, 238; assistantship, 102; and careers, 24, 26-27, 36, 42, 47-48, 67, 233, 241, 245; feedback, 124, 179; for learning, 48, 68, 70, 76-77, 79, 82, 116; mentoring, 161, 239; networking, 122, 169; publishing, 168; student government, 235; and writing, 177-178
opportunity cost, 18-21, 28, 203
optimism bias, 148, 293
oral exams. *See* exams
outlines, 115, 172, 183; chapter, 124; creating, 136-137, 180
Outlook, 144, 294
overwhelm, 28, 156; and burnout, 194; managing, 109, 137, 144, 203-204; and teaching, 112-113

Pages, 139, 290
panels. *See* conference: panels at

PaperPile, 110
papers. *See* publishing. *See also* reading
parental leave. *See* leaves of absence
parenting, 73, 94, 233, 237; conversations about, 211; and flexibility, 242-244; and graduate school, 215-223; resources about, 297-298; single, 62, 64. *See also* children; partner; pregnancy
partner, 12, 40, 121, 208, 212-214, 220; and finances, 37, 52, 61-62, 213-214; finding, 210-211; and housing, 62-64; support from your, 209. *See also* relationships
passion, 41, 129-130, 236
paternity leave. *See* leaves of absence: paternity
peers. *See* graduate students
peer mentoring. *See* mentoring: peer
peer review. *See* reviews
perfectionism, 175, 202. *See also* imposter syndrome
perseverance, 149-150, 161, 224, 285
PhD. *See* doctor of philosophy
Pink, Daniel, 160
planning fallacy, 148
play, 70, 73, 143, 193, 199, 292; and children, 199, 205-206, 221-222, 233; and flow, 73, 159; and learning, 70; pay for, 167; with robots, 143, 149, 161; and self-discipline, 159
Platt, George, 71, 191
podcasts, 2, 58, 61, 165, 181, 196, 242; recommended, 275-276, 282, 287, 293, 296, 298
policy brief, 170
Pomodoro Technique, 153
posters, conference. *See* conference: posters at
postdocs, 64, 72, 80, 87, 89-90, 178-179, 210; jobs as, 32, 35-36, 76; resources on, 279-281, 283; support from, 104-105
power, 150, 193, 210, 232, 234, 236; and advisors, 80, 97

PowerPoint, 172, 182, 207, 290
practice, 71-76, 78-79, 95, 112, 191, 234; and argumentation, 116; and asking questions, 95; and explaining research, 118, 172; and giving talks, 105, 141, 177, 181-182, 185; and interviews, 48; and meditation, 196, 200; and mindfulness, 159; and negotiation, 98; and religion (see religion); and speaking up, 201; and writing, 174
precarity, 3, 32, 37, 193, 195, 203, 299
pregnancy, 1, 3, 215-218, 231, 243; accommodations for, 217-218, 244-245; and fertility, 218; and finances, 62; and miscarriage, 218; and prenatal care, 216; resources for, 62, 216, 297; symptoms, 216. See also children; maternity; parenting
preliminary exams. See exams
preprint servers, 127, 169-170
presentations. See talks
press releases, 165, 170
principal investigator. See adviser
prioritizing, 1, 19, 23-24, 68, 78, 88, 219; and balance, 191-192, 195, 208; and marriage, 212-213; and working, 82, 154, 156; and values, 13-14, 18, 223
progress, 79, 105, 121, 138, 148; and debt, 65; and expectations, 89, 92; and goals, 68-69, 150, 158, 205; reports on, 54, 92-93, 135, 154; tracking, 145, 154, 156; works in, 169
procrastination, 41, 118, 136, 149, 153, 205; and creativity, 125; managing, 156-162, 292
productivity, 142, 201, 207; and procrastination, 125; resources about, 292-293; and scheduling apps, 69; strategies for, 152-155, 192, 196; and women, 39, 215, 244; and writing, 138, 287-288

professors. See faculty
programming, 2, 26, 114, 133-134; managing, 148
project management, 43, 116, 118, 232; software, 148; training in, 75, 86. See also schedules; time: management of
proposals. See dissertations: proposals; theses: proposals
prospectus. See dissertations
psychiatrist. See mental health professional
psychologist. See mental health professional
psychology, 72, 85, 120, 131, 168, 170; careers in, 277; and flow, 285; and theories of learning, 70-71
psychology, developmental, 67, 135
psychology, educational, 2
psychology, reverse, 69
publications, 45, 114, 133, 153, 170, 187; and CVs, 35, 44; learning about new, 126; peer-reviewed, 166; prestige of, 167-169; number of, 35, 132; and tenure-track jobs, 37. See also writing
publishers, 167-168, 187
publishing, 31, 70, 119, 165-171, 175; academic, 166-170; careers in, 10, 37-38; costs of, 166; culture of, 132; economics of, 166; nonacademic, 170-171; and resubmission, 166, 178, 203. See also books; book chapters; conferences; journals
PubMed, 126
Python, 133-134, 172

qualifying exams. See exams
quantitative, 78, 87, 132, 290
qualitative, 78, 87, 132, 271

R (programming language), 133
racism, 74, 193
Ramsey, Dave, 64, 282

reading, 73, 106, 115, 122, 133, 135-136, 138, 148, 174, 176-177, 226, 232, 240, 244; and email, 105; effectively and efficiently, 108-110; and exams, 115-118, 146-147; fun, 72, 195-197; and ideas, 126-127, 131; and notetaking, 109-110; resources about, 286; and talks, 181, 183; and teaching, 112-113, 243; time for, 118, 143, 152, 158, 192, 196, 202, 205, 217

reading groups, 126

recommendation letters, 19, 56, 95, 101-102, 122

reference letters, 34. *See also* recommendation letters

references, 109-110, 114, 136, 137, 141, 152, 176-177, 180; software for managing, 110

RefWorks, 110

rejection, 58, 149-150, 178

relatedness, 160

relationships, 4-5, 69, 150, 175, 191-193, 206, 211, 222, 229-230; and advisors (*see* advisors: relationships with); and dating, 210-211; ending, 211-212; faculty, 210, 236; and health, 193-194; long-distance, 213-214; and marriage, 209, 212-213; and motivation, 70; taking time for, 200, 207-208. *See also* careers: two-body problem

religion, 62, 198, 200, 213, 237, 298; and community, 227-228, 30; and miscarriage, 218; and values, 13

reminders, 69, 75, 105, 191-192, 224-227

replicability and reproducibility, 173; crisis of, 132

rent, 51-52, 59, 61, 63-64, 192-193

research, 4-5, 10, 24-25, 28-30; careers in (*see* careers: research); communicating, 68; costs of (*see* funding); dissemination of (*see* publishing); future, 134-135; funding for, 4, 53-55; independent, 11, 76, 100, 103, 114, 119-120, 125, 232; learning about, 126-127; and passion (*see* passion); planning and executing, 115, 153-154; quality versus quantity of, 132-133; resources for, 121, 285-287; skills, 76, 87, 285-286; staying on track with, 104; topics (*see* research, ideas); types of, 131-132. *See also* dissertations; theses

research, archival, 132

research, careers. *See* careers: research

research, deductive, 131-132

research, experimental, 131-132

research, ideas, 5, 11, 23, 69, 87, 103; communicating, 171-172; generating, 38, 48, 99, 108, 115, 124-131; judging, 11, 128-129. *See also* dissertations: topics for; research: topics; theses: topics for

research, inductive, 132

research, qualitative, 132

research, descriptive, 132

research, quantitative and survey, 131-132

research assistantships, 5, 22, 44, 52-55, 67, 97, 102-103, 114, 132, 195, 199, 235

research groups, 11, 21, 35, 79-80, 85, 87-90, 104-105, 118, 208, 210, 241, 243; culture of, 90, 103-104; support from, 76, 105, 118, 124, 127, 141, 182

research journal. *See* journals

research questions, 75, 109, 132-133, 179, 237;

ResearchGate, 126

results, 43, 93, 100, 133, 143, 152, 202; and preprints, 170; writing about, 136, 164, 176, 179, 182

resumes, 20, 23, 26, 42-46, 187, 278

reviewers, 121, 166, 175-176, 238

review, literature, 117, 123-124, 176, 286

reviews, 79-81, 105, 166, 170, 176; of graduate school applications, 238; peer, 119, 165-166, 168-169, 175, 178-179, 237, 288; reasons to write, 79; writing, 179, 289; and time management, 79-82. *See also* feedback

revision. *See* writing: revision
rewards, 156; extrinsic, 160
rhythm, 138, 143-144, 151
robots, 128-130, 143, 149, 161, 164, 170-171, 183, 217
Ronin Institute for Independent Scholarship, 245, 298
routine, 160, 197, 217
royalties, 167
Ryan, Richard, 160

SAS, 172
saying no, 68, 79-82, 98, 154, 201-202, 284
saying yes, 68, 79-82
schedules, 43, 69, 79, 100, 107, 115, 133, 152, 154; and ADHD, 162; apps for, 69, 108, 294; and children, 200, 208, 212, 217, 219-221; course, 107; defense, 140-141; and family, 211-212, 217; and leisure, 158, 196-199, 205; and meetings, 81, 100-101, 135, 143, 155; work, 3, 145, 147, 149, 151-153, 155, 158, 202; writing, 136, 138, 155
science communication, 24, 281, 289
scholarship, 124, 164-165, 234, 240
scholarships, 53-55, 66, 165-166; applying for, 55-56; finding, 66; and taxes, 56-57
school-life balance. *See* balance
Scopus, 126
self-control, 156-161
self-discipline, 159. *See also* motivation; self-control
Seligman, Amanda, 12, 22, 52, 76, 101, 108, 116, 194, 200, 224
seminars, 28, 67, 101-102, 108, 126, 234
setbacks, 2, 33, 149-151
service, 32, 34, 37, 44, 237; and time, 81, 88
sexism, 74, 86, 100, 193
Shaw, Steven R., 179
skill plan, 77-79, 82
sleep, 193, 215, 218-219; prioritizing, 1, 200; and work habits, 153, 159, 220

slides. *See* talks: slides for
SNAP, 61
social media, 77, 79, 221, 281; family, 209, 298; networking with, 169, 187, 228, 279, 281, 298; and presenting yourself on, 45-46; research dissemination via, 165, 170, 186
social sciences, 3-4, 10, 36, 87, 107, 120, 132, 134-135, 167, 182, 203, 254; resources for, 275, 277, 283, 285, 288
social support, 9, 76, 103-106, 200; and achieving goals, 69-70; from administrators, 105; from friends, 69, 156, 178, 185, 222; for idea generation, 127-128; and religion, 227; from spouses and partners, 209; from students, 103, 105, 108, 150, 240. *See also* community; support: groups
software, 148, 294; accounting, 58; graphics, 172; poster, 290; presentation, 182-183; proficiency with, 78; reference management, 109-110; statistical, 133, 172; task tracking, 144; time tracking, 149; writing, 139, 180. *See also* programming
speaking. *See* talks
spouse. *See* partner
spreadsheets, 56, 58, 144, 152, 205, 294
SPSS, 133
Stata, 133
statistics, 79, 106, 132-134
Steel, Piers, 157, 292
STEM, 3-4, 11, 12, 21, 31, 35-36, 40, 51-53, 77, 79, 86-87, 90, 104, 107, 114, 119-120, 126, 134-135, 139, 161, 179, 182, 195, 229; resources about, 276-277, 281, 283, 298
stipend, 53, 55, 58, 60, 64, 236, 241, 244; and cost of living, 63; and graduate assistantships, 110, 114; and taxes, 56-57
stories; and applications, 56; and job searches, 45-47; research, 129, 137, 141, 171-172, 174; and talks, 181

stress, 55, 98, 147, 203-204, 231, 243-244; and academic culture, 19, 90; financial, 21, 202, 243; and health, 200-203, 213; reducing, 200-203; and romantic relationships, 209, 211-213; student, 3, 5, 76, 104, 113, 193-196; and talks, 184

student governance, 198, 234-235

students, 74, 76, 79, 104, 210, 227; cohort of, 28, 69, 79, 90, 104-105, 118, 200, 210, 239; groups, 76-77, 228; questions for, 27-30, 77-78, 90-91. *See also* colleagues; doctoral students; master's students

study groups, 108; for exams, 118

success, 6, 60, 74, 91, 165, 207-209, 238-239, 247-248; and fellowships, 56; and flexibility, 242; and job applications, 46; learning from, 150; and mentoring, 86; tenure track as defining, 32; versus excellence, 71-72

supervisor. *See* adviser

support, 162, 201, 203, 229, 233, 239, 243; groups, 69, 104-105, 139, 141, 175, 200-201, 203, 218, 228, 230, 240; for student clubs and events, 234-235. *See also* community; social support

syllabi, 107, 110-111, 291; diversifying, 239-240; inclusive, 113, 291

symposia. *See* conferences

talks, 5, 44, 78, 165-166, 169; accessibility for, 183-184; in class, 181; conference, 127, 169; fear of, 185; job, 181; preparing for, 76, 105, 181-184; question-and-answer (Q&A) at, 184-185; slides for, 182-184; technology for, 186

tasks, 77-78, 151, 221, 243; and ADHD, 162; apps for tracking, 144; estimating time for, 80, 148-149, 201; management of, 134, 143-145, 148, 151-154, 156-161, 201; tracking, 69, 144

taxes, 56-57, 59, 91, 253

teaching, 6, 32, 39, 41, 61, 70, 75-76, 81, 86-87, 92, 144, 165, 234, 244, 246; assistantships (*see* teaching assistantships); careers in, 11, 32, 34, 36-37, 54, 68, 108; certificate program, 67; inclusive, 113; and pregnancy, 215, 217; and skills, 42-44, 78; strategies for, 111-113

teaching, adjunct, 32, 36-37

teaching assistantships, 1, 5, 44, 52-53, 55, 58, 67, 76, 102-103, 110-111, 187, 235, 245

teams, 5, 69, 86, 239; at companies, 44; fencing, 13, 191; undergraduate, 161; who's on your, 103-104, 106; working on, 78

temptations, 156-159; bundling, 157

tenure, 31, 37, 41, 88, 101, 208, 213, 44, 280

tenure-track, 22-24, 31-32, 34, 37, 93, 122, 215, 279-280

theory, 131, 141, 152, 171, 174, 179

theses, 2, 4-5, 11, 75, 108-109, 116, 137, 139, 118-121, 208-209; format of, 120-121; proposals for, 123-124; resources for, 288, 291; scale and scope of, 11, 119-120, 128; timelines for, 121, 145-147; topics for, 87, 97, 115, 125, 128-129, 199. *See also* research; writing

thesis committee. *See* dissertation committee

time, 143; to degree (*see* degrees: time to); estimating task, 148-149; management of, 86, 131, 142, 151-154, 156, 201, 220-222, 232, 293; nonwork, 195-197. *See also* balance; tasks; timelines

time block planning, 152

timelines, 56, 77, 140, 143, 150; advisor feedback on, 92-93, 121, 135; creating

145-148; dissertation and thesis, 119, 121, 124, 131, 135, 141, 145-148; exam, 118; and leaves of absence, 204; managing, 143-145, 149-150; and part-time funding, 245; and skill plans, 77-79

Todd, Richard, 176-177

toddlers. *See* children

training, 43, 50, 73, 159, 239; by advisers, 86; and professorship, 3, 86, 93; for research, 35-36, 75, 93, 114; teacher, 76

transcripts. *See* grades

travel, 81, 142, 149, 162, 170, 186, 230; and children, 216, 222; funding for, 53, 55, 66, 91. *See also* conferences; fieldwork

tuition, 52-53, 55, 110

tutorials, 77

two body problem. *See* careers: two body problem

uncertainty, 4, 12, 20-21, 25, 105, 195, 202-203

undergraduates, 22, 64, 104; bridge programs for, 238; dating, 210; mentoring, 31, 149-150, 161-162

underrepresented minorities. *See* minorities

unions. *See* graduate student unions

universities, public, 111, 236

universities, regional, 34

universities, research, 34

values, 5, 12-13, 30, 156, 213, 224-226, 230, 240, 247-248, 276; and advisers, 94; and balance, 208-209; and careers, 40, 203; and goals, 145, 209; and grad school, 18-19, 23-25, 203, 225; labeling, 14-18; ranking, 13-14

vacation. *See* time off

volunteering, 35, 44, 48, 50, 76-77, 81, 114, 198, 234, 236-237, 241

Voss, Chris, 49, 82, 97-98

Web of Science, 126

websites, 56, 105; committee, 237; course, 43, 110; personal, 24, 42, 45, 153, 186-187; research group and advisor, 88-89, 241; resources from, 2, 35, 111, 122, 126, 171, 241-242; student government, 235

Wegner, Daniel, 69-70

WIC, 61

wife. *See* partner

women, 208, 242, 245; in academia, 67, 80, 232, 245; and leaving academia, 21, 39, 232; and motherhood, 215-220; support from, 69, 105

Word, 121, 139-140

work; administrative, 38, 80, 105, 124, 155; algorithmic, 160; backing up your, 134; deep, 136, 152-156, 160, 197, 220; expectations for, 79, 89, 92-94, 123, 151, 195, 201, 211, 243; full-time, 3-4, 24, 32, 44, 53, 61, 68, 162, 200, 211, 220, 232, 242, 245; in groups (*see* group projects); heuristic, 160; independent, 100, 105, 120, 162, 213; in the home, 242; part-time, 4, 6, 24, 32, 37-38, 40, 44, 48, 50, 52-53, 62, 110, 114, 242, 245; quality of, 39, 132-133, 194, 244, 287; remote and asynchronous, 6, 123, 218, 220-221, 242-243; shallow, 54, 152-153, 160; and side hustles, 19, 55, 58, 61, 282

work-life balance. *See* balance

workaholism, 3, 193, 242

workload, 80, 82, 201, 216

workshops, 43, 66, 76-77, 79, 169, 181, 222, 219; blogging, 24, 68, 76; teaching, 76, 111. *See also* conferences

writing, 5, 68; audiences for, 165, 171, 173-174, 177, 234; blog (*see* blogging); campus centers for, 76, 139, 175, 201; dissertation and thesis, 43, 108, 115, 120, 135-140, 143-144, 151-154, 156, 164, 172-173, 180-181, 208, 233, 288; editors for, 139, 168, 171;

writing (*continued*)
   feedback on, 138–139, 175–179; good, 173–174; grant, 75, 172, 175, 283–284; importance of, 174; and journaling, 4; payment for, 167, 171; pitching, 170–171; starting, 135–137, 172–173; revision of, 138–139, 173, 175–178; software for, 139–140; spelling and grammar in, 176; stories in, 171–172; strategies for, 137–138, 171–174; structure of, 172, 174, 177; time for, 136. *See also* publishing

zone of proximal development, 71
Zotero, 110

GPSR Authorized Representative: Easy Access System Europe, Mustamäe tee
50, 10621 Tallinn, Estonia, gpsr.requests@easproject.com

www.ingramcontent.com/pod-product-compliance
Lightning Source LLC
Chambersburg PA
CBHW022032290426
44109CB00014B/841